The Search for the Causes of Crime

A History of Theory in Criminology

MICHAEL DOW BURKHEAD

Foreword by Michael Braswell

McFarland & Company, Inc., Publishers
Jefferson, North Carolina, and London

LIBRARY OF CONGRESS CATALOGUING-IN-PUBLICATION DATA

Burkhead, Michael Dow, 1946–
    The search for the causes of crime : a history of theory in
criminology / Michael Dow Burkhead ; foreword by Michael C.
Braswell.
        p.   cm.
    Includes bibliographical references and index.

    ISBN 0-7864-2222-X (softcover : 50# alkaline paper)

    1. Criminology — History.   2. Crime — Philosophy — History.
I. Title.
HV6021.B87   2006
364.201— dc22   2005026143

British Library cataloguing data are available

Cover image ©2005 Photodisc

Manufactured in the United States of America

*McFarland & Company, Inc., Publishers
    Box 611, Jefferson, North Carolina 28640
    www.mcfarlandpub.com*

To my wife, Jan

Because I would never have gotten this far
without her,
and because two are better than one.

Contents

Foreword

In *The Search for the Causes of Crime*, Michael Burkhead has written a stimulating and informative volume on the history of ideas regarding the causes of crime. From contemporary empirical research to the literature of Shakespeare to films like *The Silence of the Lambs*, the author examines and explores historical perspectives as well as psychological, sociological, and biological explanations of crime.

The author makes a remarkable effort to make sense of the body of knowledge and divergent views concerning crime causation theory. As he points out in a variety of interesting ways, the real struggle lies in understanding and translating the best of what we know about the nature of crime into effective judicial policies and practice. While we may collectively desire a "magic bullet" solution to crime related problems, the evidence suggests that any such transition from theory to policy to practice is unlikely to happen anytime soon, if ever.

Michael Burkhead also addresses the issue of choice. Even if we understood the root causes of crime, such understanding would not change the reality we find ourselves in, which includes a dynamic mix of research and knowledge, conventional approaches, policies and, of course, the ever present specter of political maneuvering. Choice also includes the contrast between reactive and proactive judicial strategies where the priorities of prison construction and crime prevention as well as incarceration and public education must be measured in terms of dollars both budgeted and spent. The author also points out that research is always seen and shaped through the prism of one's personal and social experience. Our choices may conform to such experiences and contexts or transcend them — both in intent and consequences. Either way, choice making has strong moral implications. As the old saying goes, "morality cannot be legislated," and, one might add, "even if it is based upon a scientifically accurate body of knowledge."

The Search for the Causes of Crime has a number of useful and

1

interesting features including tables and illustrations. Perhaps the most interesting feature throughout the text is the descriptions of interactions the author has had with various inmates in therapy groups and personal conversations. These interactions put flesh on the bones of the points he makes and the issues he raises.

In concluding his work, Michael Burkhead shares with the reader the lessons he has learned. Most importantly, he examines theoreticism and territorialism. Too often theoreticians, researchers, policy makers, and practitioners ignore and discount the value and virtue of evidence that contradicts favored theories, policies, and practice. In the search for truth, they come to more closely resemble ideological spin doctors than scholars on a quest to discover knowledge that is relevant and useful, no matter where the process leads or what it concludes. In the end, as is implicit in the author's conclusion, in a spirit of adventure and humility, we come to accept that while we "see through a glass darkly," we try to see and understand all that we can.

Michael C. Braswell, Ph.D.
East Tennessee State University

Preface

Crime is a persistent, pervasive, and costly problem in our country. Lawlessness, especially violence, is greater in the U.S. than in any other industrialized nation. In 2002, the prison and jail population in the United States was 2.16 million, with one in every 110 men a sentenced prisoner. This total is an increase of more than 1 million people since 1985. The Bureau of Justice Statistics has reported that the United States may have surpassed Russia as the country with the highest rate of incarceration in the world. In survey after survey, year after year, crime is listed as one of the most important concerns of the public in America.[1] With such a large and pressing problem on our hands, and with so many explanations and solutions competing for our attention and acceptance, what is the concerned citizen to do? The respected criminologist Edwin Sutherland said it this way: "The average citizen is confronted by a confusing and conflicting complex of popular beliefs and programs in regard to crime. Some of these are traditions from 18th century philosophy; some are promulgations of special interest groups; and some are blind emotional reactions. Organized and critical thinking in this field is therefore peculiarly difficult and also peculiarly necessary."[2] Dr. Sutherland was writing in 1976, but we would be challenged to demonstrate that precisely the same situation does not exist today, more than a quarter of a century later.

There have been so many voices in the debate about crime, so many passionate and unexamined beliefs professed, so many certain solutions proposed, so many programs enacted without results, and so many wrong turns taken along the road that the person who is listening to any of this public clamor must certainly have reached a state of confusion, if not despair. Confusion and despair, mixed with our fear of crime, can certainly drive us towards simplistic thinking. I believe that these feelings are a large part of the explanation for our stubborn, expensive, and unfruitful fixation on incarceration as the solution to crime.

The central point of this book is that we already have more knowledge

3

than we have used in addressing the problem of crime. Until we have used effectively the knowledge that we already possess, we are not very likely to discover new and useful facts or to reach new understandings. Why should we expect greater understanding of the crucial issues of crime as long as we are unable or unwilling to fully and earnestly implement what we already know? We seem to find it easier and more appealing to engross ourselves in the search for new knowledge than to struggle with the implementation of existing knowledge. It also seems to me that we desire to skip too many of the difficult steps *because* they are difficult, hoping that science and technology will somehow bail us out, any day now, with a simple and universal solution, like a new vaccine for a crippling disease.

A secondary message in this book on the causes of crime concerns our search for the root cause of crime. We often hear that scientists have mounted yet another Promethean effort to discover the root cause, or causes, of crime. Such a discovery, even if it is made, will not settle the issue once and for all, mainly because the element of choice cannot be eliminated from the equation. Criminal action is chosen; it is a personal choice. The criminologist Enrico Ferri, a student and colleague of Cesare Lombroso, was excited to write in 1917 that scientific criminology had finally destroyed all belief in a free moral agent.[3] But apparently not, since the belief in the freedom of the individual to choose between the right and the wrong is still very much with us. Dr. Ferri's certainty on this point reminds me of one of my fellow graduate students, a self-avowed radical behaviorist, who dedicated her master's thesis to the environment, since it was the environment that had produced the thesis. I suggested that, since this was the case, we should award the degree to the environment, since the environment had earned it. To my surprise, she was deeply offended and always avoided me after that.

This does not mean that scientific investigation has no role to fill in the understanding of crime. It most certainly does, and we are grateful for the light that it has provided us. Science can help us understand how the choice to act is influenced and it can help us to learn what contributes to meaningful change in a person. Scientists can help us investigate the propositions that certain types of criminal behavior may be the result of a mental disorder and that a tendency for criminal behavior may be genetic, though these propositions are far from proven. We shall have a look at the evidence so far.

Science can also be very useful in disproving specious theories of crime, which is, for example, what happened to Lombroso's theory of criminal man. Cesare Lombroso was a doctor who worked for the Italian prison service. While conducting autopsies of prisoners, he reported having discovered the clue to the cause of crime during an examination of the skull of a convicted robber. The announcement of his theory of criminal man created an international stir, and the ensuing debate about it was an important episode in the history of criminology, a debate that will be described in greater detail in Chapter 4. Dr. Lombroso turned out to be wrong, but he is often called the father of criminology for the stimulus that he provided to the investigation of the causes of crime. There are, as we shall see, other legitimate candidates for the honor, but the point that I wish to make is that putting off an earnest commitment to the knowledge that we already have about crime and criminals because we cannot act effectively until science has uncovered the root cause of crime is a mistake, an error laced with scientific hubris and false expectations, which I have chosen to symbolize as Dr. Lombroso's skull.

Professors Lilly, Cullen, and Ball have written a book on criminological theory in which they argue that the context always has its consequences. They assert that, while committed scientists let the data direct their thinking, they are not able to do so fully because they also live and work within a society and are influenced by it:

> Before ever entering academia or public service, their personal experiences have provided them with certain assumptions about human nature and the way that the world operates.... After studying crime, they often will revise some of their views. Nonetheless, few ever convert to a totally different way of thinking about crime; how they explain crime remains, if only in part, conditioned by the experiences they have had.[4]

I intend not to lose sight of this point. It certainly applies to me. I believe that the issue of crime is personal and moral and cannot be *only* a scientific investigation that leads with an unassailable certainty to a purely scientific and universal solution, like an antibiotic for immorality. Science can and does inform us about crime, but it cannot lead us. For the ultimately important decisions that must be made about crime and criminals, the old knowledge may be a better guide than the new.

These historical facts and details on the causes of crime are designed primarily for the knowledgeable reader, a concerned citizen with moral values and common sense who must cope with the problem of crime. I have not endeavored to write a textbook, nor do I claim to have the latest solution to the problem of crime. I have chosen a historical perspective and therefore I have not included the most recent developments in criminology, some of which may prove to be significant, but whose place in the history of the search for the cause of crime remains to be determined. I am not presenting any previously unpublished research nor any original theoretical ideas. I have no movement to lead, no drugs to sell, and no panacea to hype. My selection of topics is not exhaustive, since such an effort would be an encyclopedia, and I have not set out to write one. Instead, I have written what I hope is a lively and challenging critical survey of the causes of crime, a work that is accurate in its presentation of science and history but that does not presume to have examined every published theory. I have attempted to provide a context within which interesting results and findings as well as ongoing controversies can be understood and weighed by the discerning reader. I have also included in the discussion the directions in which our present knowledge should take us. I hope that this book will appeal to those persons who are interested in the problems of crime and human behavior, who are stimulated by uncertainty, and who enjoy thinking for themselves.

PART ONE

Introduction — The Explanation of Crime

It is better to prevent crimes than to punish them.
— Cesare Beccaria[1]

Criminology is not yet a science; but it has hopes of becoming one.
— Edwin Sutherland[2]

1

Setting the Stage

The Explanation of Crime

What makes bad people bad? There is a long procession of answers to this ancient question, each contingent in the parade passing in review before us with its own body of argument and supporting evidence, and accompanied by its own cadre of passionate advocates, each one claiming possession of objective truth. The marching order for this parade of explanations would include poverty, genes, gangs, climate, the full moon, brain waves, peer pressure, racism, head injury, body type, mental illness, unemployment, childhood trauma, class struggle, role models, moral insanity, vitamin deficiency, learning disabilities, poor parenting, illiteracy, substance abuse, low self control, social alienation, biological inferiority, the prison system, the shape of the skull, low self esteem, rejection, boredom, lead poisoning, labeling, neurotic guilt, TV, IQ, and the devil, or some combination of the foregoing. All of these have been candidates for the explanation of crime. Even the victims of crimes have been proposed as causes. And this is not an exhaustive list.

Among the contingents in this parade of explanations, some are current in criminology, some are absurd, others are merely out of fashion and will undoubtedly make a comeback. Body type, for example, has been in and out of fashion several times. It is currently out, but a new edition is not inconceivable. Only a few of the theories in our parade have been disproved by careful research; the shape of the skull, for instance. But with such a cavalcade of explanations and with such critical decisions waiting to be made, on what can the serious person rely?

Can criminologists help us? The situation here is somewhat better, though still far from clear. There are nearly as many approaches to the study of crime as there are explanations. A partial list of available criminologies would include structural criminology, realist criminology, chaos criminology, clinical criminology, feminist criminology, integrative criminology, postmodern criminology, constitutive criminology, classical criminology, and positivist criminology. There is also environmental criminology, radical criminology, consumerist criminology, life course criminology, and the new European criminology. There is even psychic criminology and streetwise criminology. And there are more. It appears that we are going to have to think for ourselves.

Our journey down the path of academic criminology in search of the cause of crime has been replete with traffic jams, detours, wrong turns, potholes, and dead ends. This path at times has led us into a tangled wilderness of technical and inconclusive debate, distracting us from effective crime prevention and realistic criminal rehabilitation. This journey has sometimes confused rather than enlightened us and has often diverted us from the earnest implementation of knowledge that we already possess in the name of uncovering the root cause of crime, with the supposition that the root cause can then be treated and eradicated like an infectious disease. We need only invest enough in scientific research.

But scientific research on the causes of crime is an extraordinarily territorial enterprise. Psychologists have psychological definitions of crime and look for its causes in the individual person. Sociologists have sociological definitions of crime and look for its causes in the social structure and in social forces. Biologists look for the causes of crime in genes or in neurological dysfunction; economists have economic definitions and study crime as a rational economic decision. Rarely do any of these groups communicate or collaborate with each other in any meaningful or productive way. Each group prefers its own body of knowledge, which is vigorously defended from encroachment by any other body of knowledge. Each discipline claims that the others have little to contribute to our understanding of crime and each profits very little from the reasoning and the discoveries of the others. After surveying this situation in detail, criminologists Gottfredson and Hirschi write, "We conclude that these explanations [of crime] survive more from their value to the disciplines than from their value as explanations for criminal behavior."[1] The state of our modern criminology leads the psychologist Adrian Raine to write that "it is an unfortunate reality of current academic research into criminal behavior that the majority of investigators pursue their own independent specialty lines of research, turn their backs on developments in other relevant disciplines, and closely guard their own turf."[2]

I propose that we chart our own course through these troubled waters, taking care to avoid the twin hazards of hubris and despair, taking in along the way those things that help us on our journey, and passing by those destinations that seem false, unreliable, or unhelpful. We shall try to illuminate the lessons learned from the history of criminology.

There are three basic issues that are crucial to consider. These three can serve to orient us for our journey through the causes of crime:

(1) the issue of free will, or choice, versus determinism, an issue to which I refer as *the mighty opposites*, mighty because both points of view have such strength, appeal, and endurance.

(2) the issue of a single, all encompassing root cause of crime, a single explanation versus many causes of crime, or a multicausal model of explanation, an issue to which I refer as *the one and the many*.

(3) the study of crime versus the study of criminality: are we explaining the crimes or the criminals? Do we focus on the offenses or on the offenders? The aggregate rates of crime or the individuals who commit them? Must we do both? I refer to this issue as *the acts and the actors*.

Once oriented in these three dimensions, we can begin to understand where we are, and to assess the characteristics and relative merits of theories, explanations, claims, and declarations about the causes of crime. From this starting point, we will examine the progress of the study of crime.

The Word "Criminology"

The French anthropologist Paul Topinard is often given the credit for the term *criminology*, though he gives the credit to Baron Raffaele Garofalo for his 1885 book *Criminologia*.[3] Prior to that, various terms were employed to describe what was then a new and developing science, including *moral statistics* and *criminal science*. Cesare Lombroso, whom some call the father of criminology, referred to his work as *criminal anthropology*, adopting the French fashion. *Penology* was the usual term in the nineteenth century, when the focus was on law and punishment rather than on the application of scientific methods to the causes of crime. In this book, I am using the word criminology in a more specific sense than usual, to mean *the study of the causes of crime*. The academic discipline of criminology is much larger than this. The respected criminologist C. Ray Jeffrey wrote that criminology addresses three major issues: (1) the problem of detecting the law breaker, (2) the problem of custody and treatment of the law breaker, and (3) the problem of defining and explaining criminal behavior.[4] Edwin Sutherland said that the sequence of events: law making — law breaking — reaction to law breaking, is the proper study of criminology.[5] Sue Titus Reid writes in a recent text that criminology is the scientific study of crime, criminals, and criminal behavior — and their interaction with the criminal law.[6] Thus criminology includes large areas of which the study of the causes of crime is only one branch. So I am using the word criminology in a specific, more restricted sense than is usually the case. I have chosen to do this because it is simple and convenient and less awkward than using other words or phrases.

I also intend to include in the category "criminologists" more people than those who are by training and orientation strictly criminologists. Scientists closely involved with the study of the causes of crime include biologists, economists, psychologists, psychiatrists, sociologists, anthropologists, and political scientists, among others. In fact, one of the fascinating things about our subject is how many people become involved in trying to explain crime and criminal behavior. It is testimony to the appeal and pressing nature of our subject, but it is also evidence of the confusion and uncertainty that suffuses its study. In using the word criminologist, I mean to include all those scientific workers seriously involved in studying the causes of crime irrespective of their specific academic discipline. There is probably no subject in higher education that blurs the borders of academic disciplines more than does the study of crime and criminal behavior.

A Collection of Crimes

I collect definitions of crime like archaeologists collect old bones. This may seem like an odd pursuit, but, if we are to engage in a study of the causes of crime, it is best to consider, at the beginning, what we are attempting to explain. I am interested in how serious students of crime negotiate the problems that arise from defining crime in such a way that explanations for it can be found. This is not as simple a task as it might appear at first. On the other hand, it is not so complicated as some professional theorists would have us believe. For example, here is a definition proposed by Ullman and Krassner; "Criminal behavior refers to antisocial acts that place the actor at risk of becoming a focus of attention of criminal and juvenile justice professionals."[7] Why should this be so awkward? How about "criminal behavior is arrestable behavior," an act for which you could be arrested. Susan Walklate, in a model of simplicity, defines crime as "law breaking behavior."[8] Every one knows that a crime is a violation of the law. A simple and straightforward legal definition of crime is the one favored by the classical school of criminology as represented by Cesare Beccaria and Jeremy Bentham. The classicists were not much interested in explaining why individuals committed crimes. They assumed that persons possessed free will and reason and made rational choices in terms of self interest, to gain pleasure and avoid pain. They believed in *nullen crimen sine lege*, no crime without a law. They were mainly interested in reforming the criminal law in order to make punishment both more humane and more effective. Here is an excellent example of a legal definition, one of the best specimens in the collection: "A crime is an act committed in violation of a law prohibiting it or omitted in violation of a law ordering it."[9]

I appreciate the clarity and balance of this solid legal definition. It has the virtue of simplicity and it has an appealing symmetry. It seems unassailable. But, as a basis for the study of the causes of crime, this apparently strong foundation, a strictly legal definition of crime, has unexpected ambivalence. Despite its precision I am not happy with this starting point for the study of crime because it would make criminals of both Jesus and Socrates. Dietrich Bonhoeffer, Frederick Douglass, Galileo, and Martin Luther King, Jr., would all be criminals from this point of view. Dr. King in particular would be a repeat offender and would inflate crime statistics. Those colonists who protested the Stamp Act and the Tea Tax would be criminals, the operators of the Underground Railroad during the American Civil War would be criminals, and so would the freedom riders of the 1960s. All of these groups would be the subjects of criminology. But I do not accept these persons as criminals; their acts are not the acts that we all want to prevent, and I know that they were the victims of unjust political and religious prejudices. Civil disobedience and acts of conscience are not essentially the same as rape, robbery, and murder, and the same behavioral explanation can not apply to all of these actions.

The legal definition of crime, as a starting point for scientific explanation and concerted social action, includes more types of behavior than we intend to address. In addition to those engaged in acts of conscience, civil disobedience, and political protest, we would also have to include harried citizens who accumulate parking tickets, procrastinators who delay renewing their licenses, campers who possess alcohol in a public park, and young men who fail to register for the draft. However necessary these ordinances may be, the violators of such laws are not the proper subjects of criminology. These are not offenses that "bring terror in the night" or "sorrow in the morning" and they are not deserving of our focused and intensive scientific efforts.

We must also address the problem of cultural relativity. If crime is any violation of the law, then the subject matter of criminology is different from time to time and from place to place. The history of the laws regulating mood altering substances is an especially good example of this cultural relativity. Future students and citizens will read of our twentieth century statutes on mood altering substances and wonder at our self contradictions no less than our present generation wonders at the contradictions of slavery within a democracy in nineteenth century America. Standards of sexual conduct are also a good example. Oral sex is still a crime almost everywhere in the U.S. Are those persons who engage in it the proper subjects of criminologists? The emergence of laws against dueling in the nineteenth century shows that a capital offense in one time and place is an affair of honor in another time and place. Sellin reports a horrific practice among the Khabyles of Algeria, in which the killing of an adulterous wife is a ritual committed by the father or the brother of the wife. The father or the brother has the right and the duty to kill her in order to cleanse by her blood the honor of her relatives.[10] How do these examples compare to the armed robber who kills a bank guard? Could the same behavioral explanation serve all these instances? It is superficial and false to ignore the influence of context on the definition of crime.

If a strictly legal definition of crime includes too much, fails to account for cross-cultural differences, and ignores context, and we decide to abandon it, what remains? Unhappily, what remains is Pandora's Box. "There is no agreement among criminologists as to the meaning of the term 'crime,'" concludes Jeffrey.[11] Jeffrey has fired a warning shot, for if we are not careful, we will disappear without a trace into that tangled wilderness of technical and inconclusive debate that so absorbs some academic writers and is so fruitless for public policy.

"Crime is a social fact," asserts the great French sociologist Emile Durkheim. "Crime is present not only in the majority of societies of one particular species but in all societies of all types. There is no society that is not confronted by the problem of criminality."[12] Crime is what we are all against. Durkheim asserted that "crime consists of an act that offends certain very strong collective sentiments." But these "very strong collective sentiments" change and evolve. He argued that the criminal plays a definite role in social life by contributing to the development and evolution of morality and law in a society. Writing in 1893, Durkheim reasons that crime is normal because a society exempt from it is utterly impossible. It is impossible because such a society would consist entirely of perfect human beings incapable of acting against the values of the community. Any society, in order to grow and evolve, and thereby survive, must allow individual originality, including deviation from cultural norms. Thus the originality, or deviation from the norm, of the criminal must also be possible.[13]

The criminologist Thorsten Sellin carried this line of thought a step further by declaring crime to be the violation of any cultural norm. This stance allows us to avoid the problem of cross-cultural differences by having us study the process of deviating from the norm, any norm. Thus criminology is the study of deviant behavior; anything abnormal or against cultural norms whether legally a crime or not. Every culture or society, no matter what its laws and customs, has persons who violate its norms. According to Sellin, these are the persons who are the proper subjects for criminology. Crime is undesirable social behavior, whether it is a violation of specific statutes or not. But this position has consequences, too, since mental illness, social alienation, adolescent rebellion, social change, political dissent, religious movements, dress codes, and sexual mores would all become the subjects of criminology.[14]

"Crime is conduct which offends pity or probity." Raffaele Garofalo, a proponent of the positivist school of criminology and a renowned colleague of Lombroso, proposed that we depart from legal definitions of crime and address our efforts towards explaining "natural crime." Natural crime consists of conduct that offends the moral sentiments of pity and probity. By offending the moral sentiment of pity he meant our revulsion against the infliction of suffering on other people. By probity, he meant honesty, and was referring to respect for the property rights of others. A criminal is a person who lacks the moral sentiments of pity and probity. Here, Garofalo is following Durkheim's lead, but does not go as far as Sellin, since he does not propose to study all cultural deviation.[15]

"Crimes are acts of force and fraud undertaken in the pursuit of self interest." Gottfredson and Hirschi have offered us one more distillation of the essence of crime. It includes both more and less than legal definitions of crime. This definition focuses on those antisocial behaviors for which there is strong cultural consensus and on those behaviors that we are really concerned about, crimes like rape, robbery, theft, and murder, while allowing us to eliminate those acts of civil disobedience and conscience which involve neither force nor fraud nor self interest alone. Still we cannot eliminate all ambiguity from our pursuit of crime, even with this excellent effort, since, for example, defending oneself from attack is an act of force in pursuit of self interest, but no one would consider it a crime.[16]

"Crime is a reaction to the life conditions of a person's social class," writes the radical criminologist, William Chambliss.[17] To him, criminal behavior is a result of the oppressive efforts of the ruling class to control the lower classes, to maintain their economic advantages, and to prevent nonconformity and revolutionary change. It would be unthinking to label this point of view as Marxist and summarily dismiss it. I have spent more than 25 years inside prisons of all sorts and it is indeed a very rare event to find a prison inmate from "the ruling classes." Does this mean that the upper classes are of such high moral character that criminal behavior does not occur among them except rarely? No one thinks so. Sutherland, in developing his ideas about white collar crime, reminds us of Colonel Vanderbilt's rhetorical question, "You don't suppose that you can run a railroad according to the statutes, do you?"[18] But I do not think that crime is explained by class struggle. The prosecution and punishment of criminals is without doubt class oriented, but it has never been demonstrated that the *occurrence* of crime is a class phenomenon. Therefore there is a proper place for Chambliss's point of view in the wider world of criminology, but it does not explain crime.

"Crime is a disorder," proposes Adrian Raine. "...[M]any instances of repeated criminal behavior, including theft and burglary, may represent a disorder or psychopathology in much the same way that depression, schizophrenia, or other conditions currently recognized as mental disorders represent psychopathologies."[19] This is the approach of many psychologists and psychiatrists and is based on their observations that criminals, especially repeat offenders, differ from ordinary people in important ways. It is also based on the conclusion of many average citizens that a person has got to be sick to do some of those things. Raine concludes that we need to increase our research and clinical efforts to understand and treat crime. The idea that crime is a disorder that can be treated is yet another specimen in our collection.

"Criminality is generally the result of a basic deficiency in conscience, a failure to internalize elementary inhibitions."[20] This view is proposed by the famous researchers William and Joan McCord. This effort is really only a short step away from "crime is an offense against morality." I once heard an Islamic prison chaplain respond to the question of what causes crime. His laconic reply, instantly delivered, was, "bad morals."

The study of crime cannot be "freed from subjective moral judgment" because that is precisely what it is. The behavior itself is neither criminal nor noncriminal; it is our judgment about the behavior that makes it one or the other. Jeffrey argues, "The reason we have crime, however, is not because individuals behave in the way they do, but because others think they ought not to behave in that way and have it in their power to judge their behavior."[21] This is one of the reasons that the study of crime is so interesting and also so difficult. It is an intersection where science crosses moral values. Most criminologists would like to stay on the road of science, but we cannot ignore the intersection. The argument about whether a science of crime is possible at all is an old one, and if there is "free will," science cannot account for this factor.

"Crimes are acts that may be rewarding to the actor but that inflict pain or loss on others; that is, criminal behavior is antisocial behavior," write the Canadian psychologists Don Andrews and James Bonta.[22] This is a refinement of our common sense criminology. This point of view focuses us on what we are really concerned about; antisocial acts for which there is large and widespread condemnation, historically and cross-culturally, while allowing us to take out of consideration, without getting confused, certain acts that are violations of the law in a certain time and place, but that most persons would not consider crimes; for example, acts of civil disobedience, expressions of religious freedom, and petty violations of local ordinances. Despite an abundance of variation in specific prohibitions, there is a core cultural consensus, from time to time, and from place to place, on issues of antisocial behavior such as theft, fraud, assault, rape, robbery, and murder. Sanctions against these forms of behavior are cross-cultural and the similarities are stronger and more striking than the differences.

"Crime is that behavior condemned by society," write Wilson and Herrnstein; "it occurs despite the rewards and punishments that we have devised to enforce that condemnation."[23] With this definition, the professors intend to open the door to economic and psychological explanations of crime. Stanton Samenow, author of *The Criminal Personality*, suggests that a crime is a violation of the rights of other people, and that a criminal is a person who consistently violates the rights of others.[24] This definition has the simplicity that I admire, and I think that it focuses us on the proper subjects of criminology, but what are the rights of other people?

The foregoing are only some samples from the collection, but for now, let's put up the old bones, close the lid on Pandora's Box, and consider where we are. Undaunted by academic disputes, I believe that we can refine our thinking, respect the discovery of new facts, and retain our moral values at the same time. I can decline to be confused by sweeping statements about human behavior that are not relevant to the crimes that concern the vast majority of us and the crimes to which we are almost universally opposed. I can agree with Jeffrey, who argues that a general theory of human behavior cannot explain crime because a theory of human behavior cannot tell you why the behavior is criminal.[25] I can acknowledge areas of ambiguity without abandoning moral principles altogether. I can respect data without acquiescing to the demand that a complete suspension of moral judgment is necessary in order to accurately perceive reality. Indeed, in the study of crime, I cannot suspend moral judgment.

The best course to follow is to think for ourselves. I will hold in the back of my mind that definitions of crime can fall into illegal, immoral, unconventional, and antisocial categories and that, whichever category you pick, objections will be raised by someone. I will fully acknowledge the problems that emerge from an intensive study of crime, including the criminologists' complaint, as Gottfredson and Hirschi have said it, that we do not control our own dependent variable.[26] The definition of crime is not a scientific definition, but is inevitably a moral and political one.

I will remember the legal distinction called *mala in se*, a crime which is "evil in itself," as opposed to crimes that are *mala prohibita*, prohibited within a particular cultural and historical context. I will agree with Andrews and Bonta that "[a] major task for philosophers, historians and social and behavioral scientists in criminology is to more fully understand the definitional problems associated with crime," but I will not retire from the debate in confusion.[27] When an itinerant worker robs and kills a family of five, I am sure that this is a crime. And I "mightily desire to know" what the cause of it is.

If we cannot agree on what crime is, how can we then know who is a criminal?

Who Is a Criminal?

Even criminals are against crime. Ray was a 29-year-old inmate who is a member of my treatment group at a medium security prison. I asked Ray what he would do if someone broke into his locker in the dormitory and took his belongings.

"I would stab him," replied Ray, with an angry edge to his voice. "I wouldn't let anyone do that to me. It's wrong. You can't live in here and let people do that to you."

Ray is serving his second prison sentence for breaking and entering. By his own count, he has committed 46 Breaking and Enterings (he may be bragging a little), but he has been convicted of only five of them. He is not aware of any irony in our conversation.

In the first session of a new group, I routinely ask each of the men to answer the question "Are you a criminal?" It is predictable that each one of them will say that he is not a criminal, even though the eight men in this group have a total of 54 convictions on record and have been sentenced collectively to nearly 100 years in prison. It happens again in this group, as expected, each man answering that he is not a criminal. The only exception is Charles, a 52-year-old thief who describes himself, while smiling broadly, as a "retired criminal." The next question in my routine is "Do you know anyone who is a criminal?" They report that they all know other men who are criminals and that, in fact, most of the other inmates in this prison are criminals. I disguise my amusement at this report and go on to my next question, "Who is a criminal?"

Ray answers, "Someone who does something really serious, like killing someone."

Tommy, a 20-year-old bank robber, says, "Someone who does a lot of crimes, like all the time."

Larry, a 41-year-old sex offender, replies, "A criminal is someone who rips off other people."

Charles, the 52-year-old "retired criminal," says, "I used to be a criminal because I just didn't care, but I do care now. I'm different now."

Frank, 35 years old, convicted of second degree murder, states, "A criminal would be, if you came to prison and got out, and then you came back to prison again, then you would be a criminal."

Maurice, a 25-year-old, convicted of assault, answers, "Someone who doesn't give a shit about anything."

Hinton, a 28-year-old drug dealer, offers, "Someone who hurts other people."

Mike, a 30-year-old convicted of assault, says, "Somebody who does something more than once."

As I expect from experience, each man defines "a criminal" in such a way that it does not apply to him but does apply to others at the same prison unit. This is because, as any of them will tell you, they are against crime. I next tell them that most people in society would consider them all to be criminals who should be in prison. They become visibly agitated at this declaration and the discussion becomes lively and heated. Everyone participates except for Maurice, who is silent and bristling with hostility. The session is tough, though not without its humorous moments, usually provided by Charles, who is more articulate than the others and is very pleased with his self appointed status as "retired criminal." Thus does the gritty work of treatment in prison begin again.

This group did produce the usual answers that are provided by most people, in or out of prison, to the question "Who is a criminal?" A criminal is someone who commits serious crimes, someone who commits many crimes, someone who is a prison recidivist, someone who has criminal attitudes and values, or someone whose livelihood is crime. One researcher suggests that a criminal is a person whose patterns of thinking have led to arrestable behavior.[28] These definitions seem straightforward enough, and the average citizen does not appear confused when asked "who is a criminal?" But there are some problems lurking here for the study of the causes of crime.

In a strictly legal sense, a criminal is anyone who has been convicted of a crime, any crime. But, like the legal definition of crime, the legal meaning of criminal will prove to include both too much and too little. To begin with, is a person who commits crimes and is not caught, and therefore has never been convicted of anything, a criminal? Large national surveys have consistently shown that there is a significant amount of crime not reported to the police, another large group of crimes that are reported but that do not result in an arrest, and another group that results in arrest but not in conviction. Someone once quipped that criminology is the study of the caught. Is it reasonable to assume that many criminals are not caught and that there might be something systematically different about criminals who are not apprehended as opposed to criminals who are? Certainly it is reasonable to think along these lines. We must be aware that the fact of getting caught is central to our present knowledge of the criminal. Criminologists have wrestled with this problem, and some attempts to develop a method for studying "uncaught" criminals have been made, most notably by Sutherland, who was very concerned about the problem of the nonadjudicated criminal, and by Widom.[29] These attempts have not solved the problem, however, and we should not forget about this bias when reviewing our knowledge of the criminal.

What about the mentally ill and the mentally handicapped? If they commit a crime, do we include them as criminals? Is our explanation for their criminal behavior the same as for those offenders with normal intelligence and without any sign of mental disorder? Our fixation on reducing recidivism has led us to focus on repeat offenders. Is a first offender a criminal? In prison work, *first offender* typically refers to someone in prison for the first time. But this person usually has prior arrests and convictions that did not result in incarceration. Is he a criminal, even though technically a first offender? Do we mean to exclude from our understanding of "criminal" the 30–40 percent of offenders who are incarcerated only once and do not return to prison again? This is the group of offenders that might teach us the most about preventing recidivism, but this group is rarely the object of study. What about age? Can a 10-year-old be a criminal? At what age is a person a criminal? In order to study criminality, we must decide who is a criminal, and we will have as much trouble with that decision as we had with the definition of crime.

The Mighty Opposites: Choice and Causation

I prefer to use, as a learning aid, and not with any claim that it depicts the true nature of reality, a continuum of choice. This continuum of choice has fate on one of its ends and choice on the other. These are the mighty opposites, choice and fate, free will and determinism. They are mighty because each has powerful arguments on its behalf, and because we have investigated and debated their respective contributions to criminal behavior, indeed, to all of human behavior, with much passion and for a long time.

Aristotle thought that a science of human behavior was not possible because such a science could never account for the unpredictability of free will. Herbert Spencer, a nineteenth century philosopher who is credited with extending evolutionary theory into the realm of human social behavior, argued that no free will is possible if human behavior conforms to scientific laws.[30] Stephen Hawking, the famous contemporary physicist, suggests that we say that people have free will whenever we cannot predict what they will do.[31] But, perhaps, choice is not such a sharp dichotomy and is more like a dimension. I prefer a middle path between these two extremes: that no science of human behavior is possible or that no free will exists. The continuum of choice is a visualization of this middle path; it portrays the concept that choice and causation may coexist in a single action.

Any behavior of an individual may be understood as falling at some point along this continuum, though for our purposes, we are thinking of criminal behavior. The advantage of conceiving behavior in this way is that a person's behavior may be seen as having some element of choice and some element that is not entirely under the person's control. For what behaviors are so freely chosen that there are no determining factors at all? Any behavior can be analyzed as a chain of cause and effect leading backwards through a person's life until some element not under his control is encountered, though it may be, perhaps, only a very small influence on the behavior under analysis. On the other side, what behaviors are so completely determined that there is no choice at all? There are some behaviors that we understand as completely determined, muscle reflexes for example, but it certainly has not been demonstrated that any criminal

The Continuum of Choice

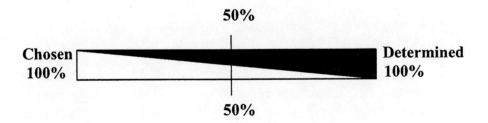

behaviors would fall in this category. Though a case might be made for some types of human behavior to fall into either extreme, complete choice or complete determination, the preponderance of criminal behavior would not fall in either extreme. Even if I could imagine a criminal act that would be an exception to this point of view, it would not destroy the usefulness of the continuum as a way of organizing our thinking about the causes of crime.

Here are two cases that illustrate the dilemma posed by the mighty opposites in ordinary lives, the twin scenarios of Gary G. and Gary F.

Gary G. is the oldest child of two wedded parents. His father, 34 years old at the time of Gary's birth, is a successful accountant. His mother, 31 when Gary is born, is an accomplished musician who has chosen to stay at home and raise a family. There is no history of alcoholism or conviction for crimes on either side of the family as far as anyone knows. The parents receive excellent prenatal care, including night classes on birthing and parenting. Gary has a normal delivery and is the healthy baby boy of proud parents.

Until the age of four, Gary G. is raised at home with the daily care and attention of his mother and father. Upon reaching age five, Gary G. is placed in a select half-day preschool program that is staffed by experienced and dedicated teachers. At age six, he enters the best public school in the city. Throughout elementary school, he is an A student in most subjects. His mother encourages his musical interests and he plays the trumpet in the school orchestra. His father encourages his athletic interests and coaches the junior soccer team on which Gary G. is a player. His family are members of a local church and Gary G. attends church camp each year. The camp stresses moral standards of behavior.

Through middle school and high school, Gary G. maintains his above average academic standing. His parents remain happily married and are financially prosperous. Gary G. continues with his interests in soccer and the trumpet. Since his parents and his friends do not smoke, Gary G. has decided that he does not like cigarettes and he does not smoke. His parents are moderate drinkers and Gary G. does try alcohol, primarily beer, while in high school. He drinks occasionally with his friends at parties. He has tried both marijuana and Ecstasy and enjoyed their effects, but he limits his drug use to occasionally on weekends. His attitude toward drug use is, "I don't want to mess up my life getting high all the time." Gary G. has had no contact at all with the police except for the driver's license examiner who gave him his driving test. He passed.

Both of Gary G.'s parents are college graduates and Gary G. also plans to attend. He is accepted at a good university and goes there after graduating from high school. He studies hard and makes above average grades. In the more permissive college environment, he continues to experiment with drugs, alcohol, and sex. He eventually rejects illegal drugs as too dangerous, drinks moderately, and spends most of his time with a steady girlfriend. His social science courses strike an interest in him and he begins to concentrate his courses in those areas.

His introductory sociology class includes a tour of a local prison, which impresses Gary G. He is reminded of some young men he knew in high school who were engaged in delinquent behavior. He begins to read about crime and criminals. He sees several excellent movies in which a criminal is the principal character. He takes a criminology course, which fascinates him. The course is taught by a dynamic and personable professor who influences and encourages him. Gary G. decides to become a criminologist and applies to graduate school in his senior year of college. His parents are very approving of his plans and offer him financial support. He is accepted by a criminology graduate program. He decides that in order to maintain his credibility and integrity as a professional criminologist, he must obey the law himself, so he does not engage in any illegal behavior, even minor drug violations. After five years of study, he is awarded a Ph.D. His dissertation is titled "Criminals from Birth: The Genetics of Crime." He is offered a full time position as a professor at one of the smaller campuses of the state university. He is 26 years old. Why did Gary G. become a criminologist and not a criminal?

Gary F. is born to an unwed mother who is 16 years old at the time of his birth and who has already dropped out of high school. His maternal grandfather is an alcoholic and he has two uncles who have served time in prison. Gary F.'s father, aged 24, is in prison serving his second sentence for larceny. Gary F.'s mother briefly considered an abortion until she received a letter from Gary F.'s father in prison. He wrote to her, "If you kill my baby, I'll never forget it." He is never involved in Gary F.'s life at any point. His mother received no prenatal care at all. The delivery is difficult and the nurses in attendance note that the mother seems less than thrilled with the baby.

Gary F.'s childhood is chaotic. His mother has a succession of live-in boyfriends, some of whom are alcoholic and some of whom are batterers. His mother frequently leaves him for days at a time with relatives or obliging neighbors. Once, when Gary F. is five years old, she leaves him in a parked car, forgetting to pull down the emergency brake. The car eventually rolls down hill and smashes into another car. Gary F., who does not have on a seat belt, is thrown against the dashboard and receives a severe concussion requiring hospitalization.

He receives no preschool education. His grandfather gives him his first taste of beer at age six. When, at the age of seven, he enters one of the poorest schools in the city, he is restless and disruptive in class, and has many absences from school. An especially dedicated third grade teacher thinks that he may have a learning disability, but this suggestion is never followed up by the overworked school staff. By middle school, he has been suspended several times for fighting and for disrupting class. Even though he has above average intelligence, he reads below the expected grade level. He does not participate in sports, having been kicked off the football team for arguing with the coach and for breaking training rules. He does not participate in any extracurricular activities. He does not attend church. After school, he associates with boys several years older who are already involved in delinquent and gang activities. He begins smoking cigarettes every day at age 13. At this age, he also has sexual intercourse for the first time, being initiated by an older girl in the neighborhood, well known for her promiscuous behavior. He is arrested for the first time at age 14 for stealing a six-pack of beer from the grocery store. He is rude and sarcastic to the police who then treat him roughly. He is released to the custody of his mother. At the end of the year, he is socially promoted to high school.

By now, his mother's drinking problem has reached alcoholic proportions. Gary F. skips school and stays away from home for days at a time. By age 15, Gary F. drinks beer every day and smokes marijuana on most days. He is sexually promiscuous, mostly with prostitutes or with girls several years younger than he is. When he reaches the age of 16, he drops out of school. He decides to make money by selling marijuana, chiefly to high school students that he knows. He lives the street life until age 18, when he is robbed of a recently acquired stash of expensive high quality marijuana given to him on credit to sell on the street. This puts him in the dangerous position of owing money to a big time drug dealer. To get out of this quandary, he decides to rob a convenience store. He is filmed robbing the store by the store's video camera. He is identified, arrested, and convicted of armed robbery. He serves eight years in the state prison and is released on parole. He has a job at minimum wage at a fast food restaurant. His total assets are several hundred dollars he managed to save while in prison. He is living in a rented apartment with his mother in the poorest section of the city. At this point, his risk for continuing criminal behavior is sky high. He is 26 years old, the same age at which Gary G. receives his Ph.D. and teaching position. Why did Gary F. become a criminal and not a criminologist?

These two case examples are hypothetical, but they are wholly plausible. Both choice and fate were involved in each of the two cases, but the weight of determining factors in both cases is heavy. Gary F. could have chosen to stay in school and he could have chosen to make money by getting a job rather than by selling marijuana or robbing a store. Gary G. could have chosen to abuse drugs and to pay for them by committing crimes. The choices that each one made were crucial in the unfolding of their lives, yet the choices that each made were not unpredictable and were not made in a vacuum empty of powerful influences. In fact, they both seemed to have been propelled in opposite directions by biological and social forces not of their choosing. So the question is not choice or fate, but how much choice and how much fate? How much freely chosen and how much predetermined? This is the reason that the continuum of choice is a more useful guide to our thinking about crime and criminals than is a simple dichotomy.

There is yet another factor that has its influence over the outcome: randomness. Suppose that Gary G.'s first criminology professor had happened to be a poor teacher, dull, arrogant and unsympathetic, and Gary G. decides that criminology is not for him. He stops going to his criminology class altogether and then fails the final exam. Making a F ruins his grade average, and he feels that his grades are beyond repair. He becomes discouraged, then restless and rebellious. His grades decline and he decides to leave college. He begins to hang out with other college dropouts, some of whom are dealing drugs to make a living. They remind him of the movies that he has seen that depicted criminals as heroes, and the street life begins to look glamorous to him. He moves gradually from the margins of the street life into the middle of the drug culture. But he is not streetwise, and soon he is snared by a police sting operation. He receives a five-year sentence in prison from an exceptionally harsh judge who was running for reelection that year on a get-tough-with-criminals platform. Gary G. is now a criminal instead of a criminologist.

On the other hand, consider again the case of Gary F., who had decided to rob a convenience store in order to be able to repay a drug dealer to whom he owed money. Suppose that when he arrives at the store for the big moment he finds a police squad car parked in front of the store, with one officer in the car and a second officer inside the store, buying a cup of coffee. Gary F. hesitates, loiters a few minutes, and then walks swiftly away down the street. The incident terrifies him. He decides that the street life is not for him. He throws his pistol in a dumpster along the street and feels great relief. He resolves to change his way of life and walks to a halfway house he passed by in the neighborhood. He goes right in and asks for help. A sympathetic and savvy counselor helps him to start a new life, including employment and night college classes. He is so impressed by his counselor that he decides to finish college and get a job like his counselor, working with down and out criminals. His first criminology class is excellent and he feels genuine excitement about it. Since he actually has no criminal record at this point (except a juvenile record), he sees no obstacle to achieving his goals. He persists through to graduation. Gary F. is now a criminologist instead of a criminal.

So to choice and fate we must add chance. It is not realistic to dismiss the influence that chance factors can have over human decisions and outcomes; yet, unlike some philosophers, I am not willing to concede that chaos is king. Criminals themselves often prefer chance explanations of their behavior ("I was in the wrong place at the wrong time") and I have spent an entire career combating this explanation for criminality, one inmate at a time, all the while knowing that chance is a indeed a factor, though not the crucial one. For our continuum of choice, chance is subsumed on the fate end. Chance is not the same as predetermination, but it is not chosen. Thus, the end of our continuum opposite to choice, or free will, might also be called "not chosen," including factors which are predetermining and factors which are attributable to chance. The crucial factor is choice, since choice is all that the person can add to the equation. Admittedly, in some circumstances, there is very little choice, but, even in those situations, there is some, and that is a crucial ingredient.

To be sure, using the continuum of choice as a way of organizing our thinking does not solve all of our problems. It raises some difficult questions of its own. Are quantitative judgments of observed behavior, such as the percentages on our continuum, really possible? It is common practice in the social sciences to make quantitative judgments about all kinds of behavior. For example, in a typical study of attitude changes, a numerical value is assigned to degrees of liking, such as Not Like At All = 1, Like Somewhat = 3, and Like Very Much = 5. These quantitative assignments enable us to apply the mathematics of probability to the results and thus justify our claim to having produced scientific evidence. If this kind of experiment is basically meaningless, then much of social science research is meaningless and we are back where we started with Aristotle's doubt. Is a science of criminology possible?

Another problem is brought out by this question: Where on this continuum does criminal culpability begin? Even if we accept this way of understanding criminal behavior, we are still left with value judgments to make. Where on the continuum must the behavior fall in order for the person to be held responsible for his crime? Jurors struggle with this kind of judgment, though they may not be thinking of it in exactly the same way as I have outlined it here. With respect to criminal behavior, there is no escape from moral judgment. And this really is to the point. "There is nothing either good or bad, but our thinking makes it so," says Horatio in *Hamlet*. A general theory of choice still cannot tell you why the behavior is criminal or where on the continuum personal responsibility begins or ends.

The continuum of choice may also be used on another level; to organize causal theories of crime. Theories of the causes of criminal behavior can be placed along this continuum according to the degree to which the theory attributes behavior to free will and choice, or to fate and determinism. On the predetermined end of our continuum will be found predispositions of all types, including biological (heredity, constitution), psychological (personality traits, learning), and sociological (social forces). On the chosen end of our continuum will be found enlightened self interest, rational calculation, moral judgment, and sin.

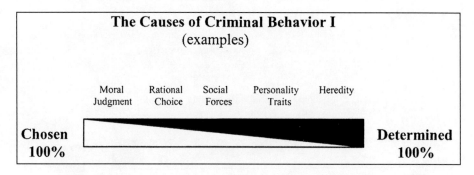

Those theories, or explanations, for criminal behavior that lend significant weight to free will and choice are generally termed as being of the classical school. Those tending strongly towards destiny and determinism are thought of as belonging to the positivist school. Some theories attempt to give significant weight to both and thus fall towards the middle

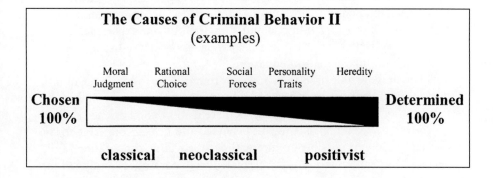

range of our continuum. Such theories are sometimes called *neoclassical* or are said to represent a *soft determinism.* (Some social scientists would argue that social forces may operate as inevitably as biological traits and therefore should be depicted on the determined end of our continuum rather than toward the middle, as I have done in the illustration above. Without rejecting this point, I have let the illustration remain as it is for the sake of simplicity.)

Lombroso's theory of the born criminal, for example, fell at the far end of the positivist dimension. However, in response to many criticisms of his theory, Lombroso gave considerable weight to social factors in his later work, moving his explanation of crime towards the center of our continuum.

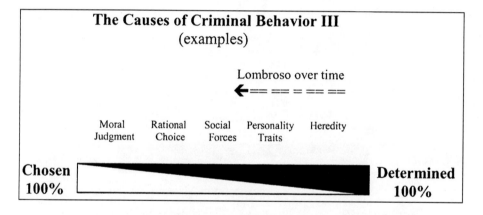

Leaning to one side or the other does have consequences. A positivist point of view certainly implies that the criminal is not at fault and that his behavior can be changed using scientific methods. It also suggests that we should be focusing our efforts and resources on the discovery of new facts, and new cause and effect relationships. It suggests that crime is both preventable and curable, though the methods for doing so remain to be discovered. This is a grand hope, not supported by our experience so far. As Hawking writes, we have not been very good at predicting human behavior from mathematical equations.[32]

For those who lean to the choice, or free will side of our continuum, there are different implications. Crime is not completely preventable, for there will be some crime for as long as there is some choice. The criminal is believed to be responsible for his behavior and held accountable for it. Change is thought possible but not without the willing cooperation of the person. Moral judgment cannot be isolated from our understanding of the behavior, for we must admit that the reason we are so concerned about this behavior is because it is criminal, that is, as Samenow puts it, it is a violation of the rights of other people.

With the continuum of choice, we have not settled the debate between the mighty opposites, but we can organize our thinking about them, evaluate theories of crime, and support our own views. We can place new announcements about the causes of crime in perspective and we can apprehend where they are leading us. Finally, we can see and appreciate explanations of crime that allow for choice and causation to coexist in a single act.

I propose no final resolution to the timeless debate between the mighty opposites; wiser heads than ours have addressed these issues with logic, wit, and eloquence, but without carrying the day for either side. I expect the debate to continue into the forseeable future, even beyond the discovery of a gene for criminality. Even if such a discovery should be made, it would not settle this argument once and for all, because even genetic predispositions do not produce certainties in behavior. For our present purposes, I recommend a healthy respect for each end of the continuum, a quick suspicion of anyone who clings too tightly to either side, and a keen sense of anticipation in the unfolding of this great debate. For my own part, I am only suggesting, in accordance with the advice of Sutherland, that we organize our thinking about the causes of crime. With the continuum of choice, we have some help in accomplishing that purpose.

The One and the Many: Models of Causation

As we have already said, the classicists were not much concerned with discovering the cause of crime as they assumed that it was a calculated choice and did not inquire further. The positivists, however, believed that criminal behavior is determined or caused by something. It is the search for this thing that causes crime that has produced the long list presented at the beginning of this chapter, but the search so far has not led to a single destination.

A profusion of problems have emerged. One of these, already discussed in an earlier section, is the definition of crime. If we are not sure what it is that we are trying to explain, it will obviously be hard to satisfactorily explain it. Another difficulty is the application of scientific method to the problem of crime. The strongest and most convincing experimental method is to randomly assign subjects to treatment conditions and then compare the effects of the various treatments on the subject of interest.

This true experimental design is the basic language of proof in the scientific sense. This experimental design, with sufficient replication, satisfies the three criteria of causation: (1) there must be a demonstrated association or connection between the cause and the effect, (2) it must be established that the cause preceded the effect, and (3) the connection between the cause and the effect must not disappear when the influences of other variables are taken into account. This means that when two variables are associated, it is possible that the preceding variable, the variable that occurs first, may not be causal. There could be a third variable, which precedes both of them, that is the real causal agent. In graduate school, we learned to refer to this possibility as "suspicion of a lurking third variable." Thus any causal inferences made from the discovery of the association between the two variables may well be spurious, that is, false or misleading.

Let's try a simple example. How would we prove the effectiveness of a medication for allergies? Is medication A more effective than no treatment at all in relieving allergic symptoms? Or, to state it somewhat differently, is medication A the cause of the relief of the allergic symptoms? The first task is to define allergic symptoms and concomitantly to define relief of those symptoms. The second task is to identify a group of subjects who have these symptoms. The next task is to assign subjects at random to one of two groups: the experimental group that receives medication A or the control group that receives no treatment at all. Then the medication is administered to the experimental group and a placebo is administered to the control group. Thus we know that the cause (medication A) preceded the effect (relief of allergic symptoms). Then we observe the results by measuring the relief of allergic symptoms for each of the subjects in each group. If the number of subjects in the experimental group (the group that received medication A) who experienced relief of the allergic symptoms is significantly higher than in the group that received no treatment at all, then medication A is the cause of the relief of the allergic symptoms. Note that this association or connection need not be perfect and hardly ever is. Some subjects in the experimental group (who received medication A) may not experience relief of allergic symptoms and conversely, some subjects in the control group (who got the placebo) might experience relief of allergic symptoms. But the effect is established if there is a significant difference between the two groups in the expected direction. What protects against lurking third variables is the random assignment of subjects to groups (assuming there was no preselection bias). Then this experiment is replicated, which means that it is repeated exactly, with different subjects randomly assigned to groups, and with the same results obtained. Thus there is scientific proof that medication A is effective for (is the cause of) the relief of allergic symptoms.

Now, how do we obtain scientific proof of the cause of crime? The thoughtful reader will already begin to see the difficulties. Let's take, for example, the popular proposition that crime is caused by broken homes. Why can't we obtain scientific proof beyond dispute regarding the truth or falsity of this proposition? Because it is quite impracticable. The first task is to define crime and we have already seen how that is not as simple as it appears at first. Especially we must keep in mind the difference between crime and criminality, between the acts and the actors. However, the definitional problem is not insurmountable, so long as we remember that whatever results we obtain are applicable strictly to crime as we chose to define it in this experiment and not to any other concept of what crime is. The reader will immediately perceive that that leaves plenty of room for argument about the results of the experiment. Next we would identify a group of subjects and randomly assign them to a broken home or a stable home. There's the difficulty. How do you assign subjects randomly to a broken home? You cannot. The best that you can do is to select subjects who came from a broken home and subjects who came from a stable home and compare them. But this opens the door wide for lurking third variables! You might be able to show that there is an association between broken homes and crime, as indeed some social scientists have, but you cannot feel confident that there is not a third variable that precedes them both and is the true cause of crime. In fact, there is good reason to suspect that this is the case, because of the large number of people who come from broken homes but who are not criminals. Therefore you cannot furnish scientific proof that broken homes cause crime. This is why Sutherland wrote that criminology is not yet a science but has hopes of becoming one.[33]

So what do you do? Some social scientists will argue that there are acceptable ways around these problems, but that point is precisely where we descend into that "tangled wilderness of technical and inconclusive debate." If it were really that easy to circumvent these problems and still obtain scientific proof beyond reasonable dispute, then we would know a lot more about the causes of crime than we know now. What we have instead are various proposals for getting around these problems, including quasiexperimental designs, nonexperimental designs, and such like. The use of these research designs results in numerous heated arguments about their validity and relevance in discovering the cause of crime in the scientific sense of proof.

There is an additional complication in identifying the cause of crime, namely, that there may be more than one. In thinking about crime, or any human behavior for that matter, there is often a strong tendency to over-simplify, to seek a single underlying principle or explanation. This is the problem of the one and the many: is there a single cause of crime or are there multiple causes of crime? And if there are multiple causes of crime rather than a single cause of crime, what is to be our method of discovery?

It is my inclination to argue against a root cause of crime. I admit that this bias is the result of my own personal experience with crime and criminals as well as my reading of the data. There have been some good efforts at a single theory of crime, most notably Sutherland's theory of differential association, mainly of historical significance now, and Gottfredson and Hirschi's self control theory, a valiant attempt at a general principle, which I admire and which has much to recommend it. Each of these theories is discussed in detail in later sections. And there have been other efforts as well. But I must admit that I am not inclined in that direction. Sutherland says, "Just as the germ theory of disease does not explain all diseases, so it is possible that no one theory of criminal behavior will explain all criminal behavior. In that case, it will be desirable to define the area to which the theory applies, so that the several theories are coordinate and, when taken together, explain all criminal behavior."[34] So we have added another level of complexity to our search — but then no one said it would be easy!

Consider this example. Suppose that we have five cases of homicide. In the first case, John L., who is a paranoid schizophrenic with a long history of treatment, shoots and kills one of his neighbors. During the shooting, John L. experiences extreme anxiety and paranoia, and hears command hallucinations in which insistent voices were telling him to kill or be killed. In the second case, Judy Y. shoots and kills her drunken and abusive husband after he had beaten her up (one of numerous beatings) and had threatened to do it again "tomorrow." In the third case, Jimmy G. gets into a fight in a local bar with another customer. Both men are intoxicated. Jimmy G. pulls out a knife and slashes his opponent a total of 16 times, and the victim dies on the way to the hospital. In the fourth case, Marvin T. accepts a contract of $50,000 to kill a potential witness in a drug trafficking case and he completes the contract. Marvin is caught when an associate is arrested on unrelated charges and "gives him up." In the fifth case, Richard D. robs a convenience store with a handgun in order to get cash to pay a drug dealer. The store clerk reaches under the counter to push a police alert button and Richard D. shoots and kills him.

Is there a single theory of crime to explain all of these behaviors? They are all crimes. They would all be included in crime statistics of all sorts:

arrest rates, conviction rates, violent crime rates, murder rates, incarceration rates. Yet it seems improbable that the same behavioral explanation would be satisfactory in each case. Still we might choose to search for the single cause of crime. Committed scientists certainly desire to discover universal laws. A unified theory of the universe is the grand challenge of physics, but who can name the Isaac Newton, the Max Planck, or the Albert Einstein of criminology? It may be that we cannot so name anyone because criminology is such a young science, but it may also be because proof in the scientific sense is not applicable to many of the problems in criminology.

We might accept that there are many causes of crime and start to make divisions in our investigations. If we take this approach, we can choose to focus on the offenses or we can choose to study the offenders. Some criminologists approach this problem by saying that we are not trying to explain all of these crimes with a general theory of crime. John L. is clearly mentally ill and needn't be included in our study. Judy Y. is guilty only of self defense and shouldn't be included as she is not really a killer or a menace to society. Jimmy G. has substance abuse problems, was in a fit of passion, and was maybe only defending himself. Only Marvin T. is a calculating, premeditating first degree murderer. And actually, a convicted contract killer is not all that common among murderers in prison. Marvin T. would be an exception in a group of incarcerated killers, and a criminologist might say we are not trying to explain the exceptions. The crime of Richard D., called a felony murder, is a more common form of homicide and, some would argue, we should be concerned only with explaining the more common forms. That's one approach to the problem: categorize the offenses in such a way as to eliminate the ones that are problematic for a single theory of crime. In other words, we could define and redefine the dependent variable, crime.

Another approach is to categorize the offenders rather than the offenses. Categorizing offenders is such a popular pastime that a good deal of the criminological literature is taken up with it. There are reasons for categorizing offenders other than explaining crime. For example, offenders might be placed into like groups in order to make prison management more efficient or in order to deliver treatment services more effectively. For now, however, it suffices to note that sometimes this is a way of organizing multiple explanations for crime. To apply our examples, we might say that Marvin T. and Richard D. are the true criminals, Judy Y. is a case of domestic abuse, Jimmy G. is a case of substance abuse, and John L. has a diagnosable mental illness. So there is a different explanation for each group. Also perhaps there is still room for some choices made by the offenders in all of these cases.

I am not suggesting that scientific investigations of the causes of crime are useless enterprises. Indeed, I believe that it is worthwhile to struggle with these problems and I believe that there are useful discoveries to be made. But I am trying to point out fundamental difficulties with which the experts struggle, to suggest some limitations that apply to the science of crime, and to help the reader to sharpen his own judgment about the current state of our knowledge of the causes of crime. I especially wish to inculcate in him a healthy skepticism concerning dramatic discoveries of the causes of crime, not to mention public policies that are based upon them. If we wait for science to discover the root cause of crime before we act decisively, later generations, who will be struggling with crime and studying its history, may very well depict our generation as sitting pensively by the roadside, as crime proliferates, turning over in our hands Dr. Lombroso's famous skull.

The Acts and the Actors: Crime and Criminality

It is important to know that crime and criminality are not the same thing and that our knowledge of the causes of crime can appear quite confused without understanding the difference. Criminality is the propensity of an individual person to commit crimes. Thus the study of criminality focuses on the individual offender, while the study of crime focuses on the offenses, such as aggregated crime rates. Having this distinction clearly in mind helps in understanding and evaluating explanations of crime, many of which are really explanations of criminality. Studying why crime increased during Prohibition and why it increased more in Chicago than in other cities results in a different kind of explanation, and suggests different courses of action, than does studying why certain individuals became bootleggers during the years of Prohibition. The first is a study of crime (crime rates) and the second is a study of criminality (the tendency of individuals to commit crimes). Lombroso is generally credited with having changed the focus of criminology from crime to the criminal, which Piers Bierne refers to as "the rise of *homo criminalis*," but neither kind of study is entirely satisfactory in isolation from the other.[35]

For example, Chaiken and Chaiken suggest the following: If a city has 3,000 burglars per 100,000 population, and on average each committed two burglaries a year, the city's burglary rate would be 6,000 per 100,000 population. Alternatively, if a city has 300 burglars per 100,000 population and each committed an average of 20 burglaries per year, the burglary rate would also be 6,000 per 100,000 population. In this example, at the level of aggregate crime rates, the two cities are nearly identical. However, this study would miss a significant difference in criminality at the level of individual analysis; criminality among the offenders in the two hypothetical cities is quite different and could very well suggest different courses of corrective action.[36]

Studying criminality in isolation from other factors is also insufficient. Hirschi and Gottfredson call this isolation "the fundamental mistake of modern theory." As an example, they summarize a theory of crime proposed by Cohen and Felson. The theory is that the commission of a crime requires (1) a motivated offender, (2) the absence of a capable guardian, and (3) a suitable target.[37] A study of the motivated offender, which would be a study of criminality, is not sufficient in itself to explain the burglary rate. We must attend to contextual and situational factors as well, such as suitability of the target and absence of a capable guardian. On the other hand, leaving out the study of the motivated offender would also lead to an insufficient understanding of the crime of burglary. "Crime and criminal behavior are confused," writes Jeffrey.[38] Are we explaining the acts or the actors? As we have seen, the classical school tended to focus on the acts and the positivist school tended to focus on the actors. To refine our thinking about the causes of crime, we must be alert to this particular confusion.

2

Schools of Criminology

Classical Criminology

The proponents of the classical school of criminology believed that human beings are moral agents possessed of free will and reason, and that people make their decisions based on a rational calculation of gain and loss. The two principal founders of this school were both eighteenth century students of law, the Englishman Jeremy Bentham and the Italian Cesare Beccaria. The ideas underlying the classical school of thought in criminology were not original with Bentham and Beccaria; the ideas and arguments were prominent in the intellectual ferment of the Enlightenment in Europe during the eighteenth century. But these two writers did produce very popular and influential books that made the debate about crime and punishment both public and urgent. The arguments presented in their writings were especially lucid and compelling. Bentham and Beccaria were primarily reformers who wanted to change a criminal justice system that they saw as harsh, discriminatory, and ineffective.

Beccaria

Properly titled, he was Cesare Bonesana, Marchese di Beccaria. But he has come down in history as simply Beccaria, a democratization of which he would certainly approve. He was a European aristocrat, born in Milan in 1748, but he was an aristocrat of the reformist type, as was his French contemporary, the Marquis de Lafayette. He was ripe for rebellion against the establishment, influenced by the chaos and cruelty of the criminal justice system of the eighteenth century, the ideas of the Enlightenment, the authoritarian dullness of his university education, and, perhaps, the opposition of his father to his marriage plans.[1] The Age of Enlightenment in Europe stretched from the philosophers Descartes and Spinoza in the seventeenth century to the French Revolution in 1789. Writers and activists of that period felt strongly that they were emerging from a time of darkness and ignorance into the light of reason, science, and respect for the common man. Impressed by new advances in science and technology, including the dramatic discoveries in physics by Isaac Newton, they were advocates for progress in all areas of human knowledge, and for the reform of political and religious institutions. It was an intellectual rebellion against religious authority and against governmental oppression. Beccaria formed his opinions by studying the leaders of this Enlightenment, especially the writings of the Baron de Montesquieu. Montesquieu was a French jurist and political philosopher who published *The Spirit of the Laws* in 1748, a work which exerted an important influence at the time.[2] He also wrote satirical pieces criticizing existing institutions. Beccaria says about Montesquieu that "truth, which is indivisible, has compelled me to follow in the shining path of this great man"[3]

Beccaria's principal foray down this shining path was his *Essay on Crimes and Punishments*, published in 1764. The great French philosopher Voltaire wrote a commentary on it in 1766 and afterwards this commentary and the *Essay* were frequently published together. In his book, Beccaria eloquently argued against the severities and abuses of the criminal law, especially capital punishment and torture. At that time, torture was a legal means of obtaining confessions and other trial evidence. The death sentence was prescribed for hundreds of crimes, including forgery, pickpocketing, counterfeiting, horse stealing, and various religious offences.[4] Beccaria's *Essay* became extremely popular and was translated into all of the European languages. His work became a guide for the reform of penal codes in many European countries. Its influence spread to the new American nation, where Beccaria's book was well known and was frequently quoted by Thomas Jefferson, Benjamin Franklin, and John Adams.[5]

If the Enlightenment in Europe was the general context for the *Essay*, then the specific context was the case of Jean Calas. In 1762 in France, the Huguenot Jean Calas was sentenced to death for the murder of his son. The prosecution argued that Calas had killed his son because the son had converted to Roman Catholicism. Voltaire took an interest in the case, and he was able to present evidence showing that the son had committed suicide. In a published work called *Treatise on Tolerance*, he argued against legally sanctioned torture and against religious intolerance. In a famous letter written to a friend, Jean d'Alembert, dated November, 1762, Voltaire again inveighed against religious persecution and against sanctioned torture in criminal trials and ended his letter with the expression "ecrasez l'infame" (stamp out the infamous thing), a phrase that later became a slogan of the French Revolution.[6] Four months after Voltaire's famous letter, Beccaria began his book.

Essay on Crimes and Punishments is a brilliantly reasoned, withering attack on the administration of justice, which Beccaria originally published anonymously, apparently for fear of retribution. He argued that the punishment should fit the crime and that a government did not have the legitimate authority to punish any more than was necessary to prevent the crime from occurring again.

"If we open our histories, we shall see that laws which are, or should be, pacts between free men, have for the most part been only the instrument of the passions of the few, or the product of an accidental and temporary need; they have never been dictated by a cool scrutineer of human nature, able to condense to one particular the activities of a multitude of men, and consider them from this point of view: *the greatest happiness of the greatest number.*"[7] What an original and appealing phrase: "a cool scrutineer of human nature"! In the "greatest happiness of the greatest number" we can see his relationship to Jeremy Bentham.

Beccaria continues in this vein, developing with persuasive reasoning and elegant, engaging prose, an argument against the criminal justice system at that time. The flavor of his famous *Essay*, the excellence of both his argument and his expression of it, can best be appreciated by digesting a sample. Below is a passage from his section on The Origin of Punishments:

> Laws are the conditions of that fellowship which unites men, hitherto independent and separate, once they have tired of living in a perpetual state of war and of enjoying a liberty rendered useless by the uncertainty of its preservation. They sacrifice a portion of this liberty so that they may enjoy the rest of it in security and peace. The sum of all these portions of liberty sacrificed for each individual's benefit constitutes the sovereignty of a nation, the sovereign is the lawful depository and administrator of these portions of liberty. But to constitute this deposit was not enough; it had to be defended from the private encroachment of each individual man, since the individual always tries not just to take back from the common store his own contributions, but to purloin that contributed by others. Palpable motive forces were therefore needed, sufficient to dissuade the arbitrary spirit of the individual from plunging society's laws once again into primitive chaos. These palpable motive forces are the punishments ordained against breakers of the law ... experience shows that the majority of men adopt no stable principles of conduct, and only evade that universal principle of dissolution, which is to be observed both in the moral and the physical world, if there exist motive forces which make an immediate impress on the senses and present themselves continually to the mind in such a way as to counterbal-

ance the strong effect of passions whose bias is opposed to the general good. Eloquence, declamation, even the most sublime truths, have not been enough to curb passions for any length of time when excited by the lively impact of present objects.

Since then it was necessity which compelled men to yield portions of their liberty, it is certain that the portion each man was willing to add to the common stock was the smallest possible — only as much, that is to say, as would induce others to defend the whole. The right to punish is the sum of these smallest possible portions. Anything above that sum is abuse, and not justice; a fact, but certainly not a right.

Punishments which go beyond the need of preserving the common store or deposit of public safety are in their nature unjust. The juster the punishments, the more sacred and inviolable the security and the greater the liberty which the sovereign preserves for his subjects.[8]

Beccaria then develops more specific arguments against the practices of his time. His arguments have a decidedly modern resonance. The law should apply equally to all regardless of social, economic or religious considerations. He argues against obscure laws, wide judicial discretion, overly severe punishments, and victimless crimes. He is very concerned about what constitutes evidence in a criminal trial and he argues for trial by jury. Concerning the deterrent power of the laws, Beccaria proposes that it is not the severity of the punishment that deters crime, but the certainty, the consistency, and the swiftness of the punishment. These ideas are the precursors of behavioral psychology and make Beccaria indeed "a cool scrutineer of human nature." He also argues that crime prevention is more efficacious than punishment of any kind.

He ends his *Essay* with this compelling sentence: "In order that punishment should never be an act of violence committed by one or many against a private citizen, it is essential that it be public, speedy, and necessary, as little as the circumstances will allow, proportionate to the crime, and established by law."[9]

As influential as the *Essay* has been, both then and now, there are dissenting voices. Graeme Newman, for example, writes that Beccaria's importance has been seriously overblown: "The majority of reforms that occurred during and soon after Beccaria's treatise can as easily be ascribed to prevailing social and political conditions as to Beccaria or his tract." Beccaria was a "pampered intellectual who had no first hand knowledge of the criminal justice system."[10] If that be true, he had something besides the principle of utility in common with Jeremy Bentham. Both had inherited wealth and could be charged with armchair criminology. David Jones writes that "Beccaria's popular success stemmed from what he wrote when and where he wrote it: he wrote on a stage prepared by Montesquieu and amplified by Voltaire. He wrote what his readership wanted to read. They adored what he wrote."[11]

And we still adore it. Beccaria is variously referred to as the leader of the classical school, the founder of the classical school, and the father of modern criminology. Jones reports that "most scholars agree that modern criminology came into being in 1764 with the publication at Liverno, Italy, of the *Trattato dei delitti e elle pena*, written by Cesare Bonesana, the Italian Marchese di Beccaria."[12] Mario Cuomo, modern day reformer and former governor of New York, quotes Beccaria thus: "[T]he most far seeing laws are those that 'resist that force by which benefits tend to become concentrated in a few hands, accumulating on the one side the utmost of power and felicity, on the other all weakness and misery.'" Cuomo then comments that this is: "[s]trong medicine for a country in which we are harder on the two bit street corner hoodlum than on the exalted pirates who roam the high seas of high finance."[13] The renowned criminologist Marvin Wolfgang writes in 1996 that Beccaria's *Essay* is "the most significant essay on crime and punishment in Western civilization."[14]

Unfortunately Beccaria had little to say on the causes of crime. Like Bentham and other writers of the Enlightenment, he held a rather simplistic view of Rational Man. His assumption was the same as Bentham's, that men seek their own self interest, and with reasoned calculation, seek pleasure and avoid pain. He assumed that crime was the inevitable result of human passions and opposing interests. All human behavior was the product of free choice by people who had the capacity for logic and reason and could choose among alternative courses of action. The classicists did not seek any other explanations for criminal behavior. Perhaps it is no coincidence that adherents of the classical school of criminology, like Bentham and Beccaria, tend to be writers and philosophers with no firsthand, in-the-trenches knowledge of crime and criminals. Persons with that kind of knowledge and experience are likely to see the problems of crime as a great deal more complicated than the classical view admits. On the other hand, perhaps we have, with the partial knowledge that our modern science has provided us, shifted our view too far towards the other extreme and created an image of crime and criminals that is more complex than is warranted and that has paralyzed us in consequence. No small part of Beccaria's power to influence reform was the simplicity and clarity of his view, a parsimony admired as much in scientific circles as in classical schools, but yet to be achieved in scientific criminology.

Two Sovereign Masters: Pleasure and Pain

Certainly one of the most famous and eloquent voices in the great debate between the mighty opposites is that of the English philosopher Jeremy Bentham. He is appropriate for consideration here because his work most directly influenced criminology and because he is given homage in every published criminology textbook. Bentham was born in 1748 in London and was a child prodigy who entered Oxford University at the age of 12. He graduated with a law degree but never practiced. He was so shy and sensitive that his fear of public criticism in court prevented him from joining his father's law practice. It is said that he proposed marriage only once in his life, at the age of 57, and that the lady said no. An inheritance from his parents enabled him to dedicate himself entirely to writing and research. So he decided eventually to focus his life's work on moral, political, and educational reform in England. He was a prolific writer and an indefatigable reformer. He died in 1832 at the age of 80, a hard worker to the end.[15] His most influential work was *The Principles of Morals and Legislation,* published in 1781 and considered to be one of the great books in Western philosophy. He wrote that he originally intended this work as the introduction to a book on the reform of the penal code in England in which he wanted to establish a rational basis for the law, to create, as he had proposed, a "science of law." He acknowledged that his work was inspired by Beccaria, whom Bentham called "my master, first evangelist of reason."[16]

Here are the famous first lines of *The Principles of Morals and Legislation*:

> Nature has placed mankind under the governance of two sovereign masters, pain and pleasure. It is for them alone to point out what we ought to do, as well as to determine what we shall do. On the one hand the standard of right and wrong, on the other the chain of causes and effects, are fastened to their throne. They govern us in all we do, in all we say, in all we think: every effort we can make to throw off our subjection, will serve but to demonstrate and confirm it. In words a man may pretend to abjure their empire: but in reality he will remain subject to it all the while.[17]

From this eloquent opening, Bentham develops a detailed and logical system for determining what action to take when confronted with moral decision making. Happiness consists of attaining pleasure and avoiding pain. These "two sovereign masters," pleasure and pain, govern the behavior of both individuals and of communities. The purpose of government is to provide the "greatest happiness of the greatest number" in the pursuit of pleasure and the avoidance of pain. All laws should be based on this principle of utility, also called the *greatest happiness principle*, the *felicity principle*, or the *pleasure pain principle*. Bentham believed that this principle could be demonstrated mathematically and he attempted to work out precise mathematical formulas for the infliction of effective punishment. For this reason, his point of view is sometimes called *hedonic calculus*.

There is debate enough in this principle of utility for a thousand philosophers and we will not indulge them here. Affirmations and refutations of this point of view would require at least a volume of its own. For our own purposes, it is sufficient to note the influence of this concept on criminology and to acknowledge its continuing presence in our efforts to understand crime and criminals. The principle of utility is a forerunner of behavioral psychology and is thus a progenitor of cognitive behavioral psychology, which is the strongest current trend in the treatment of criminal offenders. This approach to understanding human nature and human behavior underlies social learning theory and rational choice theory, both of which are contemporary and strong theories in criminology (and will be discussed in later sections).

Bentham's major purpose, however, was neither psychological nor philosophical, but political and practical. He wanted to reform the penal codes in England and to make them more rational and less harsh and discriminatory. He argued against capital punishment (except in "the most exceptional cases") on rational grounds during a time in which the death sentence was very widespread and very popular. In England in 1780, the year before the publication of Bentham's famous book, there were about 350 capital offences on the books. His energy for reform spread to include the development of a professional police service in London and to the architectural and programmatic design of prisons. The Panopticon, a polygonal, fortress like prison with a glass roof, was designed in detail by Bentham. It was unique in both architectural design and in the way in which it was to be managed. Bentham believed that prisoners should be required to engage in productive work, but also that they should be justly compensated for their labor. The Panopticon became an obsession of his, and it was widely discussed in England as well as the rest of Europe and the United States. A Panopticon was never built in England, where it was called a monstrosity and where Parliament objected to its cost. It was, however, tried in the United States three times: at Richmond in 1800, at Pittsburgh in 1821, and again in 1916 at Joliet, Illinois. These projects were eventually totally revised, as Bentham's architectural ideas were proven to be impracticable. Bentham had given careful consideration to the environment, to the architecture, to the general principles of psychology, and to the staff. However, he had left entirely out of consideration a most important element, the offender. This is why the Panopticon became known as a fine example of armchair criminology. Because Bentham was a scholar with no firsthand knowledge of offenders, he failed to understand how offenders would respond to the environment that he had created. This shortcoming resulted in the failure of his project. It is a deficiency that can still be found today, for example, in the rise of privatized prisons where entrepreneurs with excellent knowledge of business, architecture, construction, and administration, but with no knowledge of offenders, repeatedly fail to operate efficient and practical prisons.

However, some of Bentham's ideas about prisons are current today, including the proposals that prisoners should not be idle, that they should be engaged in organized work projects, and that they should receive pay for their labor. Bentham also originated the idea that prisons are schools of crime. Bentham's insistence that punishment for a criminal act should not be for revenge, but should be for the purpose of preventing a reoccurrence of the act, is the same as the "punishing smarter" thinking of today. He also anticipated our modern concern with the reintegration of the offender back into society after his sentence is completed. He recommended an intermediate stage in the process, forecasting the prerelease units of today.[18]

Though very popular and influential, both in his time and in ours, Bentham's ideas were not without severe criticism. Karl Marx wrote that "in no time and in no country has the most homespun commonplace ever strutted about in so self satisfied a way."[19] Sorokin observed that Bentham never addressed the obvious objection that what gives happiness to the greatest number of human beings does not necessarily bring the maximum of happiness to some individuals, and what gives the most happiness to some persons does not necessarily give the maximum happiness to all.[20] Bentham's vision of rational man as a free moral agent who could make choices but would always do so according to a calculation of pleasure and pain seems simplistic and superficial to twenty first century minds, who are attuned to the irrational aspects of human behavior, unconscious motivation, denial, and self deception.

Bentham placed his emphasis on the crime and not on the offender. He held to a strictly legal definition of crime — no crime without a law — and he was much more interested in the consequences of a criminal act than in the motivation for the crime. The principle of utility was sufficient, in his view, to explain crime, and he did not look further or deeper for an explanation for antisocial behavior. Our modern understanding of the psychopath does indeed see him as calculating, but very often in a short sighted and self destructive way. He is certainly not very precise and is frequently irrational in his calculations. Some twentieth century theorists of the positivist school have proposed that what is wrong with the psychopath is that he is able to focus only on the immediate gratification of his wishes and cannot engage in long term planning or delay of gratification. Perhaps what is wrong with criminals is that they see only the immediate pleasure and fail completely to see the long term calculation of pleasure and pain. If understood in this way, perhaps Bentham is not so far off after all.

His effectiveness in reforming the harshness and arbitrariness of the criminal law of his day remains his greatest achievement. He frequently chided the legal profession for not effecting change in judicial practices. Among Bentham's contributions to legal reform are the abolition of the transportation of convicted criminals to penal colonies, the mitigation of the severity of criminal punishment, removal of certain defects in jury systems, abolition of usury laws, rational opposition to the death sentence, and altering the practice of imprisonment for debts. In what became an often quoted remark, Maine wrote in 1870, "I do not know of a single law reform effected since Bentham's time which cannot be traced to his influence."[21]

The principle of utility, still a subject of earnest debate, has not answered all of our questions about the causes of crime, but for his contributions to criminology and law, Jeremy Bentham deserves a respectful acknowledgment.

Positivist Criminology

The positivists replaced the notion of free will with that of determinism. They emphasized empirical research, the individual treatment of criminals, and punishment that fit the criminal rather than the crime. They initiated the search for the cause of crime. One of the most influential progenitors of positivism in the social sciences was Auguste Comte, who published his six-volume *Course in Positive Philosophy* between 1830 and 1842. In this highly influential work, Comte introduced his "Law of Three States."[22] Civilization, as it matures, progresses through three states. The first is the theological state in which the causes of events are of divine, or demonic, origin. Eventually, this state is questioned and replaced by the metaphysical state, in which "ideas" and "forces" serve as the explanation for events. Finally, a civilization will replace the metaphysical with the positive state, in which scientific descriptions of causation are the standard of truth.

In criminology, positivism was carried into criminology by A.M.

Guerry and Adolphe Quetelet and by the Italian criminologists Cesare Lombroso, Raffaele Garofalo, and Enrico Ferri. There are earlier precursors of positivism in criminology, perhaps beginning with Jean Baptiste della Porte, who published *The Human Physiognomy* in 1586 in which he suggested that a thief is easily identified by his small ears and nose, bushy eyebrows, mobile eyes and sharp vision, large lips, and long slender fingers.[23] Sellin proposed him as "the first criminologist."[24] In any case, whoever may be first, we will follow the progress of positivist criminology in our succeeding chapters.

A University of Criminologies

As we suggested in an earlier section, "The Explanation of Crime," there are sufficient schools of criminologies to form a university of them, with departments of every description. There are as well numerous ways of organizing your thinking about them. Walklate, for example, proposes three categories for schools of thought about the causes of crime: (1) *the behavior of criminals,* positivist theories and classical theories; (2) *the criminality of behavior,* such as social disorganization theories, strain theories, and labeling theories; and (3) *the criminality of the state,* such as Marxist theory and critical theory.[25]

Lilly, Cullen, and Ball suggest that social context contributes greatly to theorizing about crime. Thus, for example, Lombroso's theory of the criminal man emerged as the theory of evolution was new and much discussed.[26] However, for this book, we have chosen a traditional and simple approach to schools of criminology. We will present them as biological, psychological, and sociological. There is some overlap in this approach; for example, Anthony Walsh proposes a *biosocial* criminology and Curt Bartol calls his book a *psychosocial* approach to criminal behavior.[27] There are groups of theories in sociology known as right realism and left realism (discussed in chapter 11). Some theories do not fit neatly into any group and there are, as we have seen, other ways of thinking about theories of crime than the academic categories of biology, psychology, and sociology. But we have promised the reader as much clear-sightedness as we can muster, and therefore we have opted for simplicity in our university of criminologies.

3

Correlates of Crime:
Age, Gender, Race, and IQ

Aging Out

Age and gender are the characteristics that have the strongest and most consistent relationship with criminal behavior. Gender is considered in the next section. As for the relationship between age and crime, there are a number of different ways of demonstrating this relationship, but the graph below is an especially clear and compelling illustration.

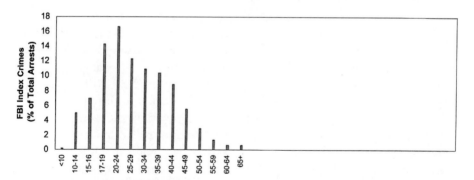

The data used in constructing this graph are from the FBI's Uniform Crime Reports for 2002. The *y* axis shows the percentage of the total arrests for 2002 for index crimes in the United States. Index crimes are the especially serious crimes that are used by the FBI to study crime trends: murder, forcible rape, robbery, aggravated assault, arson, burglary, larceny (theft), and motor vehicle theft. The *x* axis shows the age of the person at the time of arrest in categories of two years each. Each age category is labeled on the graph.

There are many interesting points that could be made from this graph; for example, 53 percent of all arrests for index crimes were of persons between 18 and 34 years of age. There were more people arrested under the age of 15 than there were arrested over the age of 54. But the main point is clear from the definite shape of the graph. Serious crime is strongly related to age, with most serious crimes being committed by persons 14 to 29 years of age. There is a decline after age 29 and another sharp and steady decline after about age 40. Though this particular graph is for one year of data, the shape of the *by age* graph for criminal statistics has remained basically the same for about 150 years.[1] This decline of crime with age is called "aging out" by some criminologists and "spontaneous desistance" by others. The relationship between crime and age remains strong even when the data is subdivided by gender and by race. Spontaneous desistance occurs across cultures and across centuries. Crime data from England and Wales in 1842, from Argentina in the 1960s, and from the United States in the 1990s all have the same basic shape.[2] It does not matter if you are looking at graphs of arrests or convictions or imprisonments. Even a graph of prison rule violations has the same shape. The data are so consistent that the English scientist Charles Goring, who was famous for having refuted Lombroso's theory, called it a "law of nature."[3] The statistician Adolphe Quetelet reported in 1835 that age was the most robust of the "constants of crime."[4]

This strikingly robust effect between age and crime is, of course, no perfect rule. Most of our young men are not criminals, despite the confusion of adolescence and the abundance of testosterone coursing through their blood vessels. On the other hand, one of the most extreme criminals with whom I was personally acquainted was 72 years old. He was as vicious, as criminally active, and as estranged from other human beings as anyone I had ever met inside the walls of a prison. Nevertheless, the relationship between age and crime is so strong and so consistent that any theory of the cause of crime is remiss not to address it in some way, even if only to admit that it does not account for it.

The phenomenon of spontaneous desistance does not prove that age is the reason for the decline in crime, only that the two are very consistently related to each other. This relationship naturally leads to the speculation that criminal activity may be a developmental or maturational issue and it suggests that biology is at least a part of the picture, as does the relationship between crime and gender. But at present there is no viable biological explanation for this effect, and most theories that have addressed aging out are social explanations. For example, Moffitt proposes that many of our teenagers are the victims of an unnaturally protracted adolescence, during which they identify with unsocialized peers rather than with positive mature adults. In place of the adult role models employed by our ancestors, modern adolescents tend to imitate the pseudoadult models provided by their more unsocialized peers.[5] This is a typical sort of social explanation which addresses the emergence, or onset, of criminality but does not actually explain its decline or desistance. What happens to cause the decline after about age 29?

In contrast, Trasler offers this explanation: The reinforcers that maintain delinquent behavior in adolescents cease to do so when the person becomes an adult. As they grow older, young men gain access to other sources of achievement and satisfaction such as a job, a girlfriend, a wife, a home, and eventually children, and they become less dependent on peer group support. This new lifestyle is inconsistent with delinquent activities. In other words, the situation changes for maturing adolescents in our society.[6] Thus, this is a situation-dependent explanation for aging out. It explains remission but does not explain onset. What causes the surge in criminal activity at about age 14? As Gottfredson and Hirschi point out, most explanations only address one side of the graph or the other; that is, they explain the emergence of criminal activity in adolescence *or* explain its decline in later life, but none explain both onset and remission, both sides of the graph.[7]

Some explanations that have been advanced are based on the idea that normal biological, social, and psychological maturation decreases criminal activity over time. As a group these are known as maturational reform theories. But these theories also have the deficiency that they do not explain the emergence or onset of criminal activity in adolescence, unless you wish to take the rather extreme position that criminal activity is a normal part of the maturation of the organism. Moffitt suggests that we look at two groups of offenders: (1) those whose behavior is antisocial in adolescence, but ceases at adulthood, called adolescence limited antisocial behavior; and (2) those whose criminal behavior continues throughout their life, called life course persistent antisocial behavior. It is suggested that these are distinct groups with separate causes underlying their behavior. This concept is extended into the idea of life course criminology, a topic discussed in chapter 11 of this book. Moffitt suggests that adolescence limited antisocial behavior is caused by social factors that encourage or entice teenagers to act out, but that most of them outgrow this stage. The life course persistent group is the result of a combination of childhood neuropsychological problems and a criminogenic environment.

Other explanations include the idea that age enables people to more accurately calculate the probability of success in crime, which leads to their rejection of it. Most criminals do not have great financial gains over time nor are they able to avoid arrest, conviction, and incarceration with great success. So, as they gain experience, they more often reject criminal activities. Another idea is that the population of offenders grows dramatically smaller with age as many active offenders are dead, sick, or incarcerated by age 40.

Matza proposes to resurrect the notion of will and to make a criminal offender, if not totally free of deterministic constraints, at least freer than he is normally pictured by theorists who espouse a deterministic point of view.[8] In other words, at least a portion of the aging out phenomenon could be explained by choice.

It seems that situation, choice, and criminality must all be included and that there is not a single explanation for the age effect. The innate tendency of a person to commit crimes is certainly the stage on which situational variables play their part. In early adolescence the opportunities to make bad choices begin to multiply and would appeal most strongly to young people who have already demonstrated their antisocial tendencies. Like Matza, we are not willing to deprive the individual adolescent of all choice in the matter, and it seems to us perfectly tenable that a person's choices would improve with age. This is true of most nonoffenders as well. It is characteristic of the psychopath that his choices do not seem to improve with age, but psychopaths are a relatively small (though very troublesome) group. The high risk lifestyle that they choose is not conducive to a fruitful old age, or even middle age, and it is plausible that some of the decline in crime with age is attributable to the diminishing number of psychopaths, many of whom are incapacitated by age 40 or so.

Gottfredson and Hirschi state that they do not think that aging out needs to be explained. It is what it is: spontaneous (that is, unexplained) remission. They point out that everyone slows down with age. They contend that useful and accurate theories of crime can be proposed and tested without explaining the crime-age relation and that some important dimensions of crime causation may be (in fact, probably are) age independent.[9] Even so, we think that it is telling that one of the few universally accepted facts in the study of crime has no satisfactory explanation. It is, perhaps, an indicator of where we really are in understanding the causes of crime.

Pragmatists would not be too concerned about explaining aging out but would be more interested in how it might be used. One psychiatrist quipped that because of the age-crime relation, our concept of sentencing criminal offenders should be revised. Instead of sentencing convicted criminals to a specific number of years based on the type of crime that they had committed, we should sentence all offenders to incarceration until they reach the age of 40, however long that might be. Then we could release them with no perceptible effect on the crime rate! Unfortunately, we cannot always agree that pragmatic decisions are *just* decisions. Therein lies another of the great dilemmas in criminology.

Why Is Criminal Man a Man and Not a Woman?

Men are always and everywhere more likely to commit crimes. Male participation in serious crimes at any age greatly exceeds that of females, regardless of crime type, source of data, level of involvement, or measure of participation. For example, here are arrests by gender from the Uniform Crime Reports of the FBI for the year 2002.

Gender by Crime

Overall Crime	Male 77.0%	Female 23.0%
Property Crime	Male 69.3%	Female 30.7%
Violent Crime	Male 82.6%	Female 17.4%

(*Source:* FBI Uniform Crime Reports, 2002)

Though the number of females arrested has increased 14.1 percent since 1993, this number still does not approach that of the males. This gender difference holds true cross-culturally and historically, wherever such data is available. Dr. Lombroso's daughter, Gina Lombroso-Ferrero, published a book in 1911 summarizing his work and repeating some of his findings on the incidence of female criminality in the latter part of the nineteenth century in Europe: Austria 15 percent, Spain, 11 percent, Italy, 8.2 percent.[10] Let's assume that the more serious offenders, the ones that we are concerned about in this book, eventually find their way to prison. Data on the composition of the prison population in the U.S. shows this gender contrast even more sharply (see top of page 51).

This strong gender contrast for criminal behavior suggests a biological cause, though the social learning of gender roles may be just as important a factor. We face two fundamental problems: (1) the gender ratio problem: why are crime rates for men so high? and why are crime rates

Prison Population by Gender

Prison Population	Male 93%	Female 7%

(*Source:* Bureau of Justice Statistics, *Source Book of Criminal Justice Statistics*, 2000)

for women so low? And (2) the generalizability problem: are the explanations for female criminality the same as explanations for male criminality, or do different explanations apply? There have been numerous explanations proposed for the observed gender difference in criminal behavior. Let's start with the "father of scientific criminology," Cesare Lombroso. He wrote a book on female criminality, one of a relatively few books on this subject. As was usual for him, he had some interesting observations, some of which can still be found in current thinking, side by side with some truly outrageous comments that, as some writers have already noted, would be "unacceptable today."[11] In *The Female Offender*, first published in 1893, he wrote that female criminality expressed itself in prostitution, and most of his work on female offenders was about prostitutes. "If cases of prostitution are included in the criminal statistics the two sexes are at once placed on an equality." He proposed that the prostitute is the genuine representative of female criminality. Characterized by a lack of "mother-sense," female criminals are, in his opinion, fewer in number than are males but are more ferocious:

> Moreover, the born female criminal is, so to speak, doubly exceptional, as a woman and as a criminal. For criminals are an exception among civilized people and women are an exception among criminals, the natural form of retrogression in women being prostitution and not crime. The primitive woman was impure rather than criminal.
> As a double exception, the criminal woman is consequently a monster. Her normal sister is kept in the paths of virtue by many causes, such as maternity, piety, weakness, and when these counter influences fail, and a woman commits a crime, we may conclude that her wickedness must have been enormous before it could triumph over so many obstacles.[12]

As his work progressed, Lombroso gave increasing importance to social factors in his theory of criminality: "Female criminality tends to increase proportionately with the increase of civilization and to equal that of men."[13] This is essentially the same as the more modern "liberation thesis." The liberation thesis is that the women's liberation movement succeeded in blurring the distinction between male and female gender roles, and that this liberation carried over into criminal activities as well as to legal activities. Women were liberated, goes the argument, to engage in all sorts of previously male behavior, both prosocial and antisocial. Thus some of Lombroso's observations are echoed today, though as we can easily read for ourselves, the father of scientific criminology was far from a feminist. Here, for example, is another quote, the content of which is more akin to the Biblical Eve than it is to modern science:

> What terrific criminals would children be if they had strong passions, muscular strength, and sufficient intelligence; and if, moreover, their evil tendencies were exasperated by a morbid psychical activity! And women are big children; their evil tendencies are more numerous and more varied than men's, but generally more latent. When they are awakened and excited they produce results proportionately greater.[14]

This argument seems even more perverted and misogynistic when we remember that crime is fundamentally a male phenomenon.

Explanations after Lombroso continued to argue the line of innate sexual characteristics. Female criminality has been related, though not very convincingly, to abnormal chromosomal configurations, body fat, the castration complex, menstruation, and the onset of puberty. Thomas in *Sex and Society*, published in 1907, argued that women are "anabolic" and men are "katabolic" (sic) by which he meant that women tended to accumulate body fat and fluid, while men tended to release such bodily characteristics. Thus women were passive and adaptable while men were aggressive and less adaptable.[15] The inherent nature of the male is to be "the hero and the criminal" while women are destined to be concerned about morality and stability and acquiescence to the roles assigned to them by men. Thus Thomas strikes out on another foray down the twisted path of biology and crime. In *The Unadjusted Girl* in 1925, Thomas argued that female delinquency begins with the wish for new experiences and excitement. Girls learn that they can have these by manipulating their "capital," that is, their sexuality. According to this line of thought, it was primarily lower class girls who were amoral and who learned to use their sexuality for personal excitement and perceived gain in status.[16]

Current explanations for female criminality tend to emphasize social learning and gender roles over innate biological characteristics, though sometimes in unusual ways. For example, Pollak argued that the difference in male and female criminality is only an apparent difference because female criminality is hidden by gender roles.[17] Another line of argument begins with the shift in the 1970s towards increased participation in the labor force for women. This change resulted in greater opportunities for women to commit crimes and also greater exposure to the frustration and stress of the workplace. It also led, as the argument goes, to increased imitation of male behavior. The feminist view is that female delinquency is a defensive reaction to male efforts to control and dominate women's lives economically, emotionally, and physically. (Feminist criminology is discussed in greater detail in chapter 11.)

Another argument says that girls are not labeled as delinquent nearly as often as boys and are not thereby set on a course for criminality, although some studies have shown that girls are actually treated more harshly than are boys for delinquent behavior.[18] It may be that girls have more self control than boys both because they are more strongly supervised by parents and because they have more innate self control. Since the consequences of their misbehavior are greater, there exist stronger deterrents for girls than for boys.

Females are freer to engage in delinquency when the mother is working. Hagan and his colleagues studied patriarchal families, in which the father worked but the mother did not; egalitarian families, in which both parents worked; and mother-only, single parent families. They omitted single parent families in which the father was the head of household because they could not find enough of these to study. Their research confirmed the prediction that female delinquency would be higher and more similar to male delinquency in the egalitarian and mother-only households than in the patriarchal families. In other words, in family structures in which the females had more opportunity to engage in delinquent behavior, more of them did so.[19]

Moffitt, Caspi, Rutter, and Silva have published interesting research on gender differences in antisocial behavior from the Dunedin Multidisciplinary Health and Development Study. The Dunedin study is a 26-year-old longitudinal study of 1,000 male and female subjects born in Dunedin, New Zealand, in 1972–73. The subjects were followed from age 3 to age 21 in their research published in 2001, though the study is continuing. Moffitt and her colleagues found that the adolescent limited versus life course persistent categories (discussed in the last section) held true for girls as well as for boys. They also report that almost all females who engage in antisocial behavior fall into the adolescence limited group, with a sex ratio of 1.5 males to 1.0 females in that group. The life course persistent antisocial female is extremely rare, with only one in 100 females falling into this group. The sex ratio in this group is ten males to one female. The males and females in the life course persistent group are very similar in terms of cognitive deficit, personality, and social environment. "Why do fewer females than males suffer the primary individual level risk factors for life course persistent antisocial behavior?" The researchers consider this to be "an unanswered question."[20]

Studies of aggression are not unequivocally helpful here. Men are more aggressive and more violent, are bigger risk takers, have more opportunity, seek more excitement, and are also, perhaps, more frustrated than are women. The problem with studies of aggressiveness is that it has never been shown that aggressiveness is the equivalent of, or inevitably leads to, criminal behavior. There are many socially acceptable ways to express aggressiveness that are not crimes, and there are certainly plenty of people who express aggressiveness in our society; for example, athletes, salesmen, politicians, and soldiers. Aggressiveness is a prominent feature of success in these professions, but these persons do not normally engage in criminal behavior and no one would consider them to be criminals.

Two books were published in 1975 that addressed "the emancipation thesis," sometimes called "the opportunity thesis," the proposition that the women's liberation movement of the 1970s, while providing greater equality and freedom for women, would also increase the female crime rate. Freda Adler proposed in her book *Sisters in Crime* that as women began to move out of traditional homemaking roles and into the competitive marketplace, they would become more masculine in orientation and that they would acquire more masculine qualities, including, among other characteristics, criminality. Liberated women would become "as capable of violence and aggression as any man."[21] In *Women in Crime*, Rita Simon wrote that as women moved into the marketplace and into positions of more power, they would have greater opportunities to commit economic and white collar crimes and that this increase in opportunity would lead to a larger number of offenses committed by women.[22] These two books stimulated much study and debate about women and crime. Since then, the data have indicated that Simon's theory had the greater validity; that is, there were larger increases in property offenses by women than there were increases in violent crimes by women, as Adler had suggested. But, overall, as Coontz and Sevigny report in 2003, the increase in female arrest rates in the last decade is more probably due to the war on drugs than to women's liberation. The increase in the female arrest rate is "largely confined to petty income generating offenses" committed by women who are multiple drug users in need of treatment. Coontz and Sevigny suggest that we need to address how gender affects both involvement in crime and involvement in drugs.[23]

It may be seen that many of these explanations address the increase in female criminality in the last years of the twentieth century but do not address the fundamental difference that has always existed between male and female criminality. In addition, some of these are really explanations for juvenile delinquency rather than explanations for adult criminality. As we shall see later, these are not the same thing, and the same explanations do not always apply. Even so, the above are a fair sample of explanations available for the gender difference in crime. We think that they show collectively that we don't know very much about it. The strongest and most consistent, not to mention obvious, fact about crime remains unexplained. As Cain has asked, "[W]hat in the social construction of maleness is so profoundly criminogenic: why do males so disproportionately turn out to be criminals?"[24] Why is criminal man a man and not a woman?

Black over White over Asian

The title of this section, "Black over White over Asian," is jargon for the consistent finding in criminology that blacks commit more crimes than whites who commit more crimes than Asians. This finding has been consistent since crime statistics have been kept in the United States. Blacks are overrepresented at every stage of the criminal justice system, from reported crimes to arrests to convictions to incarceration.[25] The same finding holds true for research conducted in the United Kingdom by Rutter and Giller.[26] The very same pattern was found by Rushton in 88 different countries.[27] Eysenck and Gudjonsson reported in 1989 that "[n]o societies were found for which this pattern has not been reported."[28]

The FBI in its Uniform Crime Reports for the year 2002 reported that for all arrests in that year, 71 percent were whites, 27 percent were blacks, and 2 percent were Asians or American Indians. This is striking since blacks are only 13 percent of the population. The situation is considerably worse if you look at serious crimes: 50 percent of all arrests for murder and manslaughter were blacks and 54 percent of all arrests for robbery were blacks. It should be also noted that African Americans are disproportionately the victims of crime.[29]

This is an emotionally charged, contentious, and politically explosive subject. In researching for this book, it was surprising to find how many otherwise detailed and comprehensive books on the causes of crime essentially ignored this subject. Walsh writes in 2002 that "[m]any shy away from dealing forthrightly with matters of race because they are aware of the tendency to label those who do as racists."[30] But this does not set the stage for objective, dispassionate science. No other topic in criminology has more need of Beccaria's "cool scrutineer" than the subject of race and crime.

The first skirmish line in this debate is that race, when carefully analyzed, is a rather bizarre concept, which appears to be a biological variable, but certainly is not. The racial or ethnic identity of someone is much less certain than age or gender. In the United States, the category of race may not explain anything more than the concept of social class explains. For example, a person with one black grandparent may be considered black, and if arrested, would appear in the category for African Americans arrested, while a person with two white grandparents and two black grandparents may not be white and may not appear in the numbers for whites arrested. A person with one Cherokee grandparent is legally a "full blood" Cherokee, and would appear in the crime statistics for Native Americans, even though he may have three white grandparents. As a biological variable, it is altogether too strange to sort out, since the DNA of all human persons is 99+ percent the same. What would be the predicted racial characteristics of an Irish-Choctaw-African-Latino? Language, religion, culture, geography, and history, none of them biological, are the factors determining ethnic identity. The fact that all of these characteristics, in certain times and places, can be trumped by the hue of one's skin is a social, not a biological, phenomenon. Raine reported, in 1993, that there is no research on genetic predisposition for crime among nonwhite groups.[31] We are not aware of any since then. Race as a social class, or social history variable, has meaning and we can begin to work with it in that context. It is well to remember that keeping statistics of all sorts by race is not a pointless exercise because doing so provides hard data about systematic discrimination against specific groups of people and directs our attention to it. The misleading part is the assumption that these racial classifications are biological rather than social.

A second skirmish line in the debate is that the statistics themselves are biased, compiled in such a way as to reflect unfavorably on minority groups. Evidence against this charge comes from victim surveys, in which the victims of crimes report the race of persons who committed crimes against them. For example, Hindelang found that 62 percent of those arrested for robbery in a single year were black and also that, in that same year, the victims of robbery described their assailants as black 62 percent of the time.[32] Data from victim surveys are generally consistent with arrest figures on the characteristic of race.[33] Furthermore, the arrest statistics are not unfavorable for all nonwhite groups. The arrest rates for Chinese Americans and Japanese Americans are much lower than for blacks *and* whites.[34] If we are able to accept the statistics on the racial characteristics of offenders as basically accurate, then, of course, the important question is why?

Attempts to explain the observation that African Americans commit crimes, especially violent crimes, at a disproportionate rate include economic disadvantage, inadequate socialization, and the evolution of a subculture of violence. There is some truth in each of these explanations. In the case of economic deprivation, the theory is that blacks have met with serious obstructions in achieving legitimate goals through legitimate means and therefore turn to crime more often in order to achieve their economic aspirations. In sociology, this is called strain theory. It is discussed in the section on sociology. In the case of inadequate socialization, the theory is that the important values that are usually taught in families are not acquired by the many young blacks who grow up in single parent families within "a culture of poverty." It has been suggested that such values include the delay of gratification in order to achieve long term goals, regard for the good opinion of the community, and self control. In the case of the subculture of violence, the theory is that blacks have acquired values that are in rebellion to the dominant culture, which has historically oppressed and abused them. To the extent that the criminal laws embody the repressive white society, they may be broken as an act of defiance and be replaced by other values. There is, however, a certain circularity in this explanation: young black males engage in excessively violent behavior, most often towards each other, *because* they live in a violent subculture where such behavior is more normal and condoned by subcultural values. But then how did this subculture of violence develop among them? And why did it not develop to the same extent among other groups who also suffered from blocked opportunities and poverty ridden environments? There is not yet a satisfactory explanation for this phenomenon, presented with convincing argument and accompanied by supporting evidence.

Constitutional, or biological explanations, such as IQ or temperament, have also been attempted, but have fallen into disrepute. Biological explanations for crime, beginning with Lombroso's "criminal man," have always been criticized as having racist implications. This is not without justification, as we shall see in the section on biology and crime. The relationship between crime and IQ has its own individual history, which we will review in the next section. At present, hardly anyone is satisfied with any of our explanations for the relationship between race and crime. It is difficult to interpret the relationship between two variables, both of which have definitions that are ambiguous, shifting, arguable, and brimming with emotion.

Crime and IQ: The Science of the Caught?

Depictions of the brilliant criminal, like the evil genius in a James Bond movie, or the real life Jeffrey MacDonald in *Fatal Vision*, will mislead us in our search for the causes of crime. Most experienced observers of the offender population have remarked on the criminal's apparent inability to learn from past experience and have noted his below average intelligence. Harry Goddard, a major figure in the debate on intelligence and criminality in the early part of the twentieth century, put it this way:

> [H]ow many of the crimes that are committed seem foolish and silly. One steals something that he cannot use and cannot dispose of without getting caught. A boy is offended because the teacher will not let him choose what he will study and therefore he sets fire to the school building. Another kills a man in cold blood in order to get two dollars. Somebody else allows himself to be persuaded to enter a house and pass out stolen goods under circumstances where even slight intelligence would have told him he was sure to be caught. Sometimes the crime itself is not so stupid but the perpetrator acts stupidly afterwards and is caught, where an intelligent person would have escaped.... Judge and jury are frequently amazed at the *folly* of the defendant — the lack of common sense that he displayed in his act. It has not occurred to us that the folly, the crudity, the dullness, was an indication of an intellectual trait that rendered the victim to a large extent irresponsible.[35]

This is a far cry from the evil genius, or even from the bright psychopath. Goddard was writing in 1914, and throughout the length of the twentieth century, scientists have made similar observations about criminals, remarking on the impulsive and self defeating qualities of their behavior, and on their consistently low scores on tests of academic ability. It is possible that our observation of the intellectual abilities of criminals is directly linked with the dynamics of getting caught; that is to say, criminals of below average intelligence are studied by social scientists because they are the ones who get caught and are available for study. The Canadian psychologist R.D. Hare wrote that this raises an "issue that urgently needs to be addressed and researched: the prevalence of psychopathy in the general population, and its expression in ways that are personally, socially, or economically damaging but are not necessarily illegal or that do not result in prosecution."[36]

Sometimes this line of thought is extended to the conclusion that criminology is simply the study of unsuccessful psychopaths while the successful psychopaths are busily running government, industry, the military, and corporations of all sorts. This possibility must be admitted, and, on any given day, after the conclusion of the evening news on TV, it seems a more than plausible proposition. But I think that, in general, this is too cynical a view, and in particular, it does not focus us on our definition of crime as a group of behaviors about which there is a strong cultural consensus, such as rape, robbery, and murder. We need not feel compelled to explain behavior about which there is considerable doubt or disagreement. Various forms of selfish corporate behavior, for example, may indeed be contrary to the public good, and may unfairly take advantage of others, but there is no widespread consensus about them as crimes; in fact, there is considerable debate in our capitalistic society about whether such business practices are good or bad. This observation is not meant to excuse corporate criminals who have committed fraud and theft, sometimes by operating deliberately in those gray areas, such as tax shelters, which might impede successful prosecution. Yet we need not be rendered helpless to address serious crime by our inability to resolve all ethical dilemmas, by a confused conception of cultural relativity, or by widely accepted capitalistic values.

Intelligent criminals exist, of course. There is no especially strong correlation between intelligence and goodness in an individual. A person may be very bright and very bad, or, conversely, a not-so-gifted person may be an extraordinarily good person, showing us once again that our intelligence alone does not necessarily advance us through the stages of moral development. But the aggregate data, gathered over the last 100 years, strongly suggest intellectual deficits in the criminal population. Much of this work, however, has been done with incarcerated populations, adding to our suspicion that we may be basing our conclusions on a subset of criminals, the less successful ones, who are apparently characterized by below average intelligence.

The debate about intelligence and criminality had an early start. The French psychologist Alfred Binet began his eventually successful efforts to measure intelligence in the 1890s. His test of mental ability was gradually improved and became widely used. However, Binet's test, based on the concept of mental age, tended to overestimate retardation when applied to adults. We shall see how this error contributed to the debate on IQ and crime.[37] The English physician Charles Goring, in his famed refutation of Lombroso's theory of crime in 1913, reported a strong correlation between intelligence and criminality. Goring found that, of the factors he studied, level of intelligence most clearly differentiated the criminals from the general community.[38]

The next year, Harry Goddard, an American physician and administrator of the New Jersey School for the Feeble-Minded, presented his data and his conclusions on criminality and intelligence. He had studied the intellectual capacities of inmates in 16 reformatories. He reported, "Every investigation of the mentality of criminals, misdemeanants, delinquents and other antisocial groups has proven beyond the possibility of contradiction that nearly all persons in these classes, and in some cases all, are of low mentality ... it is no longer to be denied that the greatest single cause of delinquency and crime is low grade mentality, much of it within the limits of feeblemindedness."[39] How suspicious we must be — and must continue to be — about such claims! Goddard's claim is overwrought, not because of the observation that there is a strong relationship between below average intelligence and incarceration in training schools and prisons, a finding which has generally held up, but because of the prideful leap that declares that we now know the single greatest cause of delinquency and crime. Goddard goes on: "The hereditary criminal passes out with the advent of feeble mindedness into the problem. The criminal is not born; he is made. The so called criminal type is merely a type of feeblemindedness, a type misunderstood and mistreated, driven into criminality for which he is well fitted by nature."[40] Goddard offered data which seemed to show that 50 percent of all criminals are mentally defective. He pointed out that whether the "feeble minded" person actually becomes a criminal depends on the interaction of his temperament and his environment against the backdrop of his mental deficiencies.

William Healy was an American psychologist and influential expert on delinquency who published, along with Franz Alexander, a book called *The Roots of Crime* in 1935. This book was widely read at the time. Healy's data convinced him that the delinquent male is five to ten times more likely than a normal boy to be mentally deficient.[41]

There was opposition to this line of thought. The U.S. Army began to administer IQ tests to draftees during World War I. Zelney reported that these tests indicated that one third of army draftees would be classified as feeble minded.[42] This was a startling result and cast doubt on the work of Goddard and others who had found so much "feeble mindedness" in reformatories and prisons. We can recall that Binet's test tended to overestimate retardation. Carl Murchison of Clark University published his book *Criminal Intelligence* in 1926 in which he reported a comparison of prison inmates and army draftees. He found *higher* intelligence among prison inmates at Fort Leavenworth than among enlisted men in World War I. Murchison was interested in eliminating what he considered to be excuses for criminal behavior and, in his book, he advocated severe penalties for crimes, including the death penalty for a third felony conviction.[43]

Sutherland reported in 1931 on 350 studies of mentality and crime and concluded that the relationship between crime and feeblemindedness is "comparatively slight. Certainly intelligence is not as closely related to crime as is age or sex."[44] The majority of prison inmates are not mentally handicapped and the mentally handicapped, as a group, are not especially inclined to committing crimes. However, both of the above observations could be true without leading necessarily to the conclusion that there is no relationship of importance between IQ and crime. Sutherland's determined attack on the link between crime and IQ, and his prestige in criminology, effectively silenced the debate for several decades. As Wilson and Herrnstein wrote in 1985, Sutherland correctly observed that, as the methods of testing improved, the apparent intellectual deficits shrank, but this did not warrant the conclusion that there were no intellectual deficits at all among the offender population.[45]

The debate reopened in the 1970s. Marvin Wolfgang's landmark Philadelphia cohort research in 1972 reported that among nearly 9,000 males in the study, the chronic offenders in the group had consistently lower IQ scores than did those without police records.[46] This result held even within social classes. In 1977, Hirschi and Hindelang determined that a low IQ is a good predictor of "official" juvenile delinquency, but an even better predictor of self reported delinquency.[47] (However, this result has a possible interpretation that is somewhat humorous: high IQ delinquents are smart enough not to self report illegal acts!) Professors Wilson and Hernnstein of Harvard University reviewed the research in 1985 in *Crime and Human Nature* and wrote that there "is a clear and consistent link between criminality and low intelligence," and they criticized criminology textbook writers for ignoring the research in this area. As estimated by Wilson and Hernnstein, the extent of the IQ deficit in delinquents was ten IQ points.[48]

Farrington published a study in 1989 as a part of the Cambridge Study of Delinquent Development, which showed that IQ at age eight predicted both self reported delinquent behavior and official measures of violence at age 32.[49] In 1995, David Lykken, of the University of Minnesota, wrote: "It is now well established that offenders, whether juvenile delinquents or adult prison inmates, have lower IQ's than nonffenders, a mean IQ of about 92 compared to the general population value of 100, or to the estimated mean for nonoffenders of about 102.... The relationship between IQ and crime is curvilinear, peaking in the borderline range of 70–80 and decreasing in both directions."[50] The Canadian psychologists Don Andrews and James Bonta agreed in their 1994 comprehensive study of the factors influencing crime: "The data are clear: delinquents tend to score lower on standardized measures of intelligence than nondelinquents."[51]

But what does this relationship mean? Its explanation cannot be entirely and neatly cut off from general issues about IQ scores, which are still very much debated: What do they really measure? Are they consistent and stable for individuals over time? Are they culturally biased? Are they racist? As Wilson and Herrnstein wrote, these issues are hotly argued, and "with more passion than understanding." It is interesting how our story of the causes of crime pushes so many of the hot button issues of our present time, as here for instance, in the meaning of IQ testing and its racial and ethnic implications.

Perhaps making a more sophisticated analysis will help us. The most frequently used test of intelligence is one of the several versions of the Wechsler Adult Intelligence Scale, designed by the American psychologist, David Wechsler. This test is divided into 11 different subtests, which measure different mental abilities. These subtests can be summed to produce two subscores called verbal IQ and performance (spatial) IQ. A review of relevant research by Quay in 1987 showed that, for criminals, performance IQ is usually significantly higher than verbal IQ and that, while the performance IQ of delinquents generally falls in the average range, the verbal IQ is 10–12 points lower than average. In other words, the 10–12 point difference in IQs between offenders and nonoffenders can be accounted for by a lower verbal IQ.[52] Aggressive psychopathic individuals are most likely to show this difference. Verbal skills deficits are associated with left hemisphere brain dysfunction, while right hemisphere dysfunction is associated with performance skills deficits. Raine suggests that "[V]erbal IQ deficits in delinquents and criminals may be the result of left hemisphere dysfunction which may be caused by environmental factors such as head injury during childhood or trauma at birth. The deficit may be genetic in nature, since verbal IQ is partly heritable."[53]

Another suggestion is found in the fact that IQ has been found to be related to type of crime. Such crimes as bribery, forgery, and embezzlement are associated with higher IQs than is average for the offender population. Assaults, homicide, and rape are associated with lower IQs. In the middle, or average, range of intelligence for offenders are property offenders, burglars, auto thieves, and alcohol and drug offenders. Low test scores are associated with impulsive crimes. This impulsiveness, or lack of self control, led Gottfredson and Hirschi to develop a general theory of crime based on the factor of self control, a theory discussed in chapter 11.

Another line of thought is that IQ does not directly affect delinquency, but that low IQ hinders academic performance, which then affects other factors that are critical to criminal behavior, such as peer associations and employment opportunities. Other important attitudes and skills are also affected by IQ, especially verbal IQ, such as goal setting, problem solving, delay of gratification, and moral reasoning. Hirschi wrote in 1969 that "hundreds" of studies showed the relationship between academic competence and criminal behavior and that the lack of relationship between school achievement and delinquency as posited by many criminologists "must be considered one of the wonders of social science."[54]

It has been best stated by Wilson and Herrnstein:

> A child who chronically loses standing in the competition of the classroom may feel justified in settling the score outside, by violence, theft, and other forms of defiant illegality. School failure enhances the rewards for crime by engendering feelings of unfairness. In addition, failure in school predicts, to a substantial degree, failure in the marketplace. For someone who stands to gain little from legitimate work, the rewards of noncrime are relatively weak. Failure in school therefore not only enhances the rewards for crime, but it predicts weak rewards for noncrime.[55]

I think that this is the best interpretation of the data that we have at present. It is not the evil genius who is the proper subject of our concern, but rather the adolescent male with average to below average intelligence who is frustrated in school and misguided at home. The problem of the successful criminal and his IQ has not been satisfactorily settled and will continue to haunt us until we are clever enough to discover some workable method for the systematic observation of noninstitutionalized criminals. And the true meaning of IQ scores will remain controversial and debatable. But these limitations need not cancel out our ability to act and to correct, based on the knowledge that we already have. At this point, the best attitude for us to adopt is one of modest persistence, with one eye on the data and the other eye on our values.

PART TWO

Biological Explanations for Crime

Positivistic physio-psychology has completely destroyed the belief in free choice or moral liberty.

— Enrico Ferri[1]

The perceived willfulness of criminal behavior is clearly an obstacle to viewing crime as a disorder.

— Adrian Raine[2]

4

The History of Biology and Crime

The Science of Lumps and Bumps

Setting the stage for Lombroso's science of criminal anthropology were a number of scholars and scientists who were connecting physiognomy and mental faculties in the nineteenth century. The most popular and fully developed of these came to be known as phrenology, a term coined by Thomas Forster in 1815 (from the Greek for "the study of the mind").[1] This theory of brain function was first put forward by Franz-Joseph Gall, an Austrian physician, who published *The Anatomy and Physiology of the Nervous System in General and of the Brain in Particular* between 1810 and 1819. The work was presented in four volumes and was coauthored by Dr. Gall's student and collaborator, Johann Spurzheim.[2]

Gall and Spurzheim believed that the traits of human character and personality, which they called "faculties," resided in particular areas of the brain. They called these areas of the brain "brain organs." They believed that the strength or "power" of each faculty was the result of the size of the brain organ for that faculty. For example, if a person practiced benevolence, then this brain organ would become larger and conversely, if it was not used, it would remain small and undeveloped. Thus the size of the brain organ indicated its development and its contribution to the person's character. They further believed that the contours of the skull conformed to the shape of the brain inside and that the faculties of an individual person could be revealed by an exterior examination of the skull, locating protuberances and depressions and measuring the size of particular areas of the skull. Gall believed the phenomenon manifested itself thus:

Striking behavior →	*Faculty* →	*Brain Organ* →	*Cranial Feature*
(such as business success)	(acquisitiveness)	(large at location of acquisitiveness)	(prominent at location of acquisitiveness)

He identified 27 faculties or organs and Spurzheim added more for a total of 37 "brain organs." The faculties included such character traits as acquisitiveness, combativeness, amativeness, secretiveness, benevolence, veneration, jealousy, conjugality, and self esteem. Gall's early work had been with criminals and the insane and his first classification reflected these interests. He claimed that there was a "murder organ" in the brain of all murderers and a developed "theft organ" in convicted thieves. Spurzheim edited out some of these early criminal classifications in his later expansions of the faculties of phrenology, but these ideas attracted penologists and, in the second half of the nineteenth century, prison inmates were often classified by their phrenological type.[3]

The ideas of phrenology became enormously popular in the Victorian era. Charts of the various faculties and their locations on the skull were produced and widely circulated. There were scientific conferences, international symposia, and professional societies. There were disciples and converts. There were scholarly journals, popular public lectures, and numerous books expanding and developing phrenology as the key to the understanding and prediction of human behavior. Phrenology received the endorsement of famous people of the time such as Ralph Waldo Emerson and Horace Mann. Instruments were developed to measure the skull, finally culminating in the psychograph, invented in 1934, a bizarre metal device that fitted over the skull, made measurements, and produced a printout of the person's character and personality.[4] Phrenological analyses of renowned people, such as Napoleon Bonaparte, Rene Descartes, Herbert Spencer, and the American chief justice John Marshall, were conducted and published. Successors to Gall and Spurzheim made increasingly expansive claims for phrenology until it evolved into a philosophy of life as much as a science of the nervous system. Parents were urged to exercise the brain organs of their children so that desirable personality traits would be developed. The well known American phrenologist Nelson Sizer wrote in 1888:

> Before phrenology was known, the wisest of men had no means of deciding, with anything like certainty, the talents or character of a stranger; and hopeful mothers looked upon their darlings as so many angelic blanks, each likely to realize her fondest expectations. Now phrenology tells her how to guide the wayward and encourage the timid, and thus

reach desired results.... There is ten times more in men and women than they realize, and their relation to business and effort could be wonderfully improved if they knew their just powers and weaknesses; and in like manner their moral and social happiness might be greatly enhanced.[5]

Though the popularity of phrenology waned in the twentieth century, belief in it can still be found in the twenty first century. There is a site on the Web devoted to the serious study of phrenology, and books on the subject continue to be published every couple of years.[6]

Though phrenology is now considered a pseudoscience, Gall and Spurzheim were not all wrong. They were certainly wrong that the skull conforms to the shape of the brain inside it, and they were wrong that the size of the brain organ is related to its "strength." They were also wrong that traits as specific as destructiveness and reverence had specific locations in the brain and that all of these traits are innate. However, they were right that the brain is the seat of mental functions and that different parts of the brain are responsible for different functions. Today this idea is known as the "cerebral localization hypothesis." The insight that there are specializations in the brain in terms of function was "a fabulous intuition since brain specialization is now a well confirmed fact," wrote the neurologist and author Antonio Damasio in 1994.[7] Gall also championed the idea that the brain is the "organ of the mind," an assertion that was contradictory to the prevailing dualistic attitude of his time, that body and mind were entirely separate. He saw that the brain was the aggregate of many organs, each with some specialized function and he recognized the difference between the white and gray matter in the brain. It is unfortunate that phrenology is mainly remembered for the ways in which it was wrong, for its "bumps on the skull," rather than for the ways in which it was right. It is unfair to blame Gall for all of the unsupportable claims and unsophisticated devotion that resulted from the expansion of phrenology into a doctrine for living.

From the beginning there were outspoken criticisms of "Dr. Gall and his skulls." The idea of cranioscopy, examining the skull for indentations and protuberances, called derisively "the science of lumps and bumps," especially met with skepticism and was easy to ridicule. The circularity of phrenological principles was also criticized. This circularity may be seen in the following example. What causes destructiveness in a person? Phrenological answer: The faculty for destructiveness. What is the faculty for destructiveness? Phrenological answer: That which produces destructiveness. The "faculties" were imaginary constructs that did not exist in the brain and did not explain specific behaviors. Another criticism was that phrenological analysis depended on measuring the size of the brain organ, but the boundaries of the brain organs were indeterminate and not based on any measurable feature.[8]

There was also, throughout its history, a disturbing connection between phrenology and racism. Phrenologists eventually began to analyze various facial characteristics as well as cranial features. It was proposed that a prognathous (protruding) jaw was a sign of lower development and of a closer relationship to primitive man. Analyses were published in England that claimed to demonstrate that the Irish and the Welsh were more prognathous than the English and that the lower classes in general were more prognathous than the upper classes. All men of genius were found to be orthaganous (having less prominent jaws), surprisingly, just like the English upper classes! It was further argued that the Irish were closer to Cro-Magnon man and thus had ties to the "Africinoid races." This argument contributed to much racial stereotyping in nineteenth century Europe and its similarity to Lombroso's "born criminal" is evident. Schlag writes, "Much phrenological work was explicitly racist, ascribing inferior physiological characteristics to non white races."[9]

There is continued suspicion, even in twenty first century circles, that biological explanations of criminality have a prejudicial and unscientific component. Raine writes that one of the burdens of biological research on crime and violence is the suggestion that such research is somehow linked to racist doctrines and may be used to justify racial policies.[10] One of the stepchildren of phrenology was anthropometry, which was used to identify criminals by facial characteristics. The Nazi government in Germany set up a Bureau for Enlightenment on Population Policy and Racial Welfare which recommended classification as Aryan or non–Aryan on the basis of measurements of the skull and other physical, primarily facial, features. Craniometric certification was required by law and decisions regarding permission to marry and work, as well as who would be sent to concentration camps, were based on these certifications.[11] Considering the history of phrenology in the nineteenth century as well as the misuse of anthropometry by the Nazis in the twentieth century, it is hardly unreasonable for members of minority groups to stay alert on this subject.

Gall was a neuroanatomist interested in explaining human behavior and dedicated to empirical methods. Later in the century, the practice of phrenology would indeed attract its share of quacks and charlatans, but Gall and his contemporaries were serious scientists. Together with his colleagues and successors, he examined and analyzed thousands of heads, skulls, and brains. Why did not they themselves, after so much examination of the cranium, see the falsity of the principle that the skull follows the contours of the brain? Schlag replies, "Part of the answer to this puzzle is that Gall and the phrenologists, despite their professed commitment to scientific examination of the empirical data, wanted to believe."[12] The phrenologists had constructed a system especially well suited for explaining away inconsistent or contrary data. For example, when it was pointed out that the great philosopher Rene Descartes did not have the cranial features associated by phrenologists with rationality, Spurzheim countered by arguing that Descartes was not such a great philosopher, which a phrenological analysis had confirmed! "Our desires attract supporting reasons like a magnet attracts iron filings," warns Macneile Dixon, a reminder of how self fulfilling our human claims to scientific objectivity can be.[13]

Given its many deficiencies, what accounts for the development, popularity, and persistence of phrenology? How did Gall's theory of brain function, supposedly based on all this empirical data, become "the guide to philosophy and the handmaid of Christianity"?

Several factors combined to propel phrenology onto the nineteenth century stage. First of all, phrenology not only "explained" behavior but also promised remedies for all sorts of problems, and such panaceas are predictably popular, at least for a time. It promised practical results in the everyday world. Next, the concepts of phrenology were very compatible with popular ideas of the time. Phrenology gave scientific wrappings to already existing folk ideas about temperament and character. Phrenology was also connected with the liberal reform movement of that period in history. Efforts to reform the care of the mentally ill and the treatment of prisoners found a supposedly scientific context for their efforts. One such reformer wrote in 1844, "Phrenology has destroyed the system of brutal torture ... [and] INSANITY, by the discovery and promulgation of Dr. Gall's system of Cerebral Physiology, has been stripped of half of its horrors."[14] Finally, the internal complexity of phrenology sustained belief and made it hard to contradict the circular arguments on which it was based. This last point, made by Schlag in a thoughtful article in the *Harvard Law Review*, deserves some development since it is relevant to present day systems of "expert knowledge."[15]

Gall and the phrenologists, convinced of the truth of the basic principles of phrenology, occupied themselves with case analyses and ever more intricate, complex, and detailed elaborations of the "faculties," their stages of development, and their combinations with each other. Some idea of the complexity is illustrated by L.N. Fowler, one of the most famous of the phrenologists. "Let anyone undertake to calculate, arithmetically, the number of changes that can be rung on the 37 faculties in all their different degrees of development, and he will find them to be inconceivably great."[16] The very complexity itself served to convince and sustain its practitioners in the belief that they were in possession of special knowledge. It also gave them nearly limitless ways of explaining away contradictory findings with ever more complicated combinations of the faculties. Schlag writes, "The internal organization of phrenology gave its practitioners what they wanted most: the belief that they knew something and that this something was useful — even good. It also gave them an elaborate construct that could be deployed to deny conflicting evidence and to counter opposition — without seriously dealing with either."[17]

For our purposes, the history of phrenology is an excellent illustration of the intense interest in biological explanations of criminal behavior more than 50 years in advance of Lombroso's theory of the born criminal. It also illustrates the degree to which even an empirical science like neuroanatomy can be misunderstood and distorted to serve nonscientific ends. And finally it reminds us of the very human tendency, even in professional scientists, to cull the evidence in favor of a dearly held theory. The thoughtful reader will recall the history of phrenology whenever new and extraordinary claims concerning the causes of crime are presented to the public for uncritical acceptance.

Dr. Lombroso's Skull

"At the sight of that skull, I seemed to see all at once, standing out clearly illuminated as in a vast plain under a flaming sky, the problem of the nature of the criminal"
— Cesare Lombroso, 1906[18]

This skull, which I have adopted as a symbol of overwrought and mistaken ideas in criminology, belonged to an infamous robber, a criminal named Vilella, described by Dr. Lombroso's daughter as "an Italian Jack the Ripper, who by atrocious crimes had spread terror in the Province of Lombardy."[19] While working with the Italian Prison Service, Lombroso had became acquainted with Vilella, and at Vilella's death in 1870, Lombroso was asked to perform the postmortem examination. He found, upon opening the skull, two distinct depressions, which were anomalous in humans and which were characteristic of lower animals. This discovery, he writes, launched him on an intensive and lifelong investigation of "criminal man." He examined a total of 383 dead prisoners and supervised the examination and measurement of 5,907 living ones. He would come to describe criminal man as "an atavistic being who reproduces in his person the ferocious instincts of primitive humanity and the inferior animals. Thus were explained anatomically the enormous jaws, high cheek bones, prominent superciliary arches, solitary lines in the palms, extreme size of the orbits, handle shaped or sessile ears found in criminals, savages, and apes, insensibility to pain, extremely acute sight, tattooing, excessive idleness, love of orgies, and irresistible craving for evil for its own sake, the desire not only to extinguish life in the victim, but to mutilate the corpse, tear its flesh, and drink its blood."[20]

In the words of his daughter, Gina, who wrote extensively about her father's ideas, "the criminal is an atavistic being, a relic of a vanished race."[21] Later, his most famous and most able student, Enrico Ferri, coined the term "born criminal."[22] Lombroso referred to this new science as "criminal anthropology." In 1876, he published the first edition of *Criminal Man* and entered a debate that continues in the twenty first century.

Lombroso's discovery was not, however, as spontaneous and unsolicited as his 1906 depiction of the event leads us to believe. The nineteenth century stage had been set for such a discovery and he was well prepared to make it.

Cesare Lombroso was born to a Jewish family in Verona in 1835. He was married in 1867 and had two daughters, who in Lombroso's later life performed many tasks for him, writing, editing, translating and answering correspondence. Lombroso had been interested in psychiatric subjects since his days as a student at the University of Vienna, and he had already studied and published articles on brain anatomy and physiology, cretinism, and epilepsy. While serving as an army doctor, he was intrigued by the apparent relationship between tattoos and character among soldiers. He reported, "The first idea came to me in 1864, when, as an army doctor, I beguiled my ample leisure time with a series of studies on the Italian soldier. From the very beginning, I was struck by a characteristic that distinguished the honest soldier from his vicious comrade: the extent to which the latter was tattooed and the indecency of the designs that covered his body."[23] This fascination led him to an extensive study of the physical characteristics of 3,000 Italian soldiers. He concluded that obscene tattooing was a characteristic of criminals.

His ideas on physiognomy had been preceded by Gall and Spurzheim, who had written on phrenology in the early nineteenth century. Havelock Ellis writes in his book, *The Criminal* that there were no less than 22 scholars in Europe who preceded Lombroso in connecting criminal behavior with the physical and mental characteristics of the criminal.[24] Much of this work was known to him. In addition, Lombroso's intellectual environment included the powerful and lasting influence of Auguste Comte, who argued persuasively for scientific description and scientific method in his *Course on Positive Philosophy*, finished in 1842; Charles Darwin, who presented the theory of evolution in *On the Origin of Species* in 1859 and

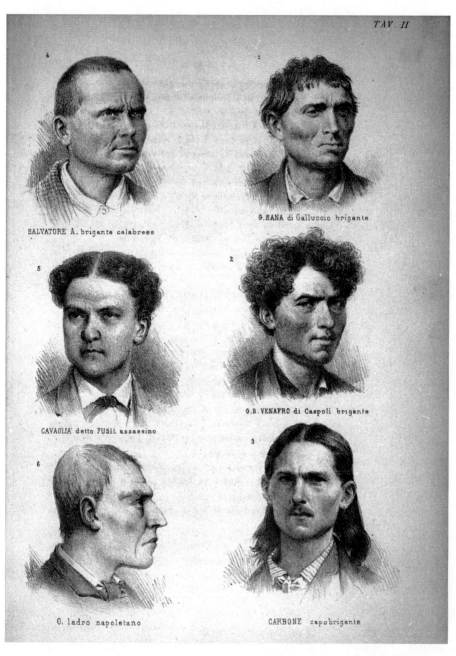

Heads of criminals, from Cesare Lombroso (1876), *L'Uomo delinquente*. Reproduced with permission from the Lilly Library, Indiana University, Bloomington, Indiana.

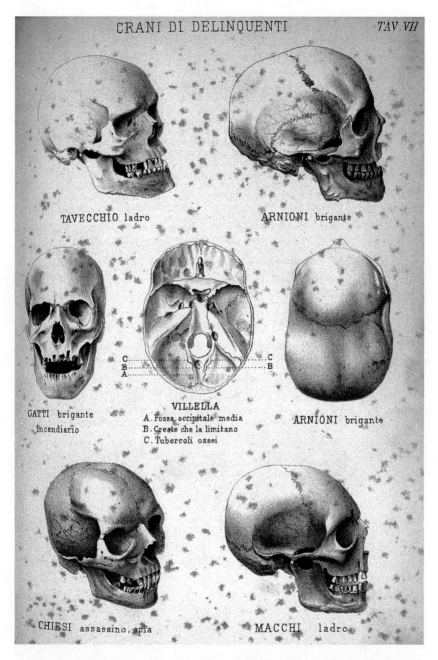

CRANI DI DELINQUENTI   *TAV. VII*

TAVECCHIO ladro   ARNIONI brigante

GATTI brigante   VILLELLA   ARNIONI brigante
incendiario   A. Fossa occipitale media
                 B. Creste che la limitano
                 C. Tubercoli ossei

CHIESI assassino, spia   MACCHI ladro

Skulls of criminals, from Cesare Lombroso (1876), *L'Uomo delinquente*. Reproduced with permission from the Lilly Library, Indiana University, Bloomington, Indiana.

The Descent of Man in 1871; and Herbert Spencer, who published *First Principles* in 1862 and eloquently expanded evolutionary theory into the realm of social life. Thus was the stage set for "the sight of that skull."

The publication of *Criminal Man* and its subsequent editions made Lombroso a well known international figure. Many visitors from around the world came to Lombroso's home in Turin to discuss and learn from him, where, according to Wolfgang, he sat surrounded by the music of Beethoven and Wagner, drawings, sketches, sculpture, and his many books. He founded a Museum of Criminal Anthropology, which contained prison items, skulls of ancient Peruvians and modern criminals, and a model of the famous penitentiary at Philadelphia.[25]

The evolution of his thought on the causes of crime is reflected in the succeeding editions of *Criminal Man*. The first edition was 252 pages. The fifth edition was published in three volumes and was over 1,900 pages. It included not only additional data but also what he had learned in response to the many criticisms of his theory of the atavistic criminal and in response to the influence of his own students, especially Ferri. He admitted into his scheme important social and environmental factors and modified his pure doctrine of the born criminal, gradually even reducing his estimate of the prevalence of the born criminal from about 100 percent to 33 percent of the criminal population.[26] He also added social factors associated with atavism: the wearing of tattoos, moral immaturity, vanity, cruelty, idleness, use of criminal slang, and high tolerance for physical pain. In the end, he left us with this classification of criminal types[27]:

1. Criminal epileptic
2. Insane criminal
3. Born criminal
4. Occasional or pseudocriminal
5. Criminaloid
6. Habitual criminal
7. Criminal by passion

To the twentieth century eye, this typology may seem awkward and dubious, with categories like "criminaloid" and "pseudocriminal." Yet in the numerous criminal classifications of the twentieth century, most of the fundamental ideas are retained (as well as the tradition of inventing awkward terminology). In Lombroso's classification, the born criminal represents about one-third of criminals. He is a genetic return to a primitive human or prehuman form. The born criminal has low self control and strong drives. He could be distinguished from the noncriminal and from other criminal types by physical features such as abnormal brain size, receding forehead, long arms, large ears, and bushy eyebrows. Eventually, Lombroso was obliged to concede causes for criminality other than atavism and so he included epilepsy and insanity (or moral insanity).

Finally, he admitted the existence of what he termed "occasional criminals," who constitute the largest group of offenders. These included (1) persons committing crimes of passion or political crimes, (2) "criminaloids," who differ from the born criminal in degree but not in kind and who are vulnerable to opportunities and temptations but are not as predisposed to crime as the born criminal. Finally he adds (3) habitual criminals, by which he meant an offender with poor education and parental example who is drawn into crime by association with other, more seriously disposed criminals.

In addition to *Criminal Man*, Dr. Lombroso wrote a valuable work on forensic science, *The Legal Medicine of the Corpse*; a book on women criminals, *The Female Offender*; a study of genius and creativity, entitled *Man of Genius*; and a summary work, *Crime: Its Causes and Remedies*.

Lombroso's work achieved wide recognition and attracted both praise and severe criticism. Wolfgang asserts that "[I]n the history of criminology, probably no name has been eulogized or attacked so much as that of Cesare Lombroso."[28] His theory was convincingly refuted by the English scientist Charles Goring in 1913 and it was partially rehabilitated by the American criminologist Earnest Hooten in 1939. He has been variously called the father of scientific criminology, the father of modern criminology, and the father of biological determinism in criminology. There are other candidates for these honors, but there is no doubt of Lombroso's seminal importance in the search for criminal man. He was idolized by many of his students and colleagues and he inspired hundreds of students and scholars around the world to conduct empirical research and to study his theories and ideas. One of his most important achievements was to focus the search for the causes of crime on the study of the offender rather than on the study of the crime.

On the other hand, he was capable of outrageous and unscientific observations. In *Crime: Its Causes and Remedies*, he reports his observation of a woman's bust, which he describes as "so full of virile angularities, and above all, so deeply wrinkled, with its Satanic leer, that it suffices of itself to prove that the woman in question was born to do evil, and that, if one occasion to commit it had failed, she would have found another."[29] He claimed that red hair was a criminal characteristic.[30] Late in his life, he became interested in spiritualism, attended seances, and wrote a book called, *After Death — What?* His theory of atavism in criminality was at best, wrong, and at worst, racist. While he was willing to modify his theory when faced with mounting evidence of the importance of social and environmental factors in criminality, he clung to a strict determinism. Eventually, his most famous student, Ferri, would write "Positivistic physio-psychology has completely destroyed the belief in free choice or moral liberty."[31] Was this a wrong turn in our search for the causes of crime?

While today the idea of the atavistic criminal may seem as quaint as phrenology, biological determinism remains as a serious and vital approach to the study of the causes of crime. The born criminal is revived again and again in the criminal types of Earnest Hooten, in the somatotypes of William Sheldon, in the research on the XYY chromosome, and in the Scandinavian twin studies. The concept has lasting appeal. Raine says in 1993 that "[a] very tentative and global estimate for the extent of heritability for crime is that genetic influences account for about half the variance in criminal behavior."[32] He writes further that "[w]hile brain imaging research must be applied to forensic issues with caution, it is argued that it holds the promise of revolutionizing our understanding of the neural networks which in part contribute to criminal and violent behavior, and therefore of understanding the causes of such behavior."[33]

The sight of that skull...

The English Convict

In 1913, Charles Goring published *The English Convict: A Statistical Study*, a work in which he employed recently developed statistical techniques to refute Lombroso's theory of the born criminal. Goring was born in 1870 in England and was educated at the University of London. Like Lombroso, he was a physician and a prison medical officer. Under the sponsorship of the British government, Goring spent 12 years studying the differences in criminal and noncriminal populations. His partner in this research was the mathematician Karl Pearson, who was famous for the creation of the Pearson correlation coefficient, still widely used in scientific research and familiar to every student of social science.[34]

Goring studied over 3,000 English convicts, making careful measurements, and comparing them with noncriminal populations such as Oxford and Cambridge University students, German army recruits, Scottish mental patients, University of London professors, British soldiers, and Scottish schoolboys. He took measurements of 37 physical traits such as hair and eye color, height, and head circumference, and measurements of six mental traits such as intelligence, temperament, and suicidal tendency.

His accumulated data disproved Lombroso's contention that criminals constituted a distinct physical type. He did find associations that were statistically significant between criminality and defective intelligence and between height and weight and criminality. Criminals were shorter and weighed less than the general population. Goring concluded that these "are the facts; and according to our inquiry, the sole facts of criminal anthropology; they are the only elements of truth out of which have been constructed the elaborate, extravagant, and ludicrously uncritical criminal doctrines of the great protagonist of the 'criminal type theory.'"[35] "The great protagonist" was, of course, Lombroso. Lombroso and his followers had never made a careful comparison of criminals and noncriminals, and they had little knowledge of the atavistic "savage" whom the criminals were supposed to resemble. In addition, they had not used precise measurement techniques or instruments, relying instead on unaided observation.

Goring made it clear that, though he found fault with Lombroso's methods and specific conclusions, he was not arguing against a biological theory of crime. Goring himself believed that criminality is inherited, and in his book he presented his own case for heredity. He found that the criminality, as measured by imprisonment, of fathers and sons was highly correlated (+.60) and that brothers also had a significant correlation for criminality (+.45). He was aware that these correlations could be the result of either heredity or environment, or both. But he argued for heredity by attempting to show that the correlations for environmental factors were very low and hence, by elimination, heredity accounted for most of criminality. He divided environmental factors into two categories: "force of circumstances" and "contagion." "Force of circumstances" meant such things as standard of living and lack of education. These circumstances produced very low correlations once defective intelligence was factored out. "Contagion" meant that the sons might have imitated the fathers in their behavior and thus their criminality was environmentally induced. Goring argued against the supposition of "contagion" by demonstrating that sons taken away from their criminal parents at an early age became confirmed criminals to the same extent as did those taken away at an later age.[36]

Goring's findings may be criticized because he did not study females at all. He restricted his study to male criminals, though he did report that the ratio of criminal brothers to criminal sisters was 102 to 6. If criminality is inherited, it should be the same for both sexes (as it is, for example, with hair color), unless it is sex linked. But Goring's argument is that criminality consists entirely of physical and mental inferiority and is thus not sex linked. So, if Goring is right, then male and female criminality should be approximately the same. Another criticism is that, in his argument against contagion, he used sons who had been removed from their parents by reason of being imprisoned. This is hardly the same as moving them from a criminal environment to a noncriminal environment. His conclusion was that the criminal is mentally inferior, but he assumed that mental ability was exclusively inherited and did not consider the role that environment plays in the development of "defective intelligence." Some of his measures were crude, the same criticism that he had leveled at Lombroso. For example, intelligence was determined by the interviewer's impression of the criminal's level of intelligence, instead of using standard measures of intelligence (which were available at the time). He studied imprisoned criminals exclusively and thus his finding regarding defective intelligence and criminality may reflect the dynamics of getting caught more than the dynamics of criminality. Piers Bierne has argued that Goring's only achievement was to replace Lombroso's criminal man with a convict born with inferior weight, stature and mental capacity.[37]

Goring made several important and lasting contributions. He was one of the first to point out the relationship between age and crime. Goring stated that persons predisposed by heredity to commit crime did so at a very young age, while those with a weaker tendency to commit crime delay longer. In an important section of his work, he writes, "[A]n individual's selection for conviction by age must be sought in the particular conjuncture of opportunity to commit crime with the intensity of the criminal predisposition—a conjuncture which obviously is highly correlated with age."[38] (The very robust relationship between age and crime was discussed in chapter 3.) His finding regarding intelligence and crime fueled a debate that continues into the present. His use of statistical argument and analysis became a standard of practice in the study of crime and criminality. *The English Convict* remains a classic example of the application of statistics to the study of the criminal.

Goring's argument against Lombroso was most convincing, though his own argument for the heritability of crime was less so. Some scholars have suggested that Goring is a more fitting candidate for the title of "father of scientific criminology" than is Lombroso, since his work was decidedly more scientific and consisted chiefly of overthrowing Lombroso's ideas. He was, in the end, rather harsh on the Italian, calling him "a traitor to science" and writing that his criminal anthropology was "an organized system of self evident confusion whose parallel is only to be found in the astrology, alchemy, and other credulities of the Middle Ages."[39] It may have been this intemperance in his criticism that eventually led the American anthropologist Earnest Hooten to become Goring's chief critic, as Goring had been Lombroso's. Hooten felt that Goring was "prejudiced against Lombroso and all of his theories" and he attempted a revival of Lombrosian theory. This work is our next subject.

The American Criminal

Earnest Hooten was an anthropologist who set out to prove once and for all the truth of Lombroso's theory of criminal man. Though he made passing acknowledgment of environmental influences, he was unequivocal in stating that "the primary cause of crime is biological inferiority."[40] His study took 12 years to complete and was well funded and supported by Harvard University. Hooten's project consisted of a massive data collection effort and a rigorous, comprehensive statistical analysis of this data. He then published a three-volume study intended for scholars and a one-volume popular book for the public.[41]

His starting point was the question "Are criminals physically different from law abiding citizens of the same ethnic origin?" Hooten and his assistants addressed this question by gathering data on 17,077 incarcerated criminals in ten states and 3,203 noncriminal civilians in four states, all male. He made elaborate physical measurements of the prisoner and non-prisoner groups. The measurements consisted of such characteristics as ear protrusion, eye folds, forehead, lips, jaw angles, and tattooing. Many of the measurements were the same as those taken by Lombroso and his collaborators. Hooten obtained a statistically significant, though slight, difference on 19 of 33 measures, including weight, stature, nose height, ear length, and cranial circumference. He divided his criminal group into subgroups for further analysis. These subgroups included what he called "Old Americans," by which he meant white men who were born in the U.S. of parents who were also born in the U.S., or as he said it, "natives of native parents." He then separated out Americans who were foreign born, Americans who were born in the U.S. of foreign born parents, and Negroes. His analysis led him to this conclusion:

> Our information definitely proves that it is from the physically inferior element of the population that native born criminals of native parentage are mainly derived. My present hypothesis is that the physical inferiority is of principally hereditary origin: that these hereditary inferiors naturally gravitate into unfavorable environmental conditions; and that the worst or weakest of them yield to social stresses which force them into criminal behavior.[42]

Some of his more specific conclusions included the claims that robbers who murder are tall and thin; men who rape are short and heavy; and men who commit burglary and theft are undersized and thin. This sounds like an early version of profiling.

The response from the scientific community at the time was distinctly unfavorable. Hooten was judged to have used good statistical procedures on bad data. There were three major criticisms: (1) His noncriminal, civilian control group was so small and so select as to be worthless as a sample of the noncriminal population. He used such groups as Nashville firemen, outpatients from Massachusetts State Hospital, and patrons of a bath house. (2) He found few significant differences between the criminal and the noncriminal groups. If his theory was correct, one would expect differences to be greater in both number and prominence. (3) He had no specific criteria for biological inferiority. He simply assumed that imprisoned persons were inferior and whatever characteristics they had were inferior characteristics. Merton and Ashley-Montague pointed out that Hooten's criminal group differed from the anthropoid apes in more respects than did the control groups; if similarity to anthropoid apes be accepted as a criterion of inferiority, the noncriminals are the inferior group and the criminals are the superior group.[43]

One of the more interesting aspects of Hooten's books were the set of drawings that accompanied the text. Hooten wrote that he began by illustrating his graphs and tables with "nasty little human figures" to make them more interesting, but he then evolved to indulging his "adolescent vice" of "drawing bad pictures." He attempted to illustrate with his drawings the physical features of the criminal types that he claimed that his data supported. There are some examples of these portraits below.[44]

Some of his observations were more discerning than were others. For example, he wrote that "[A]ntisocial tendencies manifest themselves with greatest intensity in the no man's land between childhood and maturity, and in that post adolescent stage when physical powers are fully developed, but when judgment and responsibility lag."[45] This is a well expressed observation for which there continues to be ample support. But then others were not at all persuasive: "Deficiencies of dark brown eyes and blue eyes suggest that these criminals include fewer of the relatively pure racial types and more of the mixed types than occur among civilians."[46] A "pure racial type" has crept into the discussion. Not surprisingly, the pure racial type is noncriminal, while the "mixed type" is commonly found among criminals. We've encountered this idea before.

Not an advocate of offender rehabilitation, Hooten favored banishing prisoners to some remote place. "Criminals are organically inferior. Crime is the resultant of the impact of the environment upon low grade human organisms. It follows that the elimination of crime can be effected

OLD AMERICAN CRIMINALS
MOSAIC OF CRANIAL, FACIAL, METRIC AND MORPHOLOGICAL FEATURES
NORTH CAROLINA

Longest and narrowest heads
Smallest cranial circumference
Thick eyebrows
Sparse beards
Pronounced ear protrusion
Darwins point absent
Prominent antihelix ①
Low foreheads
Extreme variation in slope
Shortest noses
High, narrow nasal roots and
    bridges ②
Concave and convex profiles
Thin nasal tips
Upward inclined septum
Frequent deflection
Thin membranous lips, but lower
    often thick ③
Compressed cheekbones
Compressed jaw angles
Bilateral chins
Full temples
Right facial asymmetry ④
Long, thin necks

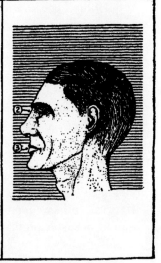

OLD AMERICAN CRIMINALS
MOSAIC OF CRANIAL, FACIAL, METRIC AND MORPHOLOGICAL FEATURES
WISCONSIN

Greatest head breadth
Straight hair
Thick beards
Longest upper faces
Vertical foreheads
Narrow nasal root and bridge
Relatively longest and narrowest
    noses
Concave and convex nasal
    profiles
Thin nasal tips
Upward inclined septum
Deflected septum
Thin cheeks
Thin membranous lips ①
Prominent antihelix ②
Median chins
Lack of asymmetry
Darwin's point absent ③

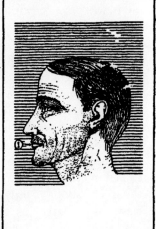

From E.A. Hooten, *Crime and the Man*, Cambridge, Harvard University Press, 1939, p. 61.

only by the extirpation of the physically, mentally, and morally unfit, or by their complete segregation in a socially aseptic environment."[47] "Extirpation" means "to eliminate" or "to destroy completely."

Hooten goes on to say, "We can direct and control the progress of human evolution by breeding better types and by the ruthless elimination of inferior types, if only we are willing to found and to practice a science of human genetics. With sound and progressively evolving human organisms in the majority of our species, problems of human behavior will be minimized, and there will be improved educability. Crime can be eradicated, war can be forgotten."[48]

It is intriguing to note the publication date of Hooten's work: 1939. This was, of course, the same year in which the Nazis ignited a world war in pursuit of their Aryan doctrines and their own program of human genetics. Perhaps this type of thinking was not as isolated in Germany as the victors of World War II seem to have claimed. In any case, the work of the Harvard anthropologist Earnest Hooten added yet another stick to that bundle of suspicion that biological theories of crime have a racist agenda.

Muffin, Horse, and Bird

There were theories of human behavior linking body characteristics and personality that preceded Lombroso's anatomical description of criminal man. Physiognomy, judging character by facial features or expressions, was practiced among the ancient Greeks and Romans. Havelock Ellis relates the story of Socrates, who was examined by just such a physiognomist, a reader of faces, who declared that Old Soc (as one of my inmates affectionately called him) was of a brutal and sensuous nature and inclined to drunkenness. Then, as now, the issue was debated. Aristotle remarked upon the connection between the shape of the head and mental disposition, but Pliny, writing in the first century A.D., thought that it was absurd to infer inner disposition from outward form. A medieval law declared that if two people came under suspicion of a crime, the uglier, or the more deformed, of the two was to be regarded as more probably guilty. As mentioned in an earlier chapter, Jean Baptiste della Porte argued in 1586 that the thief may be identified by his small ears and nose, bushy eyebrows, acute vision, large lips, and long, slender fingers.[49]

Shakespeare has Julius Caesar speak in famous lines about appearance and character: "Let me have men about me that are fat: / Sleek headed men and such as sleep o'nights. / Yond' Cassius has a lean and hungry look, / He thinks too much: such men are dangerous." In another play, Richard III, who we shall see in chapter 8 as a classic psychopath, is deformed and evil. *Dr. Jekyll and Mr. Hyde,* in which Hyde's appearance is as beastly as his behavior, is another classic example. But there are also literary rebuttals to the idea of physical type indicating inner character, contained, for example, in such works as *Beauty and the Beast* and *The Hunchback of Notre Dame.*

Lavater, in his four-volume work *Physiognomical Fragments,* published in 1775, attempted to relate the "fragments" of a person's face (chin, ears, eyes, and nose) to his behavioral tendencies.[50] But by the beginning of the nineteenth century, Franz-Joseph Gall and the phrenologists had begun to supercede the physiognomists. The phrenologists replaced the facial features used by the physiognomists with "lumps and bumps on the skull." Other variations on physical characteristics and personality followed throughout the nineteenth and early twentieth centuries. For example, Leon Rostand suggested a link between body type and personality in 1826. He proposed four body types with associated personalities: cerebral, digestive, respiratory, and muscular.[51] Other than phrenology, however, such theories received little attention until 1921 when the German Ernst Kretschmer published *Physique and Character.* This book was a popular success and went through 26 editions over the following 35 years. Kretschmer was interested in discovering the relationship between body type and mental illness, but eventually he made some observations on body type and criminal behavior. Kretschmer identified three body types, which he called the asthenic, the athletic, and the pyknic. The pyknic type was short and fat. The athletic type had well developed muscles. The asthenic type was tall and thin. Eventually he added a fourth type, a mix of the other three that he called dysplastic. He thought that the asthenic type was associated with crimes of petty theft and fraud; the pyknic type with deception and fraud; and the athletic type with crimes of violence. Kretschmer, however, did not present any evidence to support these assertions.[52]

Modern ideas about crime and physical characteristics were suggested by the phrenologists, popularized by Lombroso, discussed by the famous Kretschmer, and elaborated by Hooten's dubious studies of American criminals in the 1930s. Next in this line of work came William Sheldon, a physician who published his work on delinquent youth in 1949. Dr. Sheldon acknowledged a debt to his predecessor Hooten by writing that Hooten's underlying principle was essentially the same as his own, which ten years of observations had confirmed. "It can be summarized in a single sentence: Where essential inadequacy is present the inadequacy is well reflected in the observable structure of the organism."[53] It is hard to resist reminding the reader of how this principle was applied to the persecuted Socrates.

Sheldon advanced his theory of "constitutional psychiatry" in *The Varieties of Human Physique*, published in 1940. He developed a technique for measuring dimensions of the body from photographs taken at a fixed distance. He then measured a series of photographs of 4,000 young men of college age and concluded that physique has three major components, which he called endomorphy, mesomorphy, and ectomorphy. These terms were derived from the three layers of the skin: the endoderm, the mesoderm, and the ectoderm. When endomorphy predominates in a person, he tends to be round and soft with small bones and a tendency to put on fat. When mesomorphy predominates, the person tends to be muscular and round with large bones and a heavy chest. When ectomorphy predominates, the person tends to be thin and fragile with small bones and small features. Each of these three body types was associated with a particular temperament. The endomorph is a relaxed, sociable person. The mesomorph is an active, dynamic, aggressive person. The ectomorph is an introvert who keeps to himself and has a complaining temperament. (Wilson and Hernnstein report on one of their graduate students who, before studying Sheldon's work, used the terms *muffin, horse,* and *bird* to describe people to herself, a sort of personal classification system. How close to Sheldon's somatotypes is her system and what a refreshing change from all the pretentious and obfuscating neologisms that criminologists love to invent!)[54] Sheldon thought that every person has some degree of all three types, and he invented a three-digit rating system to indicate the relative strengths of each one in a single person. The system was based on a seven-point scale with seven meaning very strong and one meaning very weak. The system always reports the ratings in the order endomorphy, mesomorphy, ectomorphy. Thus a photograph of a person might be rated "7 1 4," which would mean that endomorphy was very strong in this person, mesomorphy very weak, and ectomorphy moderate. This person would then be generally typed as a strong endomorph. There was very little research on female body types, perhaps because researchers would have had to justify the expenditure of grant money for the minute perusal of 4,000 photos of nude college women, not to mention taking the pictures in the first place. Or perhaps there were other reasons. In any case, since by far most criminals are men, the paucity of research on female body types is not a serious problem for our purposes.[55]

It was not Sheldon's intention to explain crime, any more than it was Kretschmer's intention, but his investigations eventually led him there. Sheldon studied some 200 male delinquent youths whose behavior had led to their confinement at the Hayden Goodwill Inn in Boston between 1939 and 1949. He compared their physiques with those of a similar number of college males. He concluded that the delinquent youths were more likely to be mesomorphs and that the college men were more likely to be ectomorphs. Once again a general theory of human behavior was stretched to explain crime.[56]

Sheldon's theory did generate considerable interest, further research, and contentious dialogue among professionals. Two Harvard sociologists, Eleanor and Sheldon Glueck, replicated Sheldon's work and published their book *Physique and Delinquency* in 1956. They matched 500 "persistent" delinquents with an equal number of nondelinquents. The subjects were matched for age, race and ethnic background, intelligence, and residence in lower class neighborhoods. The Gluecks found that 60.1 percent of the delinquents were mesomorphs whereas only 30.7 percent of the nondelinquents were mesomorphs. They considered this a confirmation of Sheldon's findings. The Gluecks also reported that personality traits, such as feelings of inadequacy, and social factors, such as structured activities in the home, explained the difference between mesomorphs who became delinquents and mesomorphs who never became delinquent. This finding emphasized the inadequacy of physical factors alone to explain crime.[57]

There were additional studies by Gibbens in 1963, Cortes and Galtti in 1972, and Hartl, Monnelly, and Elderkin in 1982 that confirmed the observation that body type and criminality are related.[58] Wilson and Hernnstein were confident enough to write in 1985 that "the evidence leaves no doubt that constitutional traits correlate with criminal behavior."[59]

But not everyone was convinced. The anthropologist S.L. Washburn described Sheldon's work in 1951 as "a new Phrenology in which the bumps of the buttocks take the place of the bumps on the skull."[60] The inimitable Dr. Sutherland had found through his own research that the most delinquent youths were significantly more mesomorphic than the least delinquent youths in Sheldon's study, but he nevertheless determined that Sheldon's "data, in fact, do not justify the conclusion that the delinquents are different from the non-delinquents in general, the conclusion that the difference if it exists indicates inferiority, or the conclusion that the inferiority is inherited."[61] Gibbons argued in 1970 that a process of social selection explains the results of body type research. By social selection he means that "recruits to delinquent behavior" are likely made from the pool of mesomorphic boys because that body type is more successful in delinquent activities, just like recruits to athletic teams are likely to be mesomorphic in body build.[62] By 1986, the eminent criminologists George Vold and Thomas Bernard declared that "there is no present evidence at all of physical type, as such, having any consistent relation to legally and socially defined crime."[63]

More recent assessments of the link between body type and criminality include Raine's summary in 1993 that "there is reasonable evidence
to indicate both juvenile delinquents and adult criminals statistically differ
from controls in terms of being more mesomorphic and mesomorphic —
endomorphic and less ectomorphic than controls."[64] He adds, however,
that there are several notable failures to replicate. Shoemaker writes in
1996 that "[A]lthough officially acknowledged delinquents appear to be
disproportionately mesomorphic, a logical, biological interpretation of
this relationship has not been established, and thus the theoretical
significance of somatotypes as an explanation for delinquency remains
questionable."[65] Studies of body type and criminality continued to attract
interest throughout the twentieth century, but they have not helped us
much in explaining crime, any more than did Lombroso's contention that
red hair was a characteristic of criminal man.

It is clear that scientific criminologists have reviewed the same
research and given it different weights. It is surely no coincidence that
there is an obvious tendency for physicians and anthropologists to find
the evidence for physical types certain and clear while sociologists and
academic criminologists find it flawed and unconvincing. The anthropologist Earnest Hooten wrote bitterly in the beginning of his *Crime and the
Man*: "The anthropologist who obtrudes himself into the study of crime
is an obvious ugly duckling and is likely to be greeted by the lords of the
criminological dung-hill with cries of 'Quack! quack! quack!'"[66] A sociologist reviewer called Hooten's book "the funniest academic performance
that has appeared since the invention of moveable type."[67] This professional dialogue doesn't sound much like the objective pursuit of truth
through a strict commitment to experimental methodology, does it? Our
desires attract supporting reasons like a magnet attracts iron filings. We
must learn to view with skepticism all of those dramatic claims for the
cause of crime, as well as all of those careless assertions of scientific objectivity. The history of body type and crime is a worthy addition to the
gallery of our search for the causes of crime. It is also another poignant
example of why we must address the problem of crime by thinking for ourselves.

A Prison Snapshot

Rounding the corner of A Dorm, I walk a gravel path across the prison
yard between the infirmary and the administration building. I have finished
my morning clinic, seeing nine inmates for assessment and treatment and
holding a treatment team meeting with the unit psychiatrist and the unit

nurse. My head is swimming with unsolvable problems, some of them desperate, some of them routinely predictable. It's close to noon and the inmates are swarming from all directions, clustered in small groups, and advancing on the chow hall for lunch. I don't want to get caught up in a mob of prisoners in the middle of the yard, not because of fear for myself, but because I will have to stop while they pass by me. That means an avalanche of questions and requests. Who are you? Are you the shrink? Are you the doctor? Are you the chaplain? I need to see you today, Doc. You've got to help me. Can I talk to you? I've got to get moved, Doc. Have you got a cigarette? I'se got to talk to you, Doctor. Remember me, Doc? You're supposed to see me about parole, Doc. I'm seeing little green men in my cell, Doc. I can't sleep, Doc, I need something to help me. I'm stressed out, Doc, you need to see me before something bad happens. Five milligrams of Artane, Doc.

Some of these requests are frivolous, some are sarcastic, some are completely beyond my control. Some of them are genuine, and I do need to see them, but I cannot make that discrimination standing in the middle of the prison yard while 500 inmates are streaming by. "See the nurse and make an appointment," is my standard reply. Most of them will never do that. The few who do will get seen, but not until next week. The ones who are really desperate will make a suicidal threat or gesture and will get seen sooner. It's a control game played by prison staff and inmates; "Are You Going to See Me before I Kill Myself or Not?" But I would rather just avoid this whole scene, one I have played in many times before. So I pick up my pace, aiming for the back door to the administration building. Once inside the superintendent's domain, there are no inmates unless they have been individually summoned. I achieve this objective, deluding myself that I look like a very busy professional man in a hurry, instead of the stressed out dodger that I am. The program supervisor has left for lunch and his office is empty. So I go in, close the door, and sit down, hoping for a moment of that solitude that refreshes introverted personalities like mine. Leaning back in the dilapidated swivel chair, I can see out the window into the yard. I can see passing by, on the way to the dining hall, a small troupe of inmates. It happens that I know each one of them, though I have never seen them all together in a group like this. Danny G. is an amputee who walks by swinging his prosthetic leg in an arc and then taking a short, quick step with his good leg, then another swinging arc, then a short step, swing and step, swing and step, swing and step. Like some handicapped people do, he compensates for a missing limb by building up another part of his body. His upper body looks like that of an NFL linebacker. He often leaves his shirt unbuttoned in order to emphasize this attribute. Walking along beside him is Roger M., a mentally handicapped inmate, about 5'6" tall but weighing over 200 pounds. His short, rounded body reminds me of a porcelain Santa Claus that my mother displayed every Christmas of my childhood. Roger is easily manipulated by other inmates. The word on the yard is that he will do just about anything for a cigarette. He becomes very agitated at times and will flail with his arms at everyone within range and then begin screaming and crying. Only the unit nurse can calm him down in such circumstances. Once the story is unraveled, he usually has been mistreated by someone.

Beside Roger is Darryl H. Darryl is over six feet tall and weighs about 120 pounds. He has one eye and one arm. He poked out his eye with a ball point pen during one of his psychotic episodes. He told me that he stabbed out his eye because it says in the Bible that if your eye offends you, you should pluck it out; he said, "I couldn't stop looking at dirty magazines." Prior to his incarceration, he cut off the lower part of his left arm with a chain saw because "I couldn't stop masturbating and if your hand offends, you should cut it off." Darryl was discharged from the mental health facility as "stabilized on meds." He will last at this prison unit only until another inmate threatens him, at which point he will stop his medication, become acutely psychotic, make suicidal and homicidal threats, scare the hell out of everyone, and then be transferred back to the mental health facility.

As this trio of criminals ambulated past the window on their way to the chow hall, I was reviewing in my mind what I knew about each one of them when I had a sudden memory of my criminological studies on body type. Sheldon's somatotypes. Muffin, horse, bird, I remembered. Considering the case histories of Darryl, Roger, and Danny, body type was certainly the most trivial aspect of their lifelong journey to the state's prisons. Why do we direct our intellectual energies, not to mention our material resources, towards such investigations as body type, when the most compelling factors, like childhood abuse, neglect, diagnosable physical and mental disorders, and irresponsible models, are clearly before us, demanding our attention? Why do we stubbornly refuse to use what we already know about crime and criminals; why will we not use the light that we already possess? Is there a scientific explanation for this recalcitrance?

5

Heritability

The Concept of Heritability

Is criminality inherited? Recent advances in understanding the human genetic code have generated renewed interest in and excitement about explaining human behavior through genetics. Is there a gene for sexual preference, another for alcoholism, another for obesity? Are we "hard wired" for any number of behaviors, including violence and aggression? Is there a genetic predisposition for crime? All human traits are inherited, because they are coded in the DNA passed on to us by our ancestors. This fact does not point to genetic determinism, however, because any genetic potential requires an environment for its actualization. Walsh provides the example of seeds from a prize winning rose that are very likely to realize their maximum genetic potential in a Virginia garden but are unlikely to thrive at all if planted in the Nevada desert.[1] If you observed the thriving roses in the Virginia garden, what part of their success is genetic and what part environmental? It would be mistaken to say it's all in the genes; look what happens to them in the Nevada desert.

Heritability is a statistical expression, used by behavioral geneticists, which quantifies an estimate of the amount of variance of a trait that can be attributed to genes, and the amount that is attributable to environmental factors. A value of 1.0 means that all of the variance is attributable to genes. A value of 0.0 means that all of the variance is attributable to environmental factors. For example, if you took identical seeds of corn and planted them in two different plots of ground, the differences in the crop would be due entirely to environmental factors and the heritability coefficient would be 0.0. Conversely, if you took different strains of corn and planted them in the same plot, the observed differences in the crop would be attributable to genetics and the heritability would be 1.0. However, since it is impossible to control precisely all of the genetic and environmental factors that may be involved, the heritability coefficient typically falls somewhere between 1.0 and 0.0.

You can easily imagine how the problem of controlling all the relevant environmental factors is multiplied when you move from plant growth to human behavior. The problem of controlling genetic factors in studying heritability in humans has been addressed by using twins as subjects, a topic which is reviewed in the section below titled "The Danish Twins." Based on twin and adoption studies, Raine suggests .50 as a "tentative, global estimate" for the heritability of criminality.[2] Lykken, after a careful summary of research, thinks that the data support a heritability coefficient for criminality in the .30–.40 range.[3]

The research so far on genetics and criminal behavior has been very controversial, severely criticized by some and stoutly defended by others. Walsh pleads for a more sophisticated understanding of heritability in criminology and argues for a biosocial criminology whose basic premise is the interaction of heredity and environment, *nature x nurture*, rather than the opposition of *nature versus nurture*.[4] Consider, for example, the following situation: a child who is, by genetic inheritance, aggressive, and impulsive, with below average IQ. In the first case, he is raised by parents who are neglectful, abusive, and engaged in antisocial behavior themselves. In the next case, the same child is raised by parents who are competent, prosocial, and very involved in the child's life. In the first case, criminality flourishes and in the second case, an energetic and competitive overachiever emerges. Real cases, however, are always more complex than our simplistic explanatory scenarios, and the genetic explanation of crime is at present more hope than substance. Genetics may yet have the last word, but a modest approach is the wisest course at present, especially when considering, as we will do next, some of the history of the genetic explanation of crime.

The Saga of the Supermale

The debate on the XYY chromosome and crime may have been one of the most publicized events in criminology in the twentieth century. The public announcements on this research in the mid '60s and early '70s were widespread, dramatic, and exciting. The story of the supermale syndrome developed in the following way.

Men and women usually have 46 chromosomes in 23 pairs; one of these pairs is composed of two sex chromosomes. The X denotes the chromosome for female and the Y denotes the chromosome for male. Women usually have an XX pair of chromosomes. Men normally have an XY pair. In 1961, Sandberg and his colleagues announced the discovery of an XYY chromosomal configuration, a man who had two Y chromosomes.[5] This XYY man was of average intelligence and was not a criminal.

The discovery of this chromosomal anomaly was followed by several surveys which indicated that XYY men were disproportionately represented in maximum security mental hospitals. In the mid 1960s Scottish researchers studied 197 inmates and found that a significant number of them were XYY.[6] The descriptions of the violent crimes committed by some of these XYY men could easily be adapted for a series of horror films. These men were also described as above average height with below average intelligence. A media image quickly emerged of a large, dangerous, hulking "supermale" with unrestrained aggressiveness and murderous intent, stimulated by his extra male chromosome. This image was reminiscent of Lombroso's "criminal man." The public imagination was aroused and this image was hyped. These early surveys further suggested that, if the relationship between the XYY configuration and aggression were to be reliably established, there would be important implications for the determination of legal responsibility in criminal cases.

But other mental hospital studies contradicted these findings. Fox's review of the issues in 1971 convinced him to state that "the reality is that XYY males in an institution setting are less violent or aggressive when compared to matched chromosomally normal fellow inmates."[7] Some observers were passionately opposed to the possibility of any "internal causality" in the causes of crime, referring to the XYY research as "demonism revisited."

The debate heated up. Scientifically trained observers soon realized that the inconsistent findings resulted from the nonrandom, small sample sizes being drawn from institutional populations. There needed to be a larger, more carefully designed study. Herman Witkin and his coworkers published such a study in 1977.[8] They studied 31,436 Danish males in Copenhagen who were registered by the army for the draft in the years 1944–1947. Aware of the profiles from previous studies that XYY men were above average height, they selected from the draft files all those men who were 184 cm (6 feet) or more in height. This resulted in a population of 4,558 men. Over 90 percent of these men agreed to participate in the study. The researchers interviewed subjects, drew blood samples, and reviewed criminal and army records. This procedure yielded a total of 12 XYY men. Five of the twelve (42 percent) had a criminal record for minor offenses. Thus 42 percent of the XYY men had criminal convictions as compared to 9 percent of the normal, XY men. This difference reaches statistical significance, yet it is hard to accept that five XYY men with criminal convictions out of a sample of over 4,000 is a significant contribution to our understanding of crime. The XYY men did commit more crimes than normal controls, but they were not more likely to commit violent crimes and the types of offenses they did commit tended to be relatively minor.

The difference between the normal men and the XYY men did increase when factors of intelligence, social class, and age were considered. Witkin concluded that the XYY men had engaged in significantly more criminal behavior than did the normal men of their same age, height, intelligence, and social class, but they had not engaged in significant violent behavior. Low intelligence had the strongest relationship with criminal behavior. Many criminologists felt that a pernicious myth had been dismantled at last.

Biological researchers are careful to point out that the debunking of the supermale syndrome does not mean that biological factors are not involved in criminality. Adrian Raine reminds us that since the XYY configuration is the result of random chromosomal mutations at the time of conception and is not inherited, these results really give no information about the role of heredity in criminality.[9] The Copenhagen results do not invalidate data from twin and adoption studies. And finally these data *do* support increased criminal behavior, although not violent behavior, among the group of XYY men.

XYY males are rare specimens anyway. They are less than one percent of the general population. If a strong relationship were found between crime and this chromosomal configuration, the amount of crime accounted for would be small. The important question is whether the behavior of more commonly observed criminals is influenced by genetic factors.

There is also another lesson that can be drawn from the story of the supermale syndrome. This lesson is that we are easily distracted from doing the difficult work of implementing what we already know about crime and criminals by (1) media hype; (2) public fascination with the criminal side of our world; (3) the hope of discovering, through science, a quick and easy fix; and (4) scientific hubris, which tends to feed the hype, the fascination, and the hope. Whenever I read news of being on the verge of another scientific breakthrough in the understanding of crime, I remember the saga of the supermale syndrome, dramatically played out in public, with evocative images of demonism on the one side and Dr. Lombroso's criminal man on the other.

There is one more lesson from the saga of the supermale, a lesson supportive of a role for biology in crime. A female researcher at a large conference was heard to remark that the strongest relationship so far established between a single variable and crime is the relationship that exists between criminal behavior and a particular chromosomal configuration, namely, the XY configuration!

The Danish Twins

Twins provide an exceptional opportunity to study the influence of heredity and environment on criminal behavior. If behavior is inherited, we would expect to find the same behavior among people with identical genes. Thus, identical twins, which are the product of a single egg, should behave alike. Fraternal twins, on the other hand, are the product of two eggs fertilized by two sperms. Heredity is assumed to be identical in the former and different in the latter.

A book was published by Johannes Lange in Germany in 1919, rather dramatically titled in its English edition, *Crime as Destiny*.[10] Lange reported on a study made of 30 pairs of adult male twins, 13 identical and 17 fraternal. One member of each pair was a criminal, and whenever the twin was also criminal, the pair was termed concordant. His purpose was to determine if concordance was greater among identical twins than among fraternal twins. He found that 77 percent of the identical twins were concordant and 12 percent of the fraternal pairs were concordant. Such percentages are called concordance rates. The similarity of identical twins on the dimension of crime was thus 6.4 times greater than the similarity of fraternal twins. Lange's work was hailed at the time as proof of the heritability of criminality. The history of criminology has taught us to doubt such pronouncements, but Lange's work did launch nearly a century of research and debate on twin methodology and crime.

The most famous research on twins and crime was conducted in Denmark, partly due to this country's penchant for keeping detailed records and partly due to the size of the country, which made tracking down twin pairs easier. Karl O. Christiansen, who published his work in 1977, was able to avoid many of the methodological problems of earlier research.[11] He studied the incidence of criminal behavior among 3,586 twins in one region of Denmark between 1881 and 1910. He followed these twins through official police and court records. He defined "criminal" as a person convicted of acts roughly comparable to felonies in the U.S. He reported that if one twin engaged in criminal behavior, then the probability that his or her identical twin would be a criminal was 35 percent, compared with only 12 percent if the twins were fraternal. This result was less dramatic than Lange's findings, but it still indicated a role for heredity in the causes of crime.

Dalgaard and Kringlen in 1976 found a 26 percent concordance rate in Norway.[12] Hans Eysenck in 1977 conducted a review of nine twin studies involving 231 pairs of identical twins. He found that identical twins averaged 55 percent concordance for being criminal or antisocial and that the average concordance for fraternal twins was 13 percent.[13]

Raine reports in 1993 on 10 studies of identical twins yielding 13 separate analyses. Averaging concordance rates across all of these studies results in a concordance rate of 51 percent for identical twins and 21 percent for fraternal twins. Even when eliminating studies with specific weaknesses, concordance rates for identical twins remain nearly twice that of concordance rates for fraternal twins, indicating a definite link between heredity and criminal behavior.[14]

One criticism of this research is that it does not adequately separate the effects of the environment and heredity, since the twins were reared in the same environment. In addition, people may have responded to the twins in a very similar fashion *because* they were twins, thereby molding their behavior in very similar ways. Therefore a refinement for the study of crime and heredity is adoption research.

Adoption studies use a method commonly known as a cross-fostering design. To determine a link between crime and heredity, an analysis is made of children who were separated from their biological parents soon after birth and who were then raised by nonrelatives. The criminal behavior of these children is tracked through adulthood and is then analyzed in terms of the criminality of the biological parents and the criminality of the adoptive parents. Once again, the most famous research of this type was done in Denmark.

Sarnoff Mednick worked with a data bank that was created in Denmark and that included 14,000 children who were adopted between 1924 and 1947.[15] Court records were obtained on 65, 516 biological parents, adoptive parents, and adoptees in order to discover which had criminal convictions. The results are shown below.

Criminal Behavior in Male Adoptees in Denmark as a Function of Criminality in the Biological and Adoptive Parents[16]

	% of adoptees who were criminal	Total Adoptees who were criminal
Neither biological or adoptive parents are criminal	13.5%	2,492
Only the **adoptive parent** is criminal	14.7%	204
Only the **biological** parent is criminal	20.0%	1,226
Both the biological and the adoptive parent are criminal	24.5%	143

These data suggest that having an adoptive parent with a criminal conviction (14.7 percent) was no more significant than having *neither* a biological parent nor an adoptive parent with a criminal conviction (13.5 percent). But having a biological parent with a criminal conviction (20 percent) does have a statistically significant effect on criminality. Having *both* a biological parent and an adoptive parent with a criminal conviction (24.5 percent) had the strongest effect. The researchers also found that the more criminal convictions the biological parent had, the more convictions the adoptee was likely to have. The research of Mednick and his associates received a great deal of attention. A smaller study in Sweden in 1982 and a study of several hundred adoptees in Iowa and Missouri in 1983, both using a cross-fostering design, had similar results.[17]

Another refinement of this research would be to study identical twins who were reared apart. Though theoretically tantalizing, this rarely happens in the real world and so there are few opportunities to study it. There is one reported analysis of twins raised apart and crime, published by Grove and his colleagues in 1990.[18] They studied 32 pairs of identical twins who were raised apart and found a statistically significant effect for the heritability of antisocial behavior.

Raine summarizes the research on genetics and crime by reporting that almost all studies report some genetic predisposition to crime. Evidence for this genetic predisposition has been found by several independent research groups and in several different countries.[19]

Not everyone, however, is happy with this research. Walters and White wrote in 1989, "[O]ur review leads us to the inevitable conclusion that current genetic research on crime has been poorly designed, ambiguously reported, and exceedingly inadequate in addressing relevant issues."[20] Criticisms of twin studies include political bias, small sample sizes, inaccurate methods for determining zygosity (that is, identifying identical twins), and varying definitions of criminal behavior. Another criticism is that the criminality of a parent may be as much an environmental factor for the child as it is a genetic factor. Gottfredson and Hirschi are equally dubious in their 1990 book on crime. They write that the adoption studies do provide strong evidence that the genetic effect is minimal. "We conclude that the 'genetic effect,' as determined by adoption studies, is near zero."[21]

Raine offers a rebuttal to these critiques by pointing out that, in spite of methodological flaws, different studies by different researchers in different countries all point to the same conclusion, a result that is called *convergent validity*. He believes that the evidence does warrant the conclusion that heredity influences criminal behavior. The question not settled is how great this influence is. Raine argues that it is certainly not zero, but is probably not more than half either. Genetic factors are clearly not capable of explaining crime on their own. If you accept that identical twins have a concordance rate of 50 percent (and accepting this percentage is generous), this shows a strong effect for hereditary factors. However, it also means that identical twins are 50 percent discordant for criminal behavior, indicating the equally strong influence of environmental factors.[22]

It does not appear that the evidence for the heritability of criminal behavior is very strong, though certainly a hint is there. To biologists and statisticians, the numbers produced by the data on concordance rates stand out boldly against a background of randomness. To sociologists and criminologists, the numbers do not reflect much explanatory power, do not seem to greatly enhance our understanding of crime, and do not suggest practical steps that can be taken. If we return to the chart above on Mednick's data, it can be seen that when an adoptee had both a criminal biological parent and a criminal adopted parent, the adoptee was a noncriminal almost 75 percent of the time. Mednick wrote in conclusion that criminality is "modestly heritable" and that poor socialization by the adoptive parents has more detrimental effects on some boys whose genes make them more difficult to socialize than others.[23] This conclusion is reminiscent of Dobzhansky's statement that "what heredity determines are not fixed characters but developmental processes."[24]

Keep in mind that arguments against hereditary factors in crime are not arguments against biological factors in crime. "Genetic" does not equal "biological." For example, we might observe a specific brain dysfunction that was not inherited but was caused by injury or disease. Thus the cause of the dysfunction was not genetic, but was biological. Discrediting theories about heredity and crime do not necessarily lead to discarding all theories about biology and crime.

Finally, we must consider Sutherland and Cressey's contention that criminality cannot be inherited because crime is defined by legislatures and these definitions vary independently of the biological inheritance of criminals.[25] To see how complex this can become, contrast the Oklahoma City bombing with the bombing of Tehran during the Gulf War. In both instances, women and children were killed as the result of a deliberate bombing attack on a perceived enemy. In the case of Oklahoma City, the bombing was an atrocious crime. In the case of Tehran, the deaths were seen as an unfortunate consequence of war. What role is there for heredity to play in these differing perceptions of deadly bombing attacks? Crime, it would seem, is in the eye of the beholder and may not be susceptible to biological explanation at all.

6

Evolution and Crime

A Peacock's Feather

With his publication of *On the Origin of Species* in 1859, Charles Darwin shocked the world with a theory of evolution that contradicted the Biblical version of creation. Evolution is a process that results in heritable changes in a population and that occurs gradually over many generations. Darwin presented compelling evidence that evolution has occurred and suggested how it occurred. Evolution, he argued, proceeds by natural selection through the survival of the fittest species and the survival of the fittest members within each species. Because of a limited food supply, there is intense competition among the young born to any species. Those young that do survive tend to possess favorable natural variations, however slight the advantage may be, and these variations are passed on by heredity. Therefore, each generation will improve adaptively over the preceding generations, and this gradual and continuous process is the source of the evolution of species, of the variety of life on earth. This proposal appalled the Christian culture of the time because it contradicted the story of creation in Genesis.[1] Natural selection was only a part of Darwin's large conceptual scheme. He provided additional support for the concept that the earth itself is not static but evolving and that the earth is much older than it was previously believed to be. He introduced the concept that all related organisms are descended from common ancestors. In *The Descent of Man*, published in 1871, Darwin shocked the world again by arguing with impressive documentation that man's ancestors were animals of a lower order and that there is a continuous linkage between the most primitive forms of life and man.[2] Sexual selection, the main topic of *The Descent of Man*, is natural selection operating on factors that contribute to an organism's mating success. Darwin did not propose an explanation for the origin of life itself, but he did argue that we developed to our present stage in the following way:

random mutation → natural selection → sexual selection → species

The science of evolutionary biology today offers a much more complex view of evolution, along with various uncertainties, dilemmas, competing theories, contradictions, and contentiousness. It is now believed that evolution occurs in numerous ways, and that natural selection is only one of them. But Darwin's assertions challenged Biblical teachings that God had created man in His own image. Darwin's ideas set off another round in the debate between science and religion that had begun with Galileo and the Vatican in 1632, over the revolution of the earth around the sun. In the mid–nineteenth century, a furious debate was launched between creationists and evolutionists, exemplified by the famous public debates between the biologist Huxley and the bishop Wilberforce in London after the publication of Darwin's work. Galileo and Copernicus had displaced us from the center of the universe and now Darwin and Huxley had threatened to expel us from the Garden of Eden. A convincing deterministic explanation for crime would further erode the Biblical version of humankind because it would remove us from the concept of sin, evil freely chosen by a person who possesses knowledge of the good. From this perspective, the search for the causes of crime could be called the science of sin. Perhaps the Tree of the Knowledge of Good and Evil will be the next scriptural account to fall to the scientific ax and it is only a matter of time and research dollars before we have eliminated moral choice from the criminal equation. Darwin did not think so, however, because he wrote that science couldn't address the problem of evil and other moral dilemmas: "A dog might as well speculate on the mind of Newton. Let each man hope and believe as he can."[3]

The theory of evolution did have a profound impact on the scientific study of the causes of crime, most particularly on Lombroso, who proposed that serious, incorrigible criminals were throwbacks to an earlier stage of evolution. Darwin had written in 1871, "With mankind some of the worst dispositions which occasionally without any assignable cause make their appearance in families, may perhaps be reversions to a savage state, from which we are not removed by many generations."[4]

Lombroso's *Criminal Man* was published five years after this passage in Darwin's *The Descent of Man*. The influence of Darwin's ideas on Lombroso's theory of atavistic man, and on the field of criminal anthropology in general, is plain. Lombroso's proposal created excitement, inspired debate, and generated research, though his theory of criminal man was eventually discredited. Nevertheless, evolutionary concepts still make an appearance in criminology through the channels of social Darwinism, sociobiology, and evolutionary psychology.

Darwin's original theory of evolution was intended to explain the development of biological characteristics and mechanisms in the various species of plants and animals, but it was such an appealing theory that it was quickly extended to the explanation of human social behavior. The British sociologist Herbert Spencer invented the phrase "survival of the fittest" to describe the outcome of competition between social groups. He extended the idea of evolution from physical characteristics to human social behavior. In his books, published in the mid–nineteenth century, Spencer argued that, through competition, *social* evolution would inevitably produce prosperity and personal liberty unparalleled in human history. In *A System of Synthetic Philosophy* (1860), Spencer outlined a plan for a comprehensive system of philosophy, based on evolution, that would embrace and integrate all existing fields of knowledge. The initial installment in this project, *First Principles,* appeared in 1862.[5] Spencer was the foremost spokesman for this extension of Darwin's theory, known as "social Darwinism." This phrase was contrived in the late nineteenth century to describe the idea that humans, like animals and plants, compete in a struggle for existence in which natural selection results in the survival of the fittest. This was an interpretation of human society primarily in terms of biology, struggle, competition, or natural law, and this interpretation was ideally suited to the capitalistic countries that dominated the world at the time. Social Darwinism came to characterize a variety of past and present social policies and theories, from attempts to reduce the power of government to theories exploring the biological causes of human behavior. Some social Darwinists argued that governments should not interfere with human competition by attempting to regulate the economy or eradicate social ills such as poverty. Instead, they advocated a laissez-faire political and economic system that favored competition and self interest in social, political, and business affairs. Social Darwinists typically denied that they preferred a "law of the jungle," but most of them proposed arguments that justified imbalances of power between individuals, races, and nations because they considered some people more fit to survive than others. The most extreme type of social Darwinism was eugenics, a term coined by Sir Francis Galton in 1883 from the Greek word *eügenáv,* meaning well born. In *Hereditary Genius,* published in 1869, Sir Francis, a British scientist and Darwin's cousin, argued that biological inheritance is far more important than environment in determining character and intelligence.[6] Eugenists claimed that particular racial or social groups—usually wealthy Anglo-Saxons—were naturally superior to other groups. They proposed to control human heredity by passing laws that forbade marriage between races or that restrict breeding for various social misfits such as criminals or the mentally ill. Although social Darwinism was highly influential at the beginning of the twentieth century, it began to lose popularity and support after World War I, with one major exception. During the 1920s and 1930s these same ideas were used by the Nazis in their rise to power in Germany.

Spencer's extension of evolutionary concepts eventually led to the work of the American biologist E.O. Wilson. Wilson studied insects primarily, but extended his discoveries and insights to human society and published his landmark *Sociobiology* in 1975. He defined sociobiology as "the systematic study of the biological basis of all social behavior" and he argued that new behaviors evolve to the extent that they confer a selective advantage to those individuals who produce them.[7] During the 1960s, British biologist W.D. Hamilton and American biologist Robert L. Trivers produced separate studies showing that the self sacrificing behavior of some members of a group serves the genetic well-being of the group as a whole.[8] Wilson drew on these theories and argued that genetics exerts a greater influence on human behavior than scientists had previously believed. He claimed that human behavior cannot be understood without taking both biology and culture into account. Wilson's views became the foundations of a new field of scientific work and were later popularized in such studies as Richard Dawkins' *The Selfish Gene*, first published in 1976.[9] Dawkins argued that the history of life is a history of a mostly invisible war, a fierce competition between genetic lineages for survival and replication. It was this line of thought that eventually led to another set of theories about crime, other than Lombroso's, that were based on evolutionary thinking. The critics of the field of sociobiology have alleged that it is simply another version of social Darwinism. They claim that it downplays the role of culture in human societies and justifies poverty and warfare in the name of natural selection.

Evolutionary psychology is one of the children of sociobiology and is the grandchild of social Darwinism. According to evolutionary psychologists, the main goal of evolution is reproduction. Virtually any human behavior can be understood as an adaptation whose purpose is to increase the chances for reproduction. John Tooby and Leda Comides are a University of California husband and wife team who invented the term evolutionary psychology in 1992.[10] They have attempted to explain human behavior on a genetic basis, arguing that genes control, in more or less testable ways, specific human feelings, acts and propensities, from altruism to musical talent to rape. They propose that these and other specific behaviors have been produced by natural selection and that evolutionary theory might be both necessary and sufficient to explain much of human thought, action and culture. This is a long way from Darwin's original proposals, but not so far from Spencer's. The concepts advanced by evolutionary psychology were popular and appealing in the 1990s.

The dramatic and far reaching discoveries of Watson and Crick in the 1950s on the way in which genetic material is composed led to a great leap forward. The steady progress of geneticists in the mapping of the human genome in recent years has popularized genetic explanations for nearly everything. Evolution is supposed to explain alleged human universals, from male philandering and female coquetry to children's dislike of spinach. There are even claimed to be genes that account for differences between people — from sexual orientation to drug addiction, aggression, religiosity, and job satisfaction. It appears that Darwin, like Marx and Freud, has been dubbed the great interpreter of human existence. His ideas have been extended to explain all human phenomena, including crime, as we shall see in the next section. We shall also see in later sections that there are Freudian and Marxian theories of crime, as well as Darwinian. These extensions into the world of criminality were never intended by these original thinkers.

Criticisms of evolutionary psychology are cropping up along with its public popularity. The debate continues with books that are critical, like *Alas Poor Darwin*, published in 2000 by the British scientists Hilary and Stephen Rose, another husband and wife team.[11] Their polemical anthology brings 16 prominent scientists and philosophers together to say that evolutionary psychology's proponents are wrong. The writers in *Alas Poor Darwin* do not argue that genes have absolutely no influence over behavior, just that the advocates of evolutionary psychology take that view to the extreme. Interesting arguments by proponents of evolutionary psychology include *Are We Hardwired?* by UCLA professors Clark and Gruinstein and *The Evolution of Desire* by David Buss.[12] There are also attempts to reconcile religious and scientific views, such as John Haught in *God After Darwin* (1999) and Kenneth Miller's *Finding Darwin's God*.[13] Paul Ehrlich of Stanford University commented that evolutionary psychology appears long on psychology and short on evolution: "Biological evolution — evolution that is our genetic endowment — has unquestionably helped shape human natures, including human behavior in many ways. But numerous commentators expect our genetic environment to accomplish feats of which it is incapable. People don't have enough genes to program all the behaviors some evolutionary psychologists, for example, believe genes control."[14]

He further criticizes this approach to explaining human behavior because it is reductionist and too deterministic. He argues against the ideas that "all problems can be solved by dissecting them into ever smaller components" and that we "are slaves to our genes."[15] Contraception is evidence that we outwit our selfish genes.

We are left then with a good deal of argument and disagreement about evolution, between evolutionists, like Dawkins and Jay Gould,[16] between evolutionary biologists and evolutionary psychologists, and between religious views and scientific views. This grand theory of evolution is fully deserving of our rapt attention, if not our unconditional allegiance. The concept is simple and powerful and the evidence is impressive. Yet, if evolution is a continuous process, a chain of becoming, it appears to be so far a chain composed chiefly of missing links. The intermediate life forms in the chain, the links between the species, should be easier to find. The declaration that they will be found undoubtedly has more the ring of an article of faith than of the principles of experimental science. Then there is the peacock's feather. There are physical characteristics that are difficult to explain by evolution. One such is the peacock's tail, which appears to be a survival disadvantage. Evolutionists explain it by the concept of sexual selection. The peacock evolved his six feet of bulky, feathered appendage because, even though it makes it hard for him to run from enemies, it attracts the peahen, thus giving the peacock a greater likelihood of producing offspring. But that explanation doesn't solve the problem, for why does the peahen prefer it? How is the peahen behaving in concordance with the mechanism of evolution? Philip Johnson writes in *Darwin on Trial*:

> What I find intriguing is that Darwinists are not troubled by the unfitness of the peahen's sexual taste. Why would natural selection, which supposedly formed all birds from lowly predecessors, produce a species whose females lust for males with life threatening decorations? The peahen ought to have developed a preference for males with sharp talons and mighty wings. Perhaps the taste for fans is associated genetically with some absolutely vital trait like strong egg shells, but then why and how did natural selection encourage such an absurd genetic linkage?[17]

Darwin, with his characteristic frankness, wrote, "The sight of a feather in a peacock's tail whenever I gaze at it, makes me sick."[18] The peacock's feather, then, has become symbolic of questions that the theory of natural selection does not answer very well. Evolutionists developed other explanations for the peacock's feather, for example, the "good gene" theory, to which Johnson alluded in the previous passage. The "good gene" explanation is that the peacock's fan of feathers must be correlated with some other characteristic that is important to survival, and that somehow the peahen recognizes this correlation. There is evidence from fish that this could be so. The male stickleback fish has a red coloration on both of its sides. Milinski and Bakker showed that the intensity of this red color was correlated with both number of parasites and sexual attractiveness. The deeper red color showed that he was carrying fewer parasites than other males. Female sticklebacks preferred redder males.[19] Even if we admit that this observation could account for the peahen too, and thereby dispense with the problem of the peacock's tail, there are other problems still remaining 150 years after Darwin's first publication: the lack of transitional forms, the sudden explosion of complex life forms at the beginning of the Cambrian age, the difficulty of explaining the origin of the genetic code, the limits to change shown by breeding experiments, the punctuated equilibria controversy, and the importance of catastrophic extinctions. "Evolution is a grand, even an inspired conjecture, yet wears an unfinished air," wrote Macneile Dixon.[20] This unfinished air does not diminish the fruitfulness of Darwin's ideas nor the continuing research and debate about the mechanisms of evolution, but this incompleteness should prevent us from succumbing to an unquestioning fundamentalism, especially when evolutionary ideas are extended to the explanation of phenomena for which they were never intended. Can evolutionary theory explain crime?

Suckers, Cheats, and Grudgers

One of the basic problems in applying the concepts of evolution to human social behavior is that of explaining cooperation. Dawkins argued in *The Selfish Gene*, first published in 1976, that genes are ruthlessly selfish in their struggle for survival and that they give rise to selfish human behavior.[21] If human behavior is the result of intense competition for the survival of individuals, and if human behavior is basically selfish behavior, what explains cooperation and altruism? There are several explanations for cooperative behavior from an evolutionary perspective, but the principal one is that altruism is an illusion; that is to say, it is not truly unselfish in the survival sense. Altruistic behavior occurs because it carries a survival advantage, either through *kin selection* or through *reciprocal altruism*. An animal's direct offspring and its close kin carry copies of its genes. Therefore, unselfishly aiding one's offspring or close relatives increases the possibility of survival of one's own genes and hence it is only apparently altruistic; it is actually selfish. Here we mean "selfish" in the language of evolutionary biology, in the sense that it increases the probability of the survival of one's own gene lineage. This evolutionary explanation for cooperation is called kin selection.

Reciprocal altruism refers to those instances in which cooperative behavior occurs because it is to the survival advantage of both, or of all the animals in a group, to cooperate. For example, wolves hunting in a pack are cooperating because they are more likely to be successful and more likely to kill larger prey if they cooperate than if they hunt alone. Each individual wolf is better off cooperating so long as his share of the kill is greater than he could obtain hunting by himself, and so long as he gets his share, that is, he is not cheated by the others. There could be a survival advantage for the wolf who cheated another out of his share, and it is from this line of thought that evolutionary ideas about crime emerged. From an evolutionary perspective, crime is cheating behavior that results in a survival advantage.

John Maynard Smith is credited with having made the connection between evolutionary theory and game theory that resulted, among other things, in some evolutionary thinking about crime.[22] Dawkins explored this connection extensively in the several editions of his book. The basic game theory model, which has been used to explain human social behavior in evolutionary terms, is called the prisoners' dilemma game (PDG). The game was designed by social scientists to study cooperation and competition among people and to examine human decision making. It works like this: Imagine that there are two criminals that are arrested for bank robbery. We will name them Bonnie and Clyde. Upon arrest, Bonnie and Clyde are separated from each other and are unable to communicate with each other at all. The police are convinced that Bonnie and Clyde are guilty, but they also realize that they do not have enough evidence to convict either one of them unless somebody confesses. If neither Bonnie nor Clyde confess, the prosecutor will have to charge them with a minor firearms violation which carries a relatively light sentence of one year. Bonnie is then approached by the prosecutor and offered the following deal: if she and Clyde both confess, then they will each get a sentence of five years. If she doesn't confess, but Clyde does confess, then she will get ten years and Clyde will be set free. If she confesses, but Clyde does not, then he will get ten years and she will be set free. Bonnie's dilemma then is what to do; to confess or not to confess. The prosecutor then goes to Clyde and offers him exactly the same deal. Thus both prisoners are in the same dilemma. There are four possible outcomes, which are illustrated in the chart below.

The best outcome for both of them is if they both do not confess; however, remember that they cannot communicate with each other, and so each one does not know what the other one will do. If Bonnie decides not to confess, but Clyde does confess, then she loses. The same goes for Clyde. What then will people do when placed in this dilemma?

Bonnie

Clyde	Confesses	Doesn't confess
Confesses	Bonnie gets 5 years Clyde gets 5 years	Bonnie gets 10 years Clyde gets 0 years
Doesn't Confess	Bonnie gets 0 years Clyde gets 10 years	Bonnie gets 1 year Clyde gets 1 year

A Payoff Matrix for the Prisoners' Dilemma Game

This game model has been used in thousands of experiments and with many variations.[23] For example, sometimes money or points are used rather than years in prison. Sometimes "Bonnie" and "Clyde" are two different teams of people who make a team decision. Usually, the game is played several times so that, after the first time, the two players know what each other did the last time and can therefore make their decisions based on what the other player decided in a previous game. Successive games can continue to be played until each player has established a stable pattern of decision making. A "cooperative" player will not confess, because this decision holds the possibility of the best outcome for both players, and it also gives the best outcome to the other player, even though it is risky, because if the other player does not also cooperate (not confess), then the "cooperative player" loses. A "competitive" player will confess because it holds the least risk for him and creates the possibility that he will win and the other player will lose. This experimental design is clever and intriguing because it creates conflicting pressures to cooperate and to compete.

After many controlled experiments, the major result obtained was that most people will follow the reciprocity principle; that is, if a player perceives that the other player is cooperating with him, he will cooperate also. If he finds that the other player is competing with him, he will adopt a competitive strategy, too. It was also found that individual players may adopt a variety of strategies. As Dawkins and others analyzed the experiments, they found that some players always cooperate and are often taken advantage of by other players. They are therefore called suckers. Some players always compete, no matter what, and they are called cheats, because they always take and never give. Some players always do whatever the other player did the last time they played and these players are said to have a *tit for tat* strategy. If the other player cooperated the last time, they will cooperate this time. If the other player competed last time, they will compete this time. Some players will always cooperate on the first encounter, but if the other player competes, they will compete on subsequent encounters, as if they were holding a grudge. They are therefore called grudgers.

Dawkins and others ran computer simulations of the prisoners' dilemma game comparing the different possible strategies and their eventual effects on a given population of players. They learned that the tit for tat strategy worked the best; that is, players using this strategy accumulated the most points over a large number of encounters. The researchers equated this outcome with having a survival advantage. Other findings included that suckers do very well when encountering each other, but fare very poorly when meeting cheats. Cheats do poorly when meeting each other because neither one gains anything, but a "mutant" cheat in a population of suckers does very well indeed. Grudgers do well when meeting each other. They do poorly at first against cheats, but eventually gain ground and overcome cheats. In a population with a majority of suckers, with equally sized minorities of grudgers and cheats, the suckers were driven to extinction. The cheats peaked early on but were eventually overcome by the grudgers and became extinct themselves.

Recall that this line of thought was originally pursued in order to attempt to account for the development of cooperation within the competitive context of evolution. How does this development result in an explanation for crime? First an extension is assumed. This extension is that the cheating behavior described above is antisocial behavior and as such it is essentially the same as criminal behavior. Then it is argued that this cheating = antisocial = criminal behavior has a survival advantage under certain circumstances. These circumstances would include the existence of a large population of suckers and/or grudgers and a relatively small population of cheats who have the ability to move from one population to another when the grudgers start to exclude them. These simulations with the prisoners' dilemma game are taken to demonstrate that criminal behavior could evolve and survive as a minority behavior. It is also argued that standards of morality, guilt, and conscience may have developed as a defense against this cheating behavior.

There are also proposals for a sociobiological understanding of specific crimes, such as rape and homicide. From an evolutionary point of view, rape can be seen as a sort of cheat strategy. Thornhill and Thornhill have argued that rape is a reproductive strategy when a male lacks the resources and social status needed to attract a mate.[24] As a natural example, they report the case of the scorpion fly. The male scorpion fly attracts a female for mating by offering her a dead insect. He mates with her while she is feeding. Males who are unsuccessful in competing for a mating may grab a leg or a wing of a passing female, reposition her, and copulate. The Thornhills then argue that data on rape in humans are consistent with an evolutionary perspective (that is, a successful reproductive strategy). They cite data that shows that young women are raped more often than older women and that the age distribution of rape victims tends to follow fertility distribution in women. Their argument is not very convincing, however, because there are a substantial number of rapists with sexual dysfunction who do not succeed in impregnating their victims, and some rapists kill or seriously injure their victims, which is hardly consistent with a reproductive strategy. Rape often consists of oral and anal sex with no reproductive intent nor possible result of pregnancy. Finally, there are high status rapists who do not need to resort to force to have offspring.[25]

Daley and Wilson propose that there is an evolutionary basis for homicide. Their argument is that sociobiological theory predicts that there is an inverse relationship between genetic relatedness and homicide.[26] That means that persons are much more likely to be killed by people to whom they are not genetically related. Daley and Wilson report data that is consistent with this prediction. They found that victims are killed by relatives in less than 33 percent of the cases across large samples in the U.S. Other data from a large city showed that while 19 percent of murder victims were killed by their spouses, only 6 percent were killed by a blood relative. They looked at data for murders committed by people who lived with their victim and found that nongenetic coresidents are 11 times more likely to kill than are genetically related coresidents. Finally, they cite data that shows that children are much more likely to killed by stepparents than by natural parents. A child living in the U.S. with stepparents is over 100 times more likely to be fatally abused than a child living with its genetic parents. Raine states that "these data suggest that homicide may have its roots in evolution," but this argument seems like a very thin explanation for murder, involving only a relatively small number of homicides.[27] It hardly seems necessary to invoke evolutionary theory to predict that blood relatives are less likely to kill each other than are strangers. It sheds no light on either murder or on evolution.

There are several problems with the evolutionary explanation of crime. Since it is not possible to design experiments to test evolutionary theory, it is necessary to attempt to fit existing patterns of behavior to predictions that would be made from a sociobiological perspective, as was done, for example, in the above analyses of rape and homicide. This way of doing it gives the explanation a manipulated and suspicious flavor; the model appears retrospectively fitted to the data. Crimes include a very large range of behaviors. Which ones does evolutionary psychology propose to explain? What, for example, is the reproductive strategy behind driving while intoxicated or arson? Another problem is the assumption that competitive behavior, selfish behavior, aggressive behavior, antisocial behavior, and criminal behavior are all essentially the same thing, so that, if you explain any one of them, you have succeeded in explaining all of them. As we discussed at length in an earlier note, we must define the subject of our study and we must distinguish it from other, different subjects. It is hard to argue that an inexorable biological mechanism explains crime when the definition of crime varies according to social context. If crime is a successful reproductive strategy, why isn't there more of it?

Evolution is a very big subject. A quick Internet search produced a list of over 6,000 *recent* books with the word evolution or the word Darwin in the title or subtitle. We have not intended to argue this great subject except in regard to its direct application to the explanation of crime. This application of Darwin's "grand theory" was not at all intended by him, or by most evolutionists, and that is very much to the point. Like the theories of Freud, Marx, and others who never intended to explain crime, a powerful theory is often extended by its later followers to the explanation of crime, among several dozen other things, as if they were saying, "Oh, by the way, this probably explains crime and criminals, too." The great theorists would not approve and we should not either, unless reason and facts compel us.

7

Broken Brains and
Other Neurological Factors

The Strange Case of Phineas Gage

On September 13, 1848, a construction foreman named Phineas Gage was the victim of a bizarre accident. The consequences of this accident were to become legendary in the history of brain science. The circumstances of the case were so dramatic and its implications for the understanding of human behavior were so puzzling and intriguing that the case is still cited in textbooks on biology, psychology, and criminology.[1]

Gage was 25 years old and worked for a railroad company, laying tracks across Vermont. Part of his job was to oversee the blasting of rocks that obstructed the path of the tracks. This task was accomplished by drilling a hole in the rock, then filling the hole halfway with explosive powder, inserting a fuse, filling the rest of the hole with sand, and tamping the sand with an iron rod before lighting the fuse. On one particular job, in a moment of distraction, Gage began tamping the powder with the iron rod before his helper had poured in the sand. Consequently, he struck sparks against the rock and prematurely set off a loud explosion. The workers on the job who witnessed the accident reported a strange whistling sound that seemed to accompany the blast. The iron rod had been blown out of the hole like a miniature missile.

The rod was three feet, seven inches long and 1.25 inches in diameter. Gage had it specially made for this task. The force of the explosion sent the rod into his left cheek, drove it through the base of his skull, and then across the front of his brain. It exited through the top of his head and eventually landed more than a hundred feet away, covered in blood and pieces of his brain. Gage was thrown on his back but was still alive. He did not even lose consciousness. He lay silent for a few minutes, as if thinking hard about something, and then spoke with the members of his crew.

He was loaded onto an ox cart and carried into the nearest town, where one of the town physicians was summoned.

Gage not only survived the damage from the rod, but also survived the infection that followed it, a frequent killer in those days. In two months, he was declared cured. His youth and constitution aided him in recovery, as did the attention and efforts of his physician, Dr. John Harlow. This case, which Dr. Harlow treated early in his career, became a life-long project for him.

Gage lost the vision in his left eye, but retained perfect vision in his right. Otherwise, all of his systems seemed intact. There were no noticeable defects or disabilities; he could walk, touch, hear, and speak. There was no paralysis or loss of dexterity. His coordination was unimpaired. There were no difficulties in speech or the use of language. Yet, the changes in Gage's behavior were so obvious and so profound that his friends complained that "Gage was no longer Gage." His employers, previously so pleased with him, fired him shortly after he returned to work. He was not lacking in physical ability or skill, but the change in his character rendered him unable to perform his job.

Prior to his accident, Gage was a valuable employee. Hard working and skillful, he was respected and admired. His employers said, "[H]e was the most efficient and capable man in our employ." He was diligent and persistent, possessed "temperate habits" and had "considerable energy of character." But after the accident, Harlow wrote that Gage became "fitful and irreverent, indulging at times in the grossest profanity which was not previously his custom." Gage was now capricious, short of temper, vacillating, unable to carry out the plans that he frequently devised. He made up tales that were not true and did not seem to understand what was in his best interest. He did not follow social conventions and was not concerned at all about others. Harlow concluded that Gage was like "a child in his intellectual capacity, [but] he has the animal passions of a strong man."[2]

Gage began to drift from job to job, never staying for long anywhere. He once did a stint with Barnum's circus in New York City, describing his accident to sight seekers, showing them his scars and the iron rod that injured him; he carried the rod with him everywhere he went. He spent some years in South America working on farms and ranches but little is known of the details of his life during those years. Eventually he moved to San Francisco to live with his mother and sister. He was unable to maintain steady employment and was apparently supported by them. He died in 1861 of a seizure disorder at age 38.

No autopsy was performed after Gage's death, and Harlow did not know of his death until five years later. He petitioned Gage's sister to have the body exhumed and the skull removed as a record of the case. The sister and her husband agreed and sent the skull across the country to Harlow. The tamping iron, which had been buried alongside of Gage's body, was also retrieved and sent to Harlow. Gage's skull and his iron rod now reside in a museum at the Harvard Medical School in Boston. Therefore, we can accurately speak of Dr. Harlow's skull appearing on the scene in the U.S. just five years before Dr. Lombroso's skull in Italy.[3]

Dr. Harlow's skull was destined for a more interesting fate than was Dr. Lombroso's. Because both the skull and the rod had been collected and stored for over 130 years, they were available to provide the critical data for a computer simulation of the accident and the injuries that it caused. Such a simulation was conducted by Hanna Damasio in 1994. She concluded that it was selective damage in the prefrontal cortices of Phineas Gage's brain that led to his poor decision making and his inability to conform to social conventions.[4] Anthony Damasio reports that subsequent study of patients with neurological damage has confirmed that Gage's specific profile of symptoms occurs in other patients with similar brain damage. Damasio refers to such patients as "modern Gages." He writes, "There is no question that Gage's personality change was caused by a circumscribed brain lesion in a specific site."[5] Research in the last half of the twentieth century on the link between brain dysfunction and antisocial behavior produced results that were suggestive but inconsistent and inconclusive. Frontal lobe dysfunction, prefrontal cortex damage, left and right hemisphere dysfunction, and dysfunction in the limbic regions of the temporal lobe have all been linked with criminal behavior. It would appear that since the dramatic and intriguing case of Phineas Gage we have learned a great deal about how individual human behavior is affected by damage to specific sites in the brain. This work has not, however, illumined us regarding the causes of crime. On one pole sit criminologists such as Gottfredson and Hirschi who argue that, over the last 150 years, biology has contributed "little in the way of meaningful or interpretable research" on the causes of crime.[6] And on the other pole sit those such as someone like Raine, a neuropsychologist, who writes that biological research into crime is imperative if the scientific community is to have any chance of reaching a comprehensive understanding of the causes of crime. Raine goes on to comment that biological scientists do not integrate their findings with social scientists, and vice versa, so the two groups of scientists do not learn much from each other.[7] Consequently, there is little investigation of how social, psychological, and biological factors influence each other. Our miserable record so far of putting into practice what we already know about crime and its causes does not lead us to feel that we are on the brink of important new discoveries from the laboratory about the causes of crime.

Neurological Factors in Criminal Behavior

Neurological dysfunction, whether the result of injury, disease, hered-ity, or chemical imbalance, has been proposed as a possible cause of crim-inal behavior, especially violent behavior, since the nineteenth century. Much of this research has been aimed at explaining what, precisely, is wrong with the psychopath. Some of the research on the causes of psy-chopathy is reviewed in part 3 of this work, *Psychological Explanations for Crime*, because much of this research was conducted by psychologists. Reviewing in detail the research on neurological factors and crime, includ-ing a careful assessment of its strengths and its flaws, would require a thick volume all its own. Here we only wish to give the reader an impression of the variety of factors that have been considered and the general conclu-sions regarding such research.

There has long been the suggestion that crime, especially violent crime, may be caused, or at least, influenced, by damage or dysfunction in the brain. Electroencephalograms (EEGs) measure electrical activity in the brain. The EEGs of antisocial persons have often been found to be abnormal. The exact nature of the abnormality and the reasons for the abnormalities that are observed are still disputed.[8]

Brain sites specifically examined for links to antisocial behavior include the frontal lobe, the left hemisphere, and the limbic system. Left hemisphere dysfunction could predispose an individual to violent offend-ing by disrupting control over impulsive behavior. This is an intriguing hypothesis but is unproven.[9] Reduced lateralization for language has also been explored. The majority of people are left hemisphere dominant for language, but antisocial individuals have been shown in experiments to be less lateralized for linguistic processes. This result matches up well with the long reported observation that psychopaths use language differently than most people.[10] (Some observers would argue that this unusual use of language by the psychopath is supposed to confuse and mislead others and is entirely intentional.)

Damage to the frontal cortex has been shown to result in a pattern of deficits that include distractibility, shallowness, emotional lability, reduced ability to use symbols, and violence. There is some evidence that frontal lobe damage is linked with criminal and violent behavior, but the experimental results so far are inconsistent and not conclusive.[11] Results from studies of "psychosurgery," specifically prefrontal lobotomies and amygdalectomies, have not thus far resulted in important results for specific links to criminal behavior.[12]

Neurotransmitters are chemicals that make possible communication between cells in the brain. Because of their crucial role in communication, they underlie all types of behavior, including memory, perception, learning, eating, and drinking. Abnormal neurotransmitter levels have been shown to be related to specific mental disorders, such as increased dopamine in schizophrenia and reduced serotonin in depression. The most studied neurotransmitters are serotonin, dopamine, and norepinephrine. Scerbo and Raine conducted a summary and meta-analysis of 29 studies of antisocial behavior and neurotransmitters. Their major findings were reduced serotonin and norepinephrine in persons exhibiting antisocial behavior as compared to normal subjects, when only studies using a direct measure of the neurotransmitter levels were considered. Results also indicated that all types of violent offenders had reduced serotonin levels as compared to nonaggressives. Raine suggests that reduced serotonin and alcohol have a disinhibiting effect on behavior.[13] However, such neurochemical studies often do not control for environmental factors that could be the cause of reduced neurotransmitter levels. No clear causal inferences can be made from this work since neurotransmitter levels can be affected by a variety of factors including stress, diet, drugs, and alcohol use.

Alcoholism is associated with variations in levels of neurotransmitters and with violent behavior. The Bureau of Justice Statistics reported in 1998 that four in ten violent offenses involved alcohol use by the offender, and that among state prison inmates convicted of murder, half reported that alcohol was involved in their crimes. Studies indicate a high percentage of people who are arrested, convicted, and incarcerated have abused alcohol and illegal drugs.[14] While the association is clear, causation has not been established. The findings do not explain the large number of persons who use alcohol and drugs but do not engage in other criminal behavior. Some suggested explanations include that there is a genetic link in some people between alcohol and violence, that alcohol increases the production of testosterone, and that it affects levels of serotonin in the bloodstream, but there is little evidence for any of these proposals.[15] While there is a demonstrated relationship between alcohol and violent crime, especially among males, the reason for this relationship remains unclear. As for drug abuse, Harrison and Gfroerer, after a summary of the research on drug use and crime, concluded that

> [T]here is no firm evidence of a causal relationship between drug use and crime. The general conclusion reached by a number of researchers is that deviant behaviors such as drug use and criminal offenses occur within the

context of a general deviance syndrome. Those likely to engage in one form of deviant behavior (i.e., crime) are also likely to engage in other forms of deviant behavior (i.e., drug use).[16]

Head injury, birth complications, fetal maldevelopment, cortisol, testosterone, hypoglycemia, diet, and lead poisoning have all been linked with criminal behavior.[17] The word *linked* in this instance does not mean *caused*. For example, head injuries have been found in disproportionate numbers among violent offenders. The suggestion is that head trauma may have causal influence in acts of violence. But there are plausible alternative explanations for this finding. Violent offenders become involved in violent situations that put them at much greater risk for head injuries than nonviolent persons. In such cases, a history of head injury may be the *result* of violent behavior, not its cause. Many violent offenders come from abusive homes in which childhood injury is likely. In these cases, it is plausible that chronic maltreatment in childhood and the socialization to use violence against others contributed more to the adult violent behavior than did a specific head injury.

Sustained perinatal trauma was found more likely among seriously delinquent incarcerated children than among nonincarcerated delinquents and, in one study, minor physical anomalies, which may be the result of fetal maldevelopment in the first trimester of pregnancy, were found to be related to violent offending.[18]

There are many problems associated with this research, such as small sample size, indirect measures of variables, nonrandom control groups, absence of replication, and contradictory findings from other studies. Needless to say, significant contributions to the understanding of crime have not yet been established from this menu of possibilities, but the effort has been laudable and the suggestion of biological abnormality remains.

In *Firestorms in the Brain*, Daniel Amen reports on his observations using brain SPECT imaging.[19] SPECT (single photo emission computed tomography) is a technique that uses very small doses of radioisotopes to evaluate brain blood flow and activity patterns. The images resulting from SPECT depict relatively areas of activity and inactivity in the brain. The technique is typically used to assess brain function in cases involving strokes, seizures, dementia, and head trauma. Amen has used SPECT to assess a variety of problems including anxiety, depression, and attention deficit disorder. He has also used it to study aggression and violence. In one study, for example, he used the SPECT procedure to study the living brains of 50 murderers and 200 other violent felons. He found a consistent pattern of abnormalities in these images when compared with normal, noncriminal, nonviolent subjects. This pattern was (1) reduced activity in the prefrontal cortex; (2) overactivity in the anterior cingulate gyrus; and (3) abnormalities in the left temporal lobe. He concludes that SPECT can further our understanding of violence and aggression and that violence and aggression can be treated with medication to compensate for the above listed abnormalities: an anticonvulsant to stabilize temporal lobe abnormalities, a serotonergic agent to decrease activity in the anterior cingulate gyrus, and a psychostimulant to activate prefrontal cortex activity. He offers a series of SPECT images of violent offenders as examples.

This study is reminiscent of Raine's summary of brain imaging research over a decade ago. Raine argued in his book *The Psychopathology of Crime* that brain imaging research up to that time supported the hypothesis that frontal dysfunction may characterize violent offending. In the last chapter of his book, he is enthusiastic about the development of new and faster brain imaging techniques that will lead us closer to an understanding of crime as a psychopathological disorder: "[I]t holds the promise of revolutionizing our understanding of the neural networks which in part contribute to criminal and violent behavior, and therefore of understanding the causes of such behavior."[20]

PART THREE

Psychological Explanations for Crime

Whatever these people may be called, they are not normal.
— Hervey Cleckley[1]

Conscience, I suggested, is a conditioned response (CR) acquired according to Pavlovian principles.
— Hans Eysenck[2]

8

Psychopathy

The Psychopath

For some of us, the word psychopath is irresistibly associated with the classic film *Psycho*, in which Tony Perkins as Norman Bates is walking deliberately up the stairs wearing a malevolent, ironical smile. Or we might likewise be reminded of the calculating violence of Robert De Niro as Max Cady in *Cape Fear* or the gruesome horror beneath the brilliant charm of Anthony Hopkins as Hannibal Lector in *The Silence of the Lambs*. We are fascinated with these films and dozens of others like them, stories of vicious killers apparently normal on the surface but deadly and wicked underneath. The prototype is Robert Louis Stevenson's *Dr. Jekyll and Mr. Hyde*. These are all fictional characters, of course, but the word psychopath can as easily conjure up for us images of real people, such as Kenneth Bianchi, the Hillside Strangler; or David Berkowitz, the Son of Sam; or Ted Bundy; Gary Gilmore; Charlie Manson; Jeffrey MacDonald; or Edward Gein, the real killer who was the inspiration for *The Silence of the Lambs*.

In the media and in popular usage, *psychopath* is often employed to refer to a person who has committed an especially brutal and heinous crime, such as a sadistic murder, or a series of such murders. Sometimes the word is used incorrectly to refer to a person who is obviously mentally ill and has committed a violent crime. Sometimes the term is used to refer to a charming and sophisticated liar who easily manipulates other people, like Jack Nicholson in *One Flew over the Cuckoo's Nest*. Psychopath is one of those labels that has been applied so often and so casually in so many different contexts that its appearance in print or in conversation can be ambiguous and misleading. It means literally "disease of the mind" (psyche = mind and pathos = disease) or, as David Lykken puts it: "psychologically damaged."[1] But in professional usage, the word has evolved to a paradoxical meaning that results in much confusion. Clinicians currently apply the term psychopath to a person who is specifically *not* mentally ill, at least not in the legal or medical sense. A psychopath is a person who repeatedly commits crimes without any apparent concern for the consequences of his behavior. The notable researchers William and Joan McCord in their 1959 book *The Origins of Crime* defined the psychopath as an aggressive, impulsive person who feels little or no guilt and is unable to form lasting bonds of affection with other human beings.[2] Robert Hare wrote in 1993 that "psychopaths are social predators who charm, manipulate and ruthlessly plow their way through life, leaving a broad trail of broken hearts, shattered expectations, and empty wallets."[3]

As a measure of general popular usage of the word, *The Oxford Dictionary* defines the word psychopath as "a person suffering from chronic mental disorder with abnormal or violent social behavior."[4] This is really a good effort at accuracy and clarity, though some scientists would question whether the psychopath has a mental disorder. Some observers would object to the medical context in which the definition is presented and would comment that the psychopath does not appear to suffer at all; it is rather the victims of the psychopath who are suffering.

The word *psychopath* as a clinical label first appeared in the nineteenth century to describe a diverse and poorly understood group of mental disorders, the "psychopathic personality disorders." A belief that these disorders were hereditary resulted in the phrase "psychopathic constitutional inferiority." G.E. Partridge, an American psychiatrist, called this group of disorders a "wastebasket" category, a group of disorders lumped together because no one understood any of them.[5] In a bid for greater clarity and precision, he instead added to the confusion by adopting the term *sociopath*. This term was first introduced by Birnbaum in 1909, who believed that this disorder was the product of social learning and early environmental influences.[6] Partridge noted that this particular personality type exhibited a disposition to violate the social norms of behavior, hence the label *sociopath*. Eventually, *sociopath* became more or less interchangeable with *psychopath* in popular usage. Which label to choose seemed to depend mainly on the user's own theory about crime causation. Persons who believed that criminal behavior was the result of social problems chose the term *sociopath* while persons who favored an internal psychological or physical cause of criminal behavior selected *psychopath*. Cason reviewed the literature in 1943 and found 202 different words and phrases that were considered synonymous with *psychopath* or *psychopathic*.[7] Curran and Mallinson wrote that "the only conclusion that seems warrantable is that some time or other and by some reputable authority the term 'psychopathic personality' has been used to designate every conceivable type of abnormal character."[8]

Eventually the American Psychiatric Association settled on the term *antisocial* personality disorder.[9] This term immediately calls to mind the nineteenth century term psychopathic personality disorders. A personality disorder is a set of stable, enduring attributes and patterns of behavior that bring the person into conflict with the expectations of that individual's culture. Personality disorders are inferred from observations of a person's behavior when that person's behavior is consistently conflicted. There are ten specific personality disorders diagnosed by today's clinicians. None of them are well enough understood to have any consistently successful treatment for them. Antisocial personality disorder is one of the ten, the one that involves persistently criminal behavior. Some observers continue to agree with Partridge that personality disorder is a garbage can category for a colorful assortment of mental and emotional disturbances that no one understands.

The most recent version of the *Diagnostic and Statistical Manual (DSM-IV-TR)* of the American Psychiatric Association, published in 2000, lists the following criteria for a diagnosis of antisocial personality disorder:

A. There is a pervasive pattern of disregard for, and violation of, the rights of others occurring since age 15 years, as indicated by three (or more) of the following:
(1) *Failure to conform to social norms* with respect to lawful behaviors as indicated by repeatedly performing acts that are grounds for arrest
(2) *Deceitfulness*, as indicated by repeated lying, use of aliases, or conning others for personal profit or pleasure
(3) *Impulsivity* or failure to plan ahead
(4) *Irritability and aggressiveness*, as indicated by repeated physical fights or assaults
(5) *Reckless disregard* for the safety of self and others
(6) *Consistent irresponsibility*, as indicated by repeated failure to sustain consistent work behavior or honor financial obligations
(7) *Lack of remorse*, as indicated by being indifferent to or rationalizing having hurt, mistreated, or stolen from another
B. The individual is at least age 18 years.
C. There is evidence of Conduct Disorder (major age appropriate norms and values are persistently disregarded) with onset before age 15 years.
D. The occurrence of antisocial behavior is not exclusively during the course of Schizophrenia or a Manic Episode.[10]

Notice particularly that, in this scheme, violent behavior is not a necessary characteristic and that the *absence* of recognized mental illness is a central criterion. Hare argues that these diagnostic criteria would qualify nearly every person in prison and that all people who have committed crimes are not psychopaths.[11] Another way to make this point is to say that all psychopaths could be diagnosed with antisocial personality disorder, but not all persons diagnosed with antisocial personality disorder are psychopaths (in Hare's view). Some clinicians and researchers contend that the term *psychopath* should be reserved for the most extreme group of criminals, that is, extreme either in the number or pervasiveness of crimes committed or in the intensity or seriousness of the criminal behavior.

The confusion concerning this group of people persists into the present. The term psychopath is now most often used by clinicians to set apart and label a particular group of extreme criminals who repeatedly commit crimes. In its present and most precise usage, not all criminals are psychopaths and not all psychopaths have criminal records, though all psychopaths engage in antisocial behavior, whether they are caught or not. Some psychopaths are violent, but others are not. Psychopaths do not experience hallucinations, delusions, extreme anxiety, or loss of contact with reality. They are not considered mentally ill in the medical sense because they do not exhibit the symptoms of a known, diagnosable mental disorder of organic origin. Some researchers, Raine and Hare for instance, do argue that psychopathy *may* be a mental disorder of organic origin, but this has not been convincingly demonstrated yet and there is no medical treatment for psychopaths at present.[12] Psychopaths are not mentally ill in the legal sense because they have "substantial capacity" to appreciate the wrongfulness of their conduct and to conform their behavior to the requirements of the law. They are able to distinguish right from wrong. They persistently choose the wrong. Is such a person mad or bad? Is he possessed? Badly socialized? Mentally ill? Damaged? Evil?

The History of Psychopathy

By whatever name or label, the idea, or theory, of psychopathy is that criminal behavior, or at least some kinds of criminal behavior, are caused by mental disease or defect. This idea is usually traced to the famous French physician Philippe Pinel (1745–1826) who used the term *manie sans delire* (mania without delirium) in his classification of mental diseases published in 1801.[13] Pinel was a mental health reformer who got the opportunity to be chief of the hospital at Bicetre and later at Salpetriere as a result of the French Revolution. He had a rare compassion for the mentally ill and an intense motivation to try to understand them. He wrote, "The mentally sick far from being guilty people deserving of punishment, are sick people whose miserable state deserves all the consideration that is due to suffering humanity. One should try with the simplest methods to restore their reason."[14] He released mentally ill patients from chains and physical torment. Pinel's work eventually inspired reform throughout the Western world. In addition to instituting reforms in the treatment of the mentally ill, he also initiated the systematic keeping of records and the psychiatric case history. From his habit of carefully observing patients and taking notes, he was able to accumulate material that resulted in a publication on the classification and treatment of mental disorders. In the course of this work, he observed some patients who lashed out violently at others but who had no impairment at all in their intellectual or cognitive abilities. In referring to these patients he used the phrase *manie sans delire*. "I thought that madness was inseparable from delirium or delusion, and I was surprised to find many maniacs who at no period gave evidence of any lesion of the understanding."[15] This was the beginning of the idea of psychopathy. It was also the beginning of the idea of "mad not bad." This concept was followed by attempts to understand harmful behavior towards others, absence of remorse, and lack of conscience in medical terms, that is, in terms of disease.

In 1835, J.C. Prichard, an English psychiatrist, in his *Treatise on Insanity*, described a "form of mental derangement" in which the intellect seemed unimpaired but in which "the power of self government" was lost or lacking, so that the individual was incapable of "conducting himself with decency and propriety in the business of life."[16] Prichard called such patients "morally insane" or "morally imbecile." The American psychiatrist Isaac Ray followed shortly with his *Medical Jurisprudence of Insanity*, published in 1838, which exerted a wide influence on conceptions of criminal responsibility and mental illness. His chapter 7 is on "moral mania," about which he writes, "Thus far Mania has been considered as affecting the intellectual faculties only.... It will not be denied that the propensities and sentiments are also integral portions of our mental constitution and ... dependent on the cerebral organism.... We were bound to believe that [the brain] is liable to disease and consequently, that the affective, as well as the intellectual faculties are subject to derangement."[17]

Towards the end of the nineteenth century, the hypothesis was advanced that people who answered the description given by Prichard probably suffered from some hereditary weakness of the nervous system; hence the term *constitutional psychopathic inferiority*. This was only a hypothesis, an inference from the way in which the person behaved. Emil

Kraepelin (1855–1926), a German psychiatrist whose great textbook on mental disorders went through eight editions from 1883–1913, used the term *psychopath* and delineated seven types: antisocial, eccentric, excitable, impulsive, liar and swindler, quarrelsome, and unstable.[18]

What was happening here was the development of the theory of psychopathy: that moral judgment could be affected by disease or defect, without any obvious impairment in the intellectual functions of the person and without other classic symptoms of mental illness. As Robert White puts it, "These two ideas— a defect in the realm of socialized behavior and an innate weakness lying behind it — have continued to dominate most thinking about psychopathic personality."[19] These ideas were developing concurrently with the work of the positivists in criminology, the Italians Lombroso, Ferri, and their colleagues.

There was, inevitably, a phase of development in which psychoanalytic theories were applied to the problem of criminal behavior. Freud himself had almost nothing to say about criminals. One of the few things that he did say was that the technique of psychoanalysis was not appropriate for treating criminality.[20] This declaration did not, of course, prevent his followers from making the attempt. Franz Alexander published a widely read book in 1935, *The Roots of Crime*, in which he asserted that antisocial behavior represents an unconscious effort to obtain punishment in order to alleviate feelings of guilt.[21] Alexander adopted the term *neurotic character* to label the psychopath and this began the use of the phrase *character disorder*. This term enjoyed a relatively brief popularity but the problem of describing the difference between character and personality proved too difficult (describing the word *personality* is hard enough) and this term is no longer encountered in professional circles. The psychoanalytic point of view was popular for awhile, but most clinicians and other interested observers concluded that the psychopath's lack of remorse was perfectly genuine and was not covering anything, a point well made by Cleckley in his classic work *The Mask of Sanity*. His work laid the foundation for our present point of view on the theory of psychopathy.

The Mask of Sanity

"Whatever these people might be called," wrote Hervey Cleckley in *The Mask of Sanity*, "they are not normal."[22] Cleckley's insightful book on the psychopath was first published in 1941 and has been through five editions, the last one in 1976. Additional revised versions were published in 1982 and in 1988. The title of the book refers to the fact that the psychopath appears perfectly normal on the surface but is quite abnormal beneath his "mask of sanity."[23] *The Mask of Sanity* greatly influenced researchers in the U.S. and in Canada and it has provided the basis for most of the research on psychopathy over the last quarter of the twentieth century. Cleckley was also the author of *The Three Faces of Eve*, an engrossing and dramatic book on multiple personality disorder, which was made into a popular film.[24]

Cleckley dramatized the problem of understanding the psychopath by presenting a large collection of vividly described case histories from his own practice. In reviewing these histories, Lykken writes, "Here were people of good families, intelligent and rational, sound of mind and body, who lied without compunction, cheated, stole, casually violated any and all norms of social conduct whenever it suited their whims. Moreover they seemed surprisingly unaffected by the bad consequences of their actions, whether visited upon themselves or on their families and friends."[25]

Abundant historical and literary examples were also provided to illustrate the type of person that Cleckley wanted to identify. He offered contrasting literary examples of psychopaths and nonpsychopaths; for example, Dostoevski's elder Karamazov is a psychopath and Shakespeare's Iago is not. He also offers historical psychopaths and nonpsychopaths. The ancient Greek Alcibiades was; Adolph Hitler and the Marquis de Sade were not. From these numerous examples, selected from his own practice at a large psychiatric hospital and from history and literature, Cleckley developed a description of a particular type of personality. This description has become the definitive profile of the psychopath. The psychopath has most or all of the following characteristics:

- Superficial charm and good intelligence
- Absence of delusions and other signs of irrational thinking
- Absence of anxiety
- Unreliability
- Untruthfulness and insincerity
- Lack of remorse
- Antisocial behavior
- Poor judgment and failure to learn from experience
- Pathological egocentricity and incapacity for love
- General poverty in major affective reactions, lacks emotional depth
- Specific loss of insight
- Unresponsiveness in interpersonal relations, manipulative
- Fantastic and uninviting behavior with drink and sometimes without
- Suicide attempts rarely genuine

- Sex life impersonal and trivial
- Failure to follow any life plan[26]

The psychopath may or may not engage in violent behavior, but in either case, he differs from the "common criminal or rascal." The points of distinction between the common or typical criminal and Cleckley's psychopath are that

1. The common criminal is consistently purposive; the psychopath is not at all in comparison.
2. The common criminal can be understood by the average man; the psychopath seems to have incomprehensible motives or obscure motives; sometimes his behavior is not even for material gain
3. The common criminal tries to avoid problems and trouble, but the psychopath seems to put himself in positions of uncomfortableness and shame.
4. The psychopath usually does not commit crimes of major violence, though he sometimes does.
5. Common criminals, despite the fact that they break the laws of society, are often loyal to each other and can sometimes pursue a common cause consistently. The psychopath has no loyalty at all.[27]

Since there are differences between the common criminal and the psychopath, Cleckley makes the important point that an explanation for crime in general may not serve as an explanation for psychopathy.

A person can also be a psychopath and not a criminal. Cleckley gives numerous examples of psychopaths without criminal records, including a physician, a psychiatrist, a scientist, and a business executive. He remarks, "Some of these patients are definitely psychopaths but in a milder degree, just as a patient still living satisfactorily in a community may be clearly a schizophrenic but nevertheless able to maintain himself outside the shelter of a psychiatric hospital."[28] The difference between them and the psychopaths who are found in jails or psychiatric hospitals is that they display a better appearance of being normal. He refers to these persons as "partial psychopaths."

What is wrong with these psychopaths? Cleckley suggested that the psychopath lacks the normal affective accompaniments of experience. The psychopath experiences emotion like the color blind person experiences color. He compared this predicament to *semantic aphasia*, a condition of brain injured patients who can speak in coherent sentences but do not seem to grasp the meaning of their own words. The psychopath can talk coherently, even eloquently, about emotions, but he does not experience or know the meaning of normal emotions. He lacks the normal feelings that are necessary for learning moral values. Cleckley writes, "We have found useful the hypothesis that he has a serious and subtle abnormality or defect at deep levels disturbing the integration and normal appreciation of experience and resulting in a pathology that might, in analogy with Henry Head's classifications of the aphasias, be described as semantic."[29] The psychopath has a limitation of emotional capacity and the mechanisms of morality are ineffective because of this innate defect. "Lacking vital elements in the appreciation of what the family and various bystanders are experiencing, the psychopath finds it hard to understand why they continually criticize, reproach, quarrel with, and interfere with him."[30] This hypothesis has been criticized by some who contend that the psychopath can certainly experience at least some normal emotions, anger or delight for example.

We simply do not know the cause of the psychopath's troublesome behavior. Cleckley believes the cause to be biological, but it is well to remember that he is a physician by training. He does admit that there is no compelling evidence for this belief: "The more experience I have with psychopaths over the years, the less likely it seems to me that any dynamic or psychogenic theory is likely to be established by real evidence as the cause of their grave maladaptation. Increasingly I have come to believe that some subtle and profound defect in the human organism, probably inborn but not hereditary, plays the chief role in the psychopath's puzzling and spectacular failure to experience life normally and to carry on a career acceptable to society. This, too, is still a speculative concept and is not supported by demonstrable evidence."[31] Nevertheless, "this speculative concept" has guided research on these antisocial persons since Pinel's "manie sans delire."

What can be done with psychopaths? Cleckley is frank regarding this question. He writes in the preface to the last edition of his classic that he is himself "still in the unspectacular and perforce modest position of one who can offer neither a cure nor a well established explanation."[32] Though he cannot offer any treatment guidelines for the psychopath, he is concerned to clear up the confusion that surrounds the evaluation of these persons. "The psychopath, however, continues to be treated as a petty criminal at one moment, as a mentally ill person at the next, and again as a well and normal human being — all without the slightest change in his condition having occurred. I do not have any dogmatic advice as to a final or even a satisfactory way of successfully rehabilitating these psychopaths but believe that it is important for some consistent attitude to be reached."[33]

Finally, Cleckley is concerned to place boundaries on biological explanations of behavior. "Many types of behavior formerly regarded as voluntary wrongdoing or the just results of sin are now classed as disease. This does not prove that eventually all wrongdoing will be plainly revealed as disease and all conduct necessarily evaluated at a level at which good and bad are nonexistent.... Let us remember, however, that there are good reasons to believe that this tendency to classify wrongdoing as illness has in recent decades gone too far — perhaps in some instances to the point of absurdity."[34]

Thus even the classic work on psychopathy, which has influenced and guided nearly all of the research effort since its first publication in the 1940s, contains within it a warning about taking the disease analogy too far into the realm of wrongdoing. Though some progress in understanding these antisocial and reckless persons has been made by scientific research, Cleckley wrote that "our actual achievements should encourage profound modesty," an admission just as true now as it was 65 years ago.[35] Perhaps Dr. Cleckley caught a fleeting glimpse of Dr. Lombroso's skull.

Richard III

Studying crime and criminality through literature is not a certain route to understanding. A skillful creative writer can invent any kind of a person, influenced by any number of conditions, and motivated by any menu of reasons, but this literary invention would not necessarily be a demonstration of the truth, merely because it has been imagined and written. Nor would insight into a purely fictional criminal character be a satisfactory substitute for the scientific study of crime. Yet, on the other hand, none of the scientific disciplines — biology, sociology, psychology, or anthropology — has succeeded in presenting a full understanding of crime and criminals. This lack of wholeness does invite literary explorations of the problem. Edward Sagarin asks, "Why is it difficult to find criminologists with insights into human nature comparable to those of Shakespeare and Dostoevsky? ... [T]he criminologist takes a representative sample, the novelist creates a representative character."[36] Shakespeare's characters seem especially attractive in this regard. Books analyzing criminality through his plays can be found throughout the twentieth century, from August Goll's *Criminal Types in Shakespeare*, published in 1909, to Victoria Time's *Shakespeare's Criminals*, published in 1999.[37]

Cleckley set a precedent for this pastime himself, as discussed above. He believed that the best examples of psychopaths from Western literature are Dostoevsky's elder Karamazov, the father of the *Brothers Karama-*

zov, and Mildred from Somerset Maugham's *Of Human Bondage*. He considered the ancient Greek Alcibiades, whose life was chronicled by Plutarch, as the best example from ancient history of a psychopathic personality. But, according to Lykken, author of *The Antisocial Personalities*, Cleckley "neglected the Shakespearean character who best epitomizes the primary psychopath, Richard III, who, in the first speech of Scene I, declares himself bored, looking for action: 'Why, I, in this weak piping time of peace have no delight to pass away the time.'(I.i.24)"[38]

Cleckley may have omitted Richard III because his actions were too purposeful, too organized towards a specific end, towards the goal of gaining the throne of England. Cleckley excludes some other interesting characters for this same reason, such as Heathcliff in *Wuthering Heights*. "The personalities described in this book in contrast, show no consistent pursuit of what might be called evil," he writes; "Their exploits are fitful, buffoonish, and unsustained by any obvious purpose."[39] Cleckley argued that the psychopath's behavior is a kind of purposeless self destruction. He believed that this pattern of self destruction is a part of the essence of psychopathy and that this characteristic differentiated psychopaths from nonpsychopaths. It can be argued, however, so long as the other characteristics of psychopathy are present, this characteristic distinguishes successful from unsuccessful psychopaths. Unsuccessful psychopaths are those who wind up in mental institutions or in prisons and are therefore made accessible to earnest researchers. Observations of this group of psychopaths form the basis of most academic theorizing. There has always been, however, the suspicion that there is another whole group of psychopaths who do not flow into institutions, thereby submitting themselves to scientific scrutiny. This group is sometimes referred to as successful psychopaths. It may be that purposeful, goal directed, organized activity is what distinguishes the successful, noninstitutionalized psychopath from his incarcerated, unsuccessful brother in crime.

If you accept the proposition that following a systematic life plan, rather than distinguishing the psychopath from the nonpsychopath, is what differentiates the successful psychopath from the unsuccessful one, then Shakespeare's Richard III is indeed an excellent portrait of a violent psychopath. First published in 1597, the play is about events that occurred in England from 1471 to 1485.[40] For our purposes, it matters little if Shakespeare's Richard is true to the man who became king of England in 1483, or if his character in the play is merely an elaboration of the myth of Richard Crookback, as some historians claim, "sheer invention and romance," the efforts of Tudor historians to justify Richard's overthrow by the House of Lancaster.[41] Whether Shakespeare's Richard is fact or fiction, history or propaganda, is not our issue. What attracts our attention is this centuries-old description of the psychopathic personality, the fact that Shakespeare could produce such a character, and that he is convincing. Richard is a character who has, as Lykken puts it: "a talent for psychopathy."[42] What interests us is the comparison of psychopathic traits as portrayed by a seventeenth century dramatist and a twentieth century clinician.

In the play, Richard, the Duke of Gloucester, is deformed from birth. Shakespeare contends his physical condition, and other people's derision of Richard because of it, has resulted in hatred, jealousy, and an unbounded lust for power over others, represented by his pursuit of ultimate authority, the throne of England. Richard's physique, small statured with a hunchback and a withered arm, does not prevent him from being a successful soldier, and he fights in the War of the Roses, for the House of York. He is strong willed and energetic, and has some legitimate claims to the crown, but "many lives stand between me and home" (from 3 *Henry VI*). Therefore, he is "determined to prove a villain" and he is exceptionally murderous, even in those bloody times, in his pursuit of power. He is involved, either by conspiracy or by his own hand, in the killing of those who block his way to the English throne, or otherwise obstruct his plans, including King Henry VI; his son Edward, the Prince of Wales; Lord Hastings, the Duke of Buckingham; Richard's own brother George; and Richard's two young nephews, the sons of his brother King Edward IV, who were cruelly imprisoned in the Tower of London and later killed there. This last crime outraged the English populace and there was rebellion against Richard. Finally, Richard is killed by Henry, Earl of Richmond, at the field of Bosworth. Richmond becomes King Henry VII and is the first of the Tudor kings.

According to Holzknecht and McClure, Richard is different from Shakespeare's other flawed heroes: "His nature is not divided and there is in him little of the absorbing inner conflict of the maturer Shakespearean tragic hero— of Brutus, 'with himself at war,' of Hamlet, Macbeth, Lear, Antony, or Coriolanus, each of whom is a victim of a struggle in his own soul.... Richard has no regrets and reveals no goodness of heart that contributes to his undoing."[43]

Richard has many of the characteristics enumerated by Cleckley in his list of psychopathic traits. For example, he has a superficial charm and good intelligence. One of the most remarkable scenes in the play is Richard's seduction of Lady Anne. Richard has killed her husband and her father-in-law. He uses exceptional charm and intelligence to convince her, while at her father-in-law's funeral, to marry him. He has the psychopath's intuition for another person's weaknesses and the ruthlessness to use them to his advantage. In this case, it is Lady Anne's vanity that becomes his tool. Afterwards, he exults over his triumph of charm and deception.

> Was ever woman in this humour woo'd
> Was ever woman in this humour won?...
> Having God, her conscience, and these bars against me,
> And I no friends to back my suit withal
> But the plain Devil and dissembling looks?
> And yet to win her, all the world to nothing!
> Ha! [I.iii.228–39]

He is unreliable. He promises the Duke of Buckingham to give him the earldom of Hereford if he helps Richard to become king. When he is king, he refuses the duke's request for his payment. He is untruthful and insincere. "I clothe my naked villainy with odd old ends stol'n forth of holy writ; and seem a saint when most I play a devil"(I.iii.344–46).

He does not suffer from remorse:

> I must be married to my brother's daughter
> Or else my kingdom stands on brittle glass.
> Murder her brothers, and then marry her!
> Uncertain way of gain! But I am in
> So far in blood that sin will pluck on sin!
> Tear-falling pity dwells not in this eye [I.vii.61–6].

He engages in numerous acts of antisocial behavior, murders, assaults, and plots, but the following is an especially good example of psychopathic behavior because of the reason that he gives for his behavior:

> Edward, her Lord, whom I, some three months since,
> Stabb'd in my angry mood at Tewksbury [I.iii.241–2].

He has a pathological egocentricity and is incapable of love. He plots to kill his brother Clarence, who trusts him;

> Simple, plain Clarence! I do love thee so
> That I will shortly send thy soul to heaven
> If heaven will take the present at our hands [I.i.118–20].

He has that lack of emotional depth:

> Your eyes drop millstones, when fools' eyes fall tears
> I like you, lads; about your business straight [I.iii.353–4].

And he has a trivial and impersonal sex life: "I'll have her; but I will not keep her long" (I.iii.229).

He is unresponsive in interpersonal relations and extremely manipulative. Victoria Time writes, "By means of cunning devices and false promises, he makes almost everyone accept his disloyalty and dishonesty, and he skillfully suborns his associates to commit murder."[44]

> Plots have I laid, inductions dangerous
> By drunken prophecies, libels, and dreams
> To set my brother Clarence and the king
> In deadly hate the one against the other
> And if King Edward be as true and just
> As I am subtle, false, and treacherous [I.i.32–37].

He has a long history of uninviting behavior. His mother says of him:

> Tetchy and wayward was thy infancy;
> Thy school days frightful, desperate, wild, and furious;
> Thy prime of manhood daring, bold, and venturous;
> Thy age confirmed, proud, subtle, sly, and bloody [IV.iv.169–72].

It may be argued that Shakespeare presents a sort of pre–Lombrosian theory of crime, linking Richard's physical abnormality with his defective character. He was "rudely stamped," "Deform'd, unfinish'd, sent before my time" (I.i.20). Here is the idea of biological abnormality and criminal disposition, a general idea which is current today, though not of course in the same form as described in Shakespeare or in Lombroso.

Shakespeare also suggests a role for social learning, as Richard is ridiculed and discounted by others, creating hatred and jealousy in him. Yet he does not divest Richard entirely of free will, for Richard declares, "I am determined to prove a villain" (I.i.30). Shakespeare thus proposes what we would call in present day jargon a multicausal theory of Richard's behavior, consisting of biological anomaly, social learning, and choice.

Though Richard is, in the end, defeated and killed, he may still be called a successful psychopath. He may be called successful since he did achieve his lifelong goal, to be the king, and because his demise was not the result of his own aimless self destructiveness. He may be called psychopath because he went to the extreme of human irresponsibility, even in the context of a dark and bloody period of history. He "determined to prove a villain" and was unrepentant to the end: "Let not our babbling dreams affright our souls, For conscience is a word that cowards use" [V.iii.308–9].

This is a fitting declaration to lead us to Robert Hare's scientific work on the psychopath: *Without Conscience*. But before examining Hare's contributions to the debate, it might be helpful to the reader if we descend from the lofty heights of Shakespearean drama to the real world of the ordinary psychopath, for example, the case of Randy C.

The Case of Randy C.

Randy C. is a 31-year-old white male who has been referred to me for evaluation for promotion from medium custody to minimum custody in the state prison system. He is about six feet tall, broad shouldered and muscular, one of those prison inmates who serves his sentence lifting weights. He has blue eyes and sandy hair, worn long and tied in a ponytail. He has a handsome face, with a small scar on his right cheek. He has served three years on an eight-year total sentence that he had received for a variety of convictions including assault, possession of illegal drugs, and forgery. He has previously served a prison sentence for auto larceny and common law robbery. He was paroled from this first sentence after serving two years. By his own report, he had served a total of 18 months in juvenile detention, beginning at age 16 and being released at age 18. He states that he was "kicked out of school" at age 15 because the teachers "didn't like me." When asked to explain what they didn't seem to like about him, he responds that "I was just bored. They didn't have nothing to teach me." Thus he has been incarcerated three times so far, at age 16, at age 24, and again at age 28. His explanation for this repetition is that he was "just in the wrong place at the wrong time, I guess," and that "Nobody's perfect."

His father is a brick mason and his mother is an office worker who live in a medium sized city in North Carolina. He has a brother and a sister who lead noncriminal, conventional lives. None of his family members have ever served a prison sentence or even been arrested. "My uncle was a damn drunk though." When asked how he feels about his family, he says, "They didn't take care of me like they should have or I probably wouldn't be here now." He reports that his mother visits him in prison, but that his father and his siblings have refused to see him any more. "Not that I give a shit," he comments. Realizing that he may have made a mistake in saying that, he quickly adds, "I don't blame them, though, after all I've done." I seize upon this slight glimmer of remorse and ask him to explain what he means by "All that I've done." He answers, "You know, running with the wrong crowd, being a little wild, things like that." I ask him about the forgery charge, which involved forging checks on his parents' bank account. "Oh, that. That was just a misunderstanding. They got all upset over nothing. It was just a few bucks, that's all."

I ask him to explain the assault conviction to me and he states, "Now, I ain't no violent offender. I've just had property crimes except for this one thing, which was really just a mistake." I ask him to explain what happened and he reports that he got into a fight with a man who called him a son of a bitch and that he only did what any man would have done in that situation. The official crime version states that he beat the victim with a tire iron so badly that the victim required 14 days of hospitalization and was permanently disfigured. I ask him what he meant by saying it was "just a mistake." He replies, "It was really his fault, you know, if he hadn't said nothin,' nothin' would have happened. But I'm the one doing time, not him." Using my best reflective technique, I ask, "So what you mean by saying it was 'a mistake' is that the other guy made a mistake?" Randy answers, "Yeah, he definitely did."

He has never been married, but he proudly reports that he has fathered four children by three different women, "as far as I know," he adds. He does not, at present, have any contact with any of the children or their mothers. He can give the names of two of the children but doesn't know the names of the other two. He now has a girlfriend who visits him and writes to him every week. They plan to get married so that he can live with her when he is released on parole, which he is sure will happen because he made parole the last time he was in prison. She has a good job as an office manager and "wants to help me to readjust to society."

I ask him next what the possession of illegal drugs conviction was about. He says, "Just some weed. Everybody does that sometimes. Even lawyers and judges, people like that." The official crime version states that he had in his possession at the time of arrest over one pound of marijuana. When confronted with this report and further questioning, he eventually admits that he was originally charged with the sale of marijuana, but it was reduced to possession as a part of his plea bargain. "I gave it away to my friends most of the time. I never sold it unless I had to." "When did you have to?" I asked.

"When I needed the money."

"What about alcohol, Randy? Ever had any problems with alcohol?"

"No, I'm not what you call an alcoholic."

"How old were you when you had your first drink?"

Randy smiles broadly. "I guess about 11 or 12."

"Ever been arrested for something related to drinking, public drunk, something like that?"

"No. Not that I remember."

"How about the assault conviction. Were you drinking then?"

He looks suspicious now and answers cautiously, perhaps because he knows that I have read his criminal record, including official crime versions, and he does not know what they contain. "I might have had a couple of beers, but I don't have no drinking problem. I haven't had anything to drink for nearly three years." When I point out to him that that is the length of time that he has been incarcerated, he replies, "You can get anything you want in here," as if that proved his point.

"Randy, you beat a man almost to death in a drunken brawl and you don't think that indicates a problem?"

"No, a drinking problem is when you get drunk every day or something like that. I never do that."

"What about this prison rule violation from last year for being intoxicated on the unit?"

"Oh, that. I forgot about that. That was just some of us inmates got into some brew, that's all. There was nothin' to it."

"Randy, do you feel that you have done anything wrong in your life?"

"Oh, yeah. I've made a lot of mistakes."

"Like what, for example?"

"Like I shouldn't have been hanging around the people I was. I probably should have moved to another town."

A perusal of Randy's arrest record indicates numerous arrests that had not resulted in incarceration, for crimes like petty larceny, possession, and resisting arrest. He had already been on probation twice and parole once. His prison file includes reports from his case manager, who described him as "a complete bullshitter" and very manipulative. There was also an interview with his father, who reported that Randy had stolen and threatened him with harm so many times that he (the father) would never talk to Randy again and that Randy is just where he belongs—in prison. The prison psychologist reported that Randy scored slightly below average on a standard IQ test and had a sixth grade achievement level. Randy had reported to this psychologist that his goal in life was to go to law school so that he could be his own lawyer and get justice for all the wrongs that had been done to him.

The case of Randy C. is not as dramatic as that of a serial killer. So far as we know he has never killed anyone, though he has come close to it. He is a typical psychopath with little anxiety and no remorse, totally self focused, manipulative and deceitful, with exaggerated self esteem, and with a good deal of hostility right below the charming surface. He is not a Shakespearean character, he is a common criminal. What is wrong with him?

Without Conscience

Robert Hare has been working since the 1960s with this group of persons "whose hallmark is a stunning lack of conscience." His contributions to this field of study include the development of a method for reliably identifying psychopaths; the development of a research program to determine what makes the psychopath "tick"; and the publication, in 1993, of *Without Conscience*, a book intended to explain his research and his conclusions to the general public.[45]

Hare recognized the need to develop reliable ways of identifying psychopaths so that the risk that they posed to others could be minimized. We are safer if we can recognize with whom we are dealing. Reliable identification was also necessary so that research could be conducted with assurance that scientists were studying groups of people who were defined by the same standards. Hare took Cleckley's basic criteria and developed a sophisticated measure that he named the Psychopathy Checklist. First introduced in 1980, the checklist was extensively developed and grew in popularity among researchers and clinicians. It was eventually revised and published in 1991 as the *Psychopathy Checklist — Revised*, more commonly known as the PCL-R. A screening version was published in 1995.[46]

The PCL-R is a rating scale that produces a numerical score for psychopathy in an individual. It is designed to be administered by trained clinicians who have an experienced frame of reference. The scale consists of 20 items, rated as No (0), Maybe (1), and Yes (2). The information is obtained by interviewing the person and by reviewing official records and files. The items are closely related to the list of characteristics proposed by Cleckley. The PCL-R has become the standard practice in the field of psychopathy and it stands as a very important achievement in the study of criminal offenders.

Cleckley had proposed that the psychopath had a mental defect that he compared to semantic aphasia, a condition found in brain injured patients who can speak in coherent sentences, but do not seem to understand the meaning of their words. Cleckley meant that the psychopath could speak the words of emotion, feeling, empathy, and sensitivity to others, but that he did not experience internally, or even understand, the emotions that he verbally expressed. There appeared to be a disconnection between his speech and his emotions or some deficiency in processing language. As Johns and Quay remark a psychopath "knows the words but not the music."[47] Hare was interested in elucidating this puzzling discrepancy between what psychopaths say and what they do, a gap that seems to involve much more than simply lying, dissimulation, and hypocrisy.[48] Right at the heart of the mystery of psychopathy, he wrote, is language that is two dimensional, lacking in emotional depth. Hare adhered to the view that there was something wrong with the psychopath's brain right from the start.

To investigate this proposition, he developed a research program that has informed and stimulated the study of brain dysfunction in psychopaths for the last 35 years. The flavor of this kind of research can be found in the following example. Hare developed an experimental technique generally known as the Hare countdown paradigm. In this procedure, there are two groups of subjects, psychopaths and nonpsychopaths. Typically, these two groups are formed on the basis of their scores on the PCL-R. Each subject watches a counter slowly and inexorably moves towards a point where the subject will receive some aversive stimulus, such as an electric shock, a very loud noise, or social disapproval. While the subject is watching the counter and anticipating the "punishment," the experimenter measures one or more of the subject's physical reactions to this situation, such as heart rate, electrical conductance in the skin, or palmar sweating. This basic experiment, with numerous modifications, has been widely used in studying the differences between "normals" and psychopaths. This body of research has produced what Lykken calls "[O]ne of the most replicable findings in all of experimental psychopathology."[50] This finding is that psychopaths show relatively very little electrodermal arousal during the Hare countdown, whereas control subjects, including prison inmates who were judged to be nonpsychopaths, show higher arousal, right from the beginning of the countdown. What might this result mean?

A one to one correspondence between a specific emotion and a specific physiological response has never been established, but the inference is that the psychopaths had a lower level of arousal of the autonomic nervous system, implying that they experienced less fear and anxiety than did the normals. This finding is further enhanced by our observation of the behavior of psychopaths in which they often appear to have little or no anxiety or fear in situations that would normally cause those emotions. Anxiety and fear of consequences may be viewed as one of the principal ways in which we control our behavior; it is a part of the development of conscience. Psychopaths "have a weak capacity for picturing the consequences of their behavior."[51] They may be lacking altogether the emotional capacity for acquiring conscience. In another procedure, Hare and his colleagues found that psychopaths responded to emotional words as if they were neutral words; they reacted much less strongly to emotionally laden statements or pictures than did normal subjects. Hare proposes that "[T]he social experiences that normally build a conscience never take hold."[52]

In addition to his careful experimental research, Hare provides an especially poignant example from a famous case, that of Jack Abbott. Abbott was a long-term prison inmate who achieved notoriety by writing a book called *In the Belly of the Beast: Letters from Prison* and by becoming friends with the writer Norman Mailer, who was intrigued by him.[53] Abbott was later released from prison, stabbed and killed a young waiter who had angered him, and was returned to prison. Abbott wrote in his book, "There are emotions— a whole spectrum of them — that I know only through words, through reading and in my immature imagination. I can only *imagine* I feel these emotions (know, therefore, what they are), but *I do not*. At age thirty seven I am a barely precocious child. My passions are those of a boy."[54]

The above descriptions give the flavor of the research in this domain of study on the causes of crime, though they do not by any means summarize all of the relevant research or explicate all of the theoretical possibilities that have been suggested. Subsequent research has resulted in contradictory findings and competing explanations, some of which were discussed above in part 1. For example, some scientists believe that the psychopath's deficiencies are the result of frontal lobe damage; others have concluded that the autonomic nervous system of psychopaths is over-aroused instead of underaroused, as Hare had found. Still others suggest that the brain structures of the psychopath mature at an abnormally slow rate. Nevertheless, what the record so far does support is the existence of abnormality in the nervous system of psychopaths as compared to normals. What precisely the nature of this abnormality is and what theory serves to explain the connection between brain dysfunction and the psychopath's troubling behavior is far from established. Lykken, writing on this subject in 1995, concludes, "It may require another thirty years of research before we can decide these issues with any confidence."[55]

Hare recognized that "[M]uch of the scientific literature on psychopathy is technical, abstract and difficult to follow for those who lack a background in behavioral sciences."[56] We often encounter such statements on our journey through the scientific literature on crime. Such statements can make us feel summarily dismissed from the debate. We can only hope that these caveats lead to honest efforts to publish well written explanations, as they did for Hare, and that they are not intended to obscure the lack of important verifiable findings or a lack of skill in writing about them. Solid scientific work well communicated to the public is valuable education. Hence, Hare published in 1993 a book oriented to a more general audience. Like Cleckley's *The Mask of Sanity*, Hare's *Without Conscience* is replete with provocative anecdotes and clinical case histories as well as examples from literature and film, such as Joseph Wambaugh's book *Echoes in the Darkness*, the famous film *The Dirty Dozen*, and the classic movie *M*, with Peter Lorre. Hare used these examples to vividly illustrate the kind of person that he is calling a psychopath. It is notable that he considered examples of white collar psychopaths as well. He provided his conclusions so far on the subject of psychopathy.

Hare estimates that, on average, about 20 percent of male offenders are psychopaths and about the same percentage for female offenders. But the psychopaths are responsible for more than half of the serious crimes committed. Serial killers are very rare. Hare thinks that there are fewer than 100 in North America, but that there as many as 2 or 3 million psychopaths in North America. This means that for every serial killer, there are 20,000 to 30,000 psychopaths.[57] The movies and the media have led us to exaggerate the threat from serial killers, and this dramatic exaggeration has served to obscure the threat to communities from the more common, though less violent, psychopath. Hare also calculates that the recidivism rate of psychopaths is about twice that of other offenders and the violent recidivism rate is about triple that of other (nonpsychopathic) offenders.

Hare's research indicated that the quality of family background was a good predictor of criminal behavior among nonpsychopaths but had no effect on the emergence of criminality in psychopaths, who appeared in court at an average age of 14, regardless of family background. He concluded that he could find no evidence that psychopathy is the direct result of social or environmental factors. He does propose that social factors and parenting practices influence the way the disorder develops and the way that it is expressed in behavior:

> Thus an individual with a mix of psychopathic personality traits who grows up in a stable family and has access to positive social and educational resources might become a con artist or white collar criminal, or perhaps a somewhat shady entrepreneur, politician or professional. Another individual, with much the same personality traits but from a deprived and disturbed background, might become a drifter, or a mercenary, or violent criminal.[58]

Hare believes that psychopaths can be identified at a very early age. The parents of children later diagnosed as psychopaths are usually aware that something is wrong before the child begins school. There are particular signs that the child is departing from normal development:

- repetitive, casual, and seemingly thoughtless lying
- apparent indifference to, or inability to understand, the feelings, expectations, or pain of others
- defiance of parent, teachers, and rules
- continually in trouble and unresponsive to reprimands and threats of punishment
- petty theft from other children and parents
- persistent aggression, bullying, and fighting
- a record of unremitting truancy, staying out late, and absences from home
- a pattern of hurting or killing animals
- early experimentation with sex
- vandalism and fire setting[59]

Psychopaths do not exhibit the typical symptoms of major mental disorders. They are not disoriented, out of touch with reality, or experiencing delusions and hallucinations. They are not feeling intense anxiety or internal distress. Unlike psychotic individuals, psychopaths are rational and conscious of what they are doing and why they are doing it. Hare boldly states, "Their behavior is the result of choice, freely exercised."[60]

So here, even within one of the most biological of theories, we find that the foremost researcher is unwilling to abandon free will entirely and is unequivocal in placing the psychopath, whatever might be wrong with his nervous system, on the choice end of our continuum.

According to Hare, over 50 years of research has not advanced our understanding of this group of people very much. "[I]n spite of more than a century of clinical study and speculation and several decades of scientific research, the mystery of the psychopath still remains."[61]

The biologists and the experimental psychologists may, indeed, one day unravel the tangled threads of psychopathy, but we do not know enough yet even to assume that they will eventually succeed — and we cannot wait to act decisively. We know that psychopaths are the ones who do the greatest damage among us and that they can be identified early. Early identification makes possible early intervention — and this is the light that we already possess.

The Criminal Personality

Crime resides within the person and is caused by the way he thinks, not by his environment, propose Samuel Yochelson and Stanton Samenow. They prefer the term *criminal personality* because it avoids the confusion that is usually raised with terms like psychopath, sociopath, antisocial personality disorder, and dyssocial offender. They also prefer to avoid what they regard as the "usual euphemisms" for a criminal, such as offender, client, violator, resident, delinquent, or inmate. Samenow points out that using the word *criminal* focuses us on what we are really concerned about, that is, the person who commits crimes, and on the behavior that we wish to change, that is, criminal behavior. In contrast to Lykken, they would place most serious offenders on the opposite end of our continuum, the choice end.

Samenow, a psychologist who is now in private practice in Virginia, worked for 15 years at St. Elizabeth's Hospital in Washington, D.C. He, together with the psychiatrist Samuel Yochelson, began treating patients who had been committed to the hospital by the courts as not guilty by reason of insanity. Their project, the Program for the Investigation of Criminal Behavior, was carried out in the 1960s and '70s. Their original group consisted of 255 males. Gradually, over the years, they expanded their efforts to include offenders of all types. Together they published the results of their work in *The Criminal Personality*, which eventually became three volumes and nearly 1,500 pages.[62] Dr. Yochelson died of a heart attack in 1976 while, on his first out-of-town speaking trip. Samenow has continued work on the criminal personality until the present time, lecturing tirelessly across the U.S., and publishing additional books and articles.

Samenow began with an examination of the historical and current theories of the cause of crime and found all of them inadequate. "When I first began this work, I believed that criminal behavior was a symptom of buried conflicts that had resulted from early traumas and deprivations of one sort or another. I thought that people who turned to crime were victims of a psychological disorder, an oppressive social environment, or both."[63] But he writes that as he became experienced with criminals in treatment and as he searched through the literature on the causes of crime and the treatment of criminals, he and his colleague became "reluctant converts" to a new point of view. They concluded that sociological explanations were too simplistic. If these theories were accurate, that social conditions cause crime, then there should be many more criminals then there are. Criminals cause crime — not bad neighborhoods, inadequate parents, television, schools, drugs, or unemployment. They saw criminals not as victims but as victimizers who had freely chosen their way of life. They concluded that focusing on forces outside of the individual is futile for understanding the criminal and for engaging him in a change process. So they abandoned the search for causes and launched their treatment program, based on the proposition that, for unknown reasons, hard core criminals simply choose, from childhood, to engage in antisocial behavior.

Samenow and Yochelson propose that a criminal is a person whose patterns of thinking have led to arrestable behavior. Their approach to the understanding of the criminal is "phenomenological," by which they mean "thinking about thinking." Like Pinel and Cleckley before them, they are astute observers of human behavior who carefully document their observations. Their intensive work, including hundreds of interviews, led them to describe the criminal as a person who reveals himself when the thinking by which he supports his actions is uncovered. Samenow and Yochelson describe what they call "thinking errors" that exist in the criminal's mind and that inevitably lead to criminal actions. The concept of thinking errors is not an original contribution; it is an idea that can be traced throughout the development of cognitive psychology. It can be found in the rational emotive therapy of Albert Ellis and in the cognitive therapy of Aaron Beck, among others. But no one has applied this idea to the criminal person so specifically and with such deliberation and thoroughness as have Yochelson and Samenow.

For example, one of the thinking errors is called the "victim stance." The criminal constantly attempts to blame others or anything at all except himself for his crimes. In this mode of thinking, the criminal attempts to convince others that he is really the victim and is not responsible for what he has done. This is a common trait among criminals. It might be said that self justification is a common human characteristic and not confined to criminals alone. But with the criminal, this trait, or thinking error, is extreme, both in the frequency with which he exhibits it, applying it to virtually every behavior, and in degree, in the lengths to which he will carry it. One example of this extremity is the inmate I interviewed who had shot to death a convenience store clerk during a robbery. His explanation of his behavior was that he had been fired from his job and had no money. Therefore, he had no choice but to rob. When the store clerk reached for a weapon from behind the counter, he had no choice but to shoot. "Really," my inmate explained, "if he hadn't done that, he would be alive today. He killed himself by doing that. I had no choice." Therefore, my inmate had concluded that it was his employer's fault that he had no job, it was society's fault that he had no money, and it was the clerk's own fault that he was killed. What a tidy explanation for armed robbery and felony murder. Furthermore, the inmate felt that he was the victim now because he was forced to serve life in prison just for "being in the wrong place at the wrong time." This type of extreme thinking, extreme both in frequency and in degree, is what Samenow calls a "thinking error"; it is clearly beyond the common human tendency towards self justification. Other examples of thinking errors include the "I can't" attitude, "lack of a concept of injury to others," "superoptimism," and "sentimentality."

Samenow and Yochelson identify and describe in detail a total of 52 thinking errors, a study which is both exhaustive and exhausting. Nevertheless, professionals who are very experienced with criminals find these personality descriptions to be very accurate. Their use of the methods of group therapy with criminals to correct the errors in thinking is regarded by many professionals as a very useful treatment technique. Samenow has published a condensed version of *The Criminal Personality*, titled *Inside the Criminal Mind*, which is very helpful reading for anyone directly involved with the identification, care, or treatment of criminals.[64]

Another helpful contribution made by Samenow and Yochelson is the Continuum of Criminality.[65] In developing this continuum, they emphasize the thinking processes in the individual that inevitably lead to irresponsible behavior. The irresponsible but nonarrestable person, the petty thief, the professional criminal, the white collar criminal, and the illiterate bank robber all have thought patterns in common, though they differ in degree, in intensity, in pervasiveness, and in the consequences that their behavior incurs. On one end of the continuum, is the basically responsible person. The responsible person has a lifestyle of hard work, fulfillment of obligations, and consideration for others. He derives self respect and the respect of others through his achievements. Desires to violate the law do occur in such a person, but they usually disappear quickly and without much effort. The responsible person does have moments of anger, of vindictiveness, of deceit, but even these moments do not result in serious injury to the person or to the rights of others.

Some people do not violate the law, but they can be considered irresponsible. These are the people who are chronically late, perform poorly at work, or fail to fulfill their obligations. They do not consider other people or the effects that their behavior has on other people. They are frequently untruthful. However, they cannot be arrested for these shortcomings and we do not call them criminals. Yet they are defaulters, liars, excuse givers, and are generally unreliable and very self centered in their personal relationships. People referred to as arrestable criminals have all the thinking patterns and irresponsible behavior of the hard core criminals, but their crimes are less extreme and less serious in terms of the injuries that are inflicted on others. They are minor violators. People in this category have strong recurrent desires to violate the law, but they can be deterred from committing serious crimes.

Finally, at the opposite end of the continuum from the basically responsible person is the extreme criminal. He is the one that we refer to as a criminal personality. His criminal thought processes are operative at an early age. Although he is member of a relatively small group of offenders, he poses the greatest problems in terms of the heavy injuries that he inflicts. He violates the rights of others as a permanent lifestyle. He commits literally hundreds of violations of the law and is convicted for only a small portion of what he has done. He thinks constantly of crimes and is totally inconsiderate of others. He is deceitful in the extreme and is almost completely devoid of empathy. Lying is a way of life to him. His life goals are excitement and power over others. He has a chessboard view of life in which everyone is an opponent. One wins by making calculated moves that are as deceitful as possible and that result in the elimination of threats to his position. We are not calling "criminal" anyone who has ever told a lie or been irresponsible or violated the law. All of us have behaved irresponsibly at some time or been deceitful at some time, perhaps in order to avoid some difficult situation. But the extreme criminal is very different in the intensity and the frequency of his criminal thinking patterns. He appears, as Samenow asserts, "morally retarded." His style of life, his attitude towards others, and his choices are different from that of responsible persons. He has freely chosen an irresponsible lifestyle and he supports this lifestyle with thought processes that justify these choices. He is not a victim; he is a victimizer. If this extreme criminal also chooses to abuse drugs and alcohol, he becomes even more extreme in his thinking and behavior.[66]

The Continuum of Responsibility

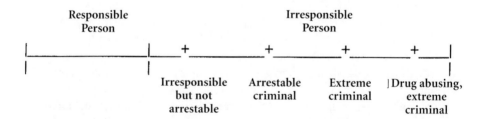

In a sense, the work of Yochelson and Samenow does not belong in a review of the causes of crime because they have no theories to propose nor any research to report regarding the causes of crime. Samenow writes, "[T]he essence of this approach is that criminals choose to commit crimes."[67] But they have made some very useful additions to our understanding of crime and criminals, including their plain language categories and resistance to the temptation (so common in psychology) to invent obscure, tongue tying terminology. The continuum of criminality is a helpful way to think about offenders, to see their errors in thinking as different in degree and intensity from the average person's errors in thinking. The detailed descriptions of the criminal personality and the errors in thinking that characterize them lead to a deeper understanding of the criminal's actions and decisions. This approach to understanding the criminal person results in a specific and practical treatment method that can be applied to all levels of offenders, from minor violators to extreme criminals.

The treatment consists of a group process, led by a therapist with a firm and directive stance, in which the criminal is led through patient and repetitive corrections of his errors in thinking. The goal of the treatment is to move him along the continuum towards being a more responsible person, both in word and in deed. Has this treatment approach proved effective? Samenow and Yochelson report data indicating that they were successful (as defined by no rearrests) with one out of three. Some of the men in the original treatment group of 255 were followed up for as long as 12 years.[68] Considering that they were working with the most extreme criminals, a success rate of approximately 33 percent is very good. It is useful to know that not all trained and experienced scientists and clinicians are settled on a deterministic point of view towards criminals, including even serious repeat offenders, and that at least some careful observers in the field of crime are not hesitant to assert that their understanding of the criminal is "unapologetically moralistic."

The Psychopathic Mind

Reid Meloy has written a very thick volume on the origin, dynamics and treatment of the psychopath, which is based on Sigmund Freud's theory of psychoanalysis.[69] Meloy is an able forensic psychologist who has testified in numerous court cases, including, among others, *United States v. Timothy McVeigh*, where he worked for the prosecution. He has spent considerable time interviewing and assessing criminals. Unfortunately, his writing is hardly accessible to an audience untrained in psychoanalytical thought and language. This may be just as well, since, applying the test of Occam's razor, Meloy's explanation would not be the best choice for the cause of crime. Parts of his book are fascinating, for example, when he recounts how one of the Hillside Stranglers, Kenneth Bianchi, feigned multiple personality disorder and how he was found out by the wily and skilled hypnotherapist Dr. Orne. But when it comes to the explanatory sections of his opus, Meloy's speculations are rough going for the uninitiated. And now that we are more knowledgeable about the history of criminology, we have every right to be suspicious on that count alone.

According to Meloy, there are five developmental themes that coalesce in the psychopathic process:

> The developmental origins of the psychopathic personality are characterized by a precocious separation from the primary parent during the symbiotic phase of maturation; failures of internalization that begin with an organismic distrust of the sensory-perceptual environment; a predominate, archetypal identification with the stranger self object that is central to the conceptual self and object fusions within the grandiose self structure during the period of separation-individuation; a failure of object constancy and a primary narcissistic attachment to the grandiose self; [and] states of relatedness ... that are aggressively and sadomasochistically pursued with actual objects. This co-existence of benign detachment and aggressively pursued, sadistically toned attempts to bond is pathognomonic of the psychopathic process.[70]

How will we separate the wheat from the chaff in such a convoluted and abstruse explanation? The effort is considerable and even some outstanding psychologists claim to have abandoned the attempt. The inimitable Dr. Lykken, for one, writes, "This psychodynamic approach seems to rely for its confirmation largely on clinical impressions and the Rorschach Test. I do not attempt to characterize these theories further because I frankly do not understand them."[71] Lykken is pulling our leg, of course, and he is saying, without further ado, that psychoanalytic theory explains nothing to him about crime.

Freud himself had little to say about criminals. The little that he did say, however, drew the sharp focus of some of his followers and was used by them enthusiastically for decades. Freud believed that everyone carries some oedipal guilt from early childhood, from competition with the father over the attention of the mother, but that this guilt is largely unconscious. Freud observed that children will often be naughty in order to provoke punishment which, in turn, assuages their guilt. He wrote, "In many criminals, especially youthful ones, it is possible to detect a very powerful sense of guilt which existed before the crime, and is therefore not the result but its motive."[72] This "criminality from a sense of guilt" was the idea seized by Freudian disciples wanting to explain criminal behavior. We can see here another example of a theory not intended to explain crime being stretched to do so. Alexander and Staub proclaimed in 1931 that the reasons for crime are unconscious and the cure consists of making the unconscious known; to discover the reasons for committing crimes.[73] Glover, writing in 1960, flatly states that this concept is "the key to all problems of delinquency."[74]

Freud did not think that psychoanalysis was appropriate for criminals and juvenile delinquents because they had not developed the psychic structures and the particular attitude necessary for that form of treatment. He proposed that "something other than analysis" be used for this population. Nonetheless, Meloy supports long-term psychoanalytic psychotherapy although it does "present major countertransference and resistance issues to the mental health professional."[75] By these major issues, he means the well known observations that psychopaths usually do not want to change and that psychotherapists think that they will not change. But, Meloy writes, "I am not going to propose a new model for treating the psychopath."[76] Alas!

Meloy believes that there is a "psychobiological predisposition" for psychopathy. In his book, he reviews the literature in four areas that indicate differences between psychopaths and normal persons: neuroanatomical differences, neurochemical differences, differences in autonomic reactivity, and differences discovered through twin and adoption studies. We have seen this literature already in the section on biology and nothing new is added here.

In fact, as far as the explanation of crime goes, Lykken and Meloy land in essentially the same place. Lykken says a biological predisposition that results in little or no fear and anxiety plus poor parenting, a combination he summarizes with the pithy phrase "no fear and no father," together produce psychopaths. Lykken's theory is discussed in the next chapter. This is, at the core, hardly different from Meloy, who reviews the same body of research literature on biology and crime as does Lykken and who, instead of saying "poor parenting," posits his five developmental themes (listed above). "My theoretical and clinical hypothesis is that psychopathy is psychobiologically predisposed, but there are necessarily deficient and conflictual primary object experiences that determine its phenotypic expression."[77] This is a simply an obscure way of saying the same thing that Lykken has said and is no more of an explanation than his. Both Lykken and Meloy in the end espouse some unspecified combination of nature and nurture, both gone awry in the case of the psychopath, with little or no helpful explanation other than this. Nor can we call it a scientific explanation since it is hard to think of how to conduct specific experiments that would disprove the proposal that criminal behavior is some unspecified combination of biological, psychological, and social factors.

In one of his chapters, Meloy poses a question that is of the utmost interest to us in our study of the causes of crime: "What is the relationship between conscious choice and unconscious determination in human behavior?"[78] He recognizes that this question has an especially sharp edge when applied directly to criminal behavior. Meloy takes the thoroughly reasonable position that both conscious choice and unconscious determination, especially in the form of defense mechanisms, exist in the psychopath. For example, he points to the existence of both conscious deception, which the psychopath uses to manipulate and gain control over others, and unconscious denial, which is a defense against external sources of displeasure and anxiety. He relates a very common form of denial in criminals which we encountered above in our own section, "Who Is a Criminal?" "The most common expression I have heard in forensic settings is 'I am not a criminal ... I do not belong with these individuals.'"[79] Meloy reminds us of a very famous example of this denial, angrily uttered by then-president Richard Nixon in 1974: "I am not a crook." Anyone who challenges this distorted self concept of the criminal will likely be met with an aggressive display of righteous anger or with acid disdain.

Unfortunately, Meloy follows these interesting points with more psychoanalytic obfuscation. For example, he writes that "the conscious act of deception 'sets up' the actual object to receive and contain the purged psychic material that threatens to devalue the grandiose self if not projected. This continuous process of deception, to facilitate the unconscious purging cycle, is endogenous to the psychopathic character."[80] Undoubtedly we, along with Lykken, simply do not understand what he is saying.

For now, the last word on psychoanalysis and crime is from the irrepressible Dr. Freud himself, who wrote in *Psychoanalysis and the Ascertaining of Truth in the Courts of Law* (1906), "With the neurotic, the secret is hidden from his own consciousness; with the criminal, it is hidden only from you."[81]

The Problem of Classification

It appears that personality classification started with Hippocrates in the fifth century BC. He believed that there were four humors, or bodily fluids; black bile, yellow bile, phlegm, and blood. If any one of these humors dominated in an individual, then a particular temperament would result. Thus the dominance of black bile would produce a melancholic temperament, associated with sadness and depression. A phlegmatic temperament, associated with calm dispassion and, in the extreme, apathy, was the result of an excess of phlegm. When blood was the dominant fluid, then a sanguine temperament was produced, an attitude of cheerfulness and optimism. A choleric temperament, bad tempered, irritable, and, in the extreme, angry, was caused by an excess of yellow bile. This theory had a strong influence in medicine even into the nineteenth century.[82]

The Roman statesman and philosopher Seneca argued in the first century A.D. that a person with a choleric temperament is the one most inclined to crime, since a person with that temperament is frequently in the grip of anger, a passion that creates a kind of temporary insanity. Seneca, whom Drapkin calls the greatest criminologist of the ancient world, had many insightful remarks on crimes, penalties, and passions. He believed that crime is the outcome of a person's submission to passion rather than reason and that this submission would most likely happen if the person has a choleric temperament. Thus the biology of the individual results in a particular personality or temperament, which predisposes the individual to criminal behavior.[83] Similar theories about criminals are being proposed and researched as we enter the twenty first century, but this way of thinking about the cause of crime is some 2,000 years old. Seen in this light, our progress seems quite small.

Theophrastus, who lived circa 372–287 B.C., was a devoted student of Aristotle and took over from him as head of the Peripatetic School. He had wide ranging interests and he is considered by some to be the father of botany. Among his many works is a book called *Characters*, which consists of 30 ethical sketches with titles like *loquacious man*, *boastful man*, and *mean man*. His style was often copied by later writers and observers so that he might legitimately be called the father of personality types as well as the father of botany. One of his sketches is called *The Unscrupulous Man*: "The unscrupulous man will go and borrow more money from a creditor he has never paid ... when marketing he reminds the butcher of some service he has rendered him, and standing near the scales, throws in some meat, if he can, and soup bone. If he succeeds, so much the better; if not, he will snatch a piece of tripe and go off laughing."[84] This sketch by Theophrastus is one of our earliest descriptions of the con artist. So we can see that such persons are not merely a modern problem. By 1998, this person is called by Theodore Millon *the unprincipled psychopath*.[85]

Psychopathy was the first personality disorder to be recognized in psychiatry. Koch, a German psychiatrist, proposed in 1891, that "psychopathic inferiority" replace the earlier concept of "moral insanity." Koch believed that a physical basis existed for these impairments. "They stem from a congenital or acquired inferiority of brain constitution."[86] There followed a century of classifying psychopaths. Below is just a sampling of the smorgasbord of classifications.

Kraepelin began classifying psychopaths in 1904 and by 1915 had developed and described seven classes of psychopathic personalities: the excitable, the liars and swindlers, the antisocial, the unstable, the eccentric, the quarrelsome, and the impulsive.[87] D.K. Henderson proposed in 1939 three subtypes of psychopath: (1) aggressive, (2) passive inadequate and (3) creative. By "creative psychopath," he meant such memorable characters as Lawrence of Arabia: a brilliant, aggressively active, but erratic and moody person.[88] Needless to say, the idea of a "creative" psychopath was controversial.

Edwin Megargee (1979) developed ten types of offenders (Able, Baker, Charlie, etc.). He used such category names in order to avoid labeling effects. These types were identified by profiles on the Minnesota Multiphasic Personality Inventory (MMPI). Each profile had its own description of characteristics and its own treatment recommendations.[89] Herbert Quay (1984), using several psychological tests, developed typologies for the purpose of managing prison inmates. Quay's five types are: (1) aggressive-psychopathic, (2) manipulative, (3) situational, (4) inadequate-dependent, and (5) neurotic-anxious.[90] I can't help but think of old Hippocrates right here. These typologies may help to make housing and treatment decisions in prison, but they do not advance our understanding of the causes of crime.

By 1998, Millon had proposed understanding subtypes of psychopaths in terms of their relationships with the prominent features of other personality disorders such as borderline personality disorder, histrionic personality disorder, paranoid personality disorder, and dependent personality disorder. He classified ten subtypes of psychopathic personality disorder, which are listed and briefly explained below.

Unprincipled psychopath—con artists and charlatans, related to narcissistic personality disorder.

Disingenuous psychopath—veneer of friendliness and sociability overlying a flagrant deceitfulness, related to histrionic personality disorder.

Risk taking psychopath—treacherous thrill seekers, related to histrionic personality disorder.

Covetous psychopath—driven by envy and a drive for retribution, and aggrandizement, related to antisocial personality disorder.

Spineless psychopath—caricatures of swaggering tough guys, related to avoidant and dependent personalities.

Explosive psychopath—sudden and unpredictable emergence of hostility, rages, and violent outbursts; related to borderline personality disorder.

Abrasive psychopath—intentionally antagonistic and fractious, oppositional, related to paranoid personality disorder.

Malevolent psychopath—murders and serial killers, related to paranoid and sadistic personality disorders.

Tyrannical psychopath—unmerciful and inhumane, intimidating with or without physical violence, considered the purest type of classic psychopath.

Malignant psychopath—mistrust and resentment of others with desire to seek revenge on others for past wrongs with callous force or cunning revenge, related to paranoid personality disorder.[91]

Millon readily admits that these classifications are derived from direct experience, clinical lore, and a reading of the research literature. We have not come far from the choleric temperament of Hippocrates and Seneca. Hans Toch, a curmudgeon in the classification debate, contends that the construct of psychopathy has generally served to allow us to dismiss individuals who are difficult to work with. Such psychopathic categories are often not based on any theory of the causes of criminal behavior and do not enable us to make useful and meaningful discriminations among groups of offenders. There are too many people who can too easily be placed under too many "constellations of psychopathic traits." Subtypes of psychopaths highlight groups or combinations of characteristics, but do not help us to understand them.[92]

John Gunn takes this thought further and asserts that psychopathic disorder does not exist. The equating of abstract concepts with real objects is called *reification*. Clustering together various personality traits (which are themselves abstractions) and then giving a name to this cluster of traits, or symptoms, is an example of reification. It may be useful in terms of making the conversation go more smoothly, but it does not in itself increase our understanding of the causes or the mechanisms underlying the pathology. If we use the term long enough, we tend to forget its abstract origin and come to assume that it actually exists and that we have discovered it and that we understand it, at least partially. This reification is especially a problem with psychopathy because it has such moral connotations. Gunn has argued that the term *psychopathic disorder* is a largely moral term and acts as a "trigger for rejection," allowing us to regard psychopaths as suffering from an untreatable disorder; thus we may wash our hands of them. Blackburn calls psychopathy "a mythical entity." A disorder that is defined by a past history of socially deviant behavior is a fixed category and is "little more than a moral judgment masquerading as a clinical diagnosis." In his view, it is a term that should be discarded.[93]

The concept of psychopathy has promoters and detractors. The promoters say that there exists a meaningful description of the psychopathic person, and most clinicians who work with offenders claim to recognize psychopathic characteristics in at least some of the persons that they see and assess in the justice system. There is some evidence from twin and adoption studies that there is a heritable component to criminality. Brain imaging techniques have identified dysfunctions in the temporal and frontal regions of the brain. The lack of anxiety and failure to respond to aversive consequences may also have biological explanations. Millon reports in his summary of the research that maternal deprivation, having a sociopathic father, and lack of affectionate bonds in the family are predictive of psychopathy. Lykken and others have shown that children from disorganized, chaotic, and neglectful families will become adult criminals in significant numbers. However, even the most ardent promoters of psychopathy do not claim that psychopathy, even if thoroughly understood, is the explanation for crime. At best, it explains some chronic offenders. If there are many routes to crime, a personality disorder is merely one of them.

Some of the detractors argue only against the *term* "psychopath" because it has been so used and abused as a label. They argue that it means too many different things to too many different people and ought to be tossed out of the vocabulary in favor of more precise and less abused terms. Others argue against the concept of psychopathy itself. Perhaps we have discovered nothing by grouping together a set of behavioral characteristics that are troublesome, and not well understood, then giving this group of personality characteristics a name, then going out to find some persons who will exhibit at least some of these characteristics, and falling gradually into the delusion that we have explained something about crime. There is also the problem that all of our research is limited to unsuccessful psychopaths, those who have been caught and adjudicated in some way, usually incarcerated. Some have suggested that the study of psychopathy is nothing other than the study of the dynamics of getting caught. We know nothing about successful psychopaths except that many of us know that we have met some and seen them in action.

On balance, I think that the psychopathic personality is an accurate description of a particular type of person who will persistently engage in criminal behavior of various sorts, both violent and nonviolent, but it is not at all clear how he came to be like this. It is more useful to think of this tendency to antisocial behavior as existing in degrees. For example, Yochelson and Samenow propose degrees of irresponsibility, and Andrews and Bonta suggest different levels of risk.[94] Some detractors have argued that thinking of it in this way is not helpful; it reminds them of degrees of pregnancy: either you are or you're not. But this is not a fair analogy since disorders of all types can and do exist in degrees of severity (and pregnancy is a normal, healthy condition, not a disorder at all).

Perhaps it is from the psychopath's anomalous behavior that we have the most to learn, but 2,000 years of personality classification has not led us to the cause of crime.

9

Learning Theory and Crime

Professor Bandura's Bobo Dolls

Social learning theory is the proposition that we learn social behavior by observing and imitating, and by being rewarded and punished. One of the classic experiments of social learning theory was conducted in the 1960s by Albert Bandura and his colleagues.[1] Bandura wanted to know if imitative learning could explain aggressive behavior in children. This experiment, which generated hundreds of other experimental studies on social learning, included two adult role models, one male and one female, one female experimenter, and 36 children who were attending the Stanford University Nursery School Program. The children included 36 boys and 36 girls. They ranged in age from 37 to 69 months.

There were three experimental conditions: one in which the subjects were exposed to an aggressive adult model, one in which they were exposed to a nonagressive, subdued adult model, and one in which there is not an adult model at all (the control group). In the first experimental procedure, a child was put to work on an interesting art project. An adult is in another part of the room where there are tinker toys, a mallet, and a big, inflated doll, called a Bobo doll. After a minute of working with the tinker toys, the adult gets up and for almost ten minutes attacks the inflated doll, pounding it with a mallet, kicking it and throwing it, all the while yelling such remarks as "sock him in the nose ... hit him ... kick him." After observing the outburst, the child is then taken to a different building and placed in a room that has many attractive toys. But after two minutes the experimenter interrupts, stating that these are her best toys and she has decided to save them for other children. The frustrated child now goes into an adjacent room containing a variety of toys, two of which are a Bobo doll and a mallet.

The second condition is the same except that the adult model acts in nonaggressive, subdued ways. In the third condition, there is no adult model at all. In some of the conditions, the children saw adult models of the same gender as themselves and in other conditions they saw an adult of the opposite gender.

Those children who were in the control group and who had not been exposed to the aggressive adult model rarely did anything aggressive. The children who had been exposed to the aggressive adult model were many more times more likely to act aggressively. Not only did they act aggressively, but they used the exact words and actions of the adult model. The report of these experiments included photographs that really made the point. Children subjects were shown attacking the Bobo doll in remarkably similar ways to the adult models.

In some of the experiments, the children saw the adult model rewarded for her aggression by being called "a strong champion" and being given candy and soft drinks. In another condition, the child saw the adult model punished for aggression. Those who saw the rewards were significantly more aggressive than the ones who saw the model punished. In addition there was evidence that the male model influenced both male and female children more than the female model did. Bandura thought that this was because physical aggression is a highly masculine typed behavior and therefore the male model was more influential to the children.

Psychology has offered four traditional views of aggression. Freud saw it as an instinctual urge which, under the constraints of civilization, builds up and ultimately demands discharge in some way.[2] Dollard and Miller proposed what became known as the frustration-aggression hypothesis.[3] They argued that aggression was always a consequence of frustration and that frustration always leads to some form of aggression. Behavioral psychologists taught that aggression is learned by the reinforcement of aggressive responses. Bandura and other social learning theorists demonstrated that aggressive behavior can be learned by observation alone.

The experiments of Bandura and his colleagues on aggression became classic in psychology because of the stimulus they provided for hundreds of experiments on social learning. They are not revered because they explained crime. Is aggressive behavior the same as criminal behavior? Can we just treat them as if they were synonymous and whatever explains one explains the other? This is a common, though very dubious, premise in discussions on what the research says about criminal behavior. It is not the aggressive behavior in itself, but our judgment of it that makes it criminal. The same aggressive behavior can be instrumental, even praiseworthy, in one context, and criminal in another. Consider whether the following actions are all the same and the same mechanisms explain them all: (1) a soldier shoots and kills another soldier in combat; (2) a policeman shoots and kills a fleeing felon; (3) a man shoots and kills a clerk in the course of an armed robbery. These are all highly aggressive actions; in fact, the same action. But our judgments about these actions render them entirely different. The study of aggressive behavior apart from context, however valuable that study may be in other ways, cannot lead to an understanding of crime.

The learning theory research on aggression most certainly leads to the daunting proposition that support for the expression of violence in a culture is teaching violence to its members by observational learning. But moral judgment cannot be left out of the explanation of crime, because it is our moral judgment and the cultural context that makes the behavior criminal rather than merely aggressive.

The attempt to forge a link from learning theory to aggression to crime can be traced back to another one of psychology's classic experiments, the conditioning of Little Albert.

Little Albert

Learning theory is one of the ways in which psychologists attempt to explain crime. One of the most famous experiments in psychology was conducted by the American behaviorist John B. Watson shortly after the First World War.[4] Though it was not intended to explain crime, its results did lead to attempts to explain crime. Little Albert was a boy, aged 11 months, who was the subject of the experiment. Watson conditioned a fear of white rats in Little Albert, who had previously liked white rats and often played with them. Watson did this by pairing a loud, upsetting noise with the presentation of the white rats. Every time Little Albert reached out towards the rats, Watson hit a metal bar with a hammer. The noise caused Albert to whimper, cry, and withdraw. (This experiment would not meet ethical standards of research today, which is one of the problems in learning about criminal behavior from scientific experiments.) After a few such pairings, Little Albert would cry and try to crawl away every time the rats were introduced even without the loud noise. This conditioned fear reaction to the white rats persisted over a long time and even generalized to other furry objects such as rabbits and teddy bears. This phenomenon is called stimulus generalization. Watson's experiment resulted in an explosion of research on human learning.

Working in London, England, Hans Eysenck took the findings of this body of theory and research and applied it to the problem of crime.[5] He reasoned that when we ask why people commit crimes and other antisocial acts, we are putting the cart before the horse. It is our natural inclination to act selfishly and to take what one needs or wants. Babies and young children act this way and so do animals. Therefore, the crucial question, argues Eysenck, is why people do *not* commit crimes. What is it that stops us from acting with selfish aggression and with complete disregard for others?

Eysenck believes that it is conscience that prevents most people from acting in antisocial ways and that conscience is a conditioned emotional response acquired in childhood, just like Little Albert's fear of white rats. A conditioned response like this is acquired according to specific principles. These principles were first put forward by the great Russian psychologist Ivan Pavlov. Pavlov demonstrated learning in which a stimulus comes to evoke a response that it did not previously evoke. For example, if an animal is given an electric shock immediately following the presentation of a particular sound, then after a number of such pairings, the sound alone will produce the reactions that before only the electric shocks produced, such as muscle tension, fear, anxiety, and so on.[6]

Because his parents or caretakers punish antisocial behavior, after which stimulus generalization occurs, the child comes to experience anxiety, fear, tension — "unpleasure" — towards antisocial activities of many kinds. Some people are autonomically prone to this kind of conditioning, argued Eysenck, while others are not.

If conscience is acquired in this way, and it is conscience that prevents antisocial behavior, what has happened when conscience is absent or defective? There are three possibilities: (1) the child has lax parenting in which the necessary conditioning experiences do not happen; (2) the wrong experiences are reinforced; (3) low cortical arousal makes certain individuals extremely hard to condition. Cortical arousal means a state of the organism in which the brain is wide awake, concentrating, focusing, attentive, and working at maximum capacity. Low arousal is like sleepiness, lack of attention, or lack of interest. Low arousal can lead to the sensation seeking that we often find in psychopaths. Low arousal also makes learning by Pavlovian principles extremely hard. Psychopaths condition slowly and therefore in contrast to normals are able to acquire the values and inhibitions of their social group only to a minimal degree. Eysenck writes that these observations about conscience explain a great deal of the known facts about antisocial conduct and have strong experimental support.[7] He presented research to support this, which he regarded as strong, but which other scientists have regarded as weak. Also, as we have seen in a previous section, there is evidence for *over* arousal in psychopaths, too. What seems to be consistent in the nervous system of psychopaths is abnormality, but exactly what abnormality remains elusive.

Whether or not it applies very well to criminal behavior, social learning theory remains an important area of modern psychology and has generated a very large body of experimental literature on human learning. Watson was working in the early part of the twentieth century in the U.S. and Eysenck did his work on crime in England in the middle part of the twentieth century. In last decade of the century, two Canadian psychologists, Don Andrews and James Bonta, presented their application of social learning theory to criminal behavior. They call their work "the psychology of criminal conduct," and it is the subject of our next section.

The Psychology of Criminal Conduct

In science, one endeavors to discover cause by employing the classical experimental design. In this design, subjects are selected that do not differ from each other in any way that would be important. The subjects are then randomly assigned to two different groups. One of the groups receives an intervention and the other group (the control group) does not. If, after the intervention, the two groups differ from each other on an important characteristic, this difference is directly attributable to the intervention. The intervention caused it. This is so because the random assignment of subjects to the two groups controlled all of the variation between them, except for the intervention. A major obstacle to discovering the cause of crime is the ironic ethical predicament that immediately presents itself when we attempt to use the classical experimental design to discover the causes of crime. It is ironic because the application of objective science is prevented by our moral standards, our subjective judgment of the wrongness of such an application in this case. Take for example, a hypothetical experiment to determine the cause of crime. First we select a group of perfectly normal adolescent boys. Next we randomly assign them to one of two groups. Then we expose the subjects in one of the two groups to negative criminal role models for an extended period of time. The other group does not receive this intervention. We then follow up on the subjects for a significant length of time and discover (or not) that criminal offenses among the subjects in the intervention group is significantly higher than among the members of the second, or control, group. Of course, in the scientific course of things, further experimentation would be undertaken to replicate the experiment, to confirm the results, and to refine the findings. You might already be thinking of ways to refine the original experiment. For example, what would happen if you varied the length of the exposure to the criminal role models? But the point is that this series of experiments could be a definitive study on the cause of crime, except that it would be clearly unethical to conduct it. We could not agree to do anything to the subjects that might instigate or increase criminal behavior. This is ironic since to apply objective scientific methods to determine the cause of immoral behavior is, we have decided, immoral. Thus we are again warned that the explanation of crime is not entirely a scientific matter.

There are, however, ways around this dilemma that can provide useful information. One way to escape the dilemma is to start with a group of adolescents who have already engaged in criminal behavior, then randomly assign them to two groups. Next one of the groups receives an intervention that is designed to *reduce* criminal behavior; for example, exposure to positive, prosocial role models. Then, after a follow-up period, any significant differences in criminal offenses between the two groups could be attributed to the intervention. We could then infer that role models and criminal behavior are related, even that role models have an effect on criminal behavior, but we have not found the cause of crime with the same confidence that we would have if we had conducted the unethical classical experiment described above. In fact, much of the research on the causes of crime is of this second type. Another type of research employed to circumvent the ethical dilemma is to compare groups of offenders with groups of nonoffenders and try to discover the differences between them. This type of research produces lists of variables, or characteristics, that are related, or associated, with criminal behavior, but this research does not demonstrate the cause of anything, not in the scientific sense. Since most of the research on criminal behavior is of these last two types, it is not hard to see why there is so much disagreement about what the research has actually proven about the causes of crime.

Don Andrews and James Bonta, of Carleton University in Ottawa, Canada, have produced a tremendous review of the research literature on criminal behavior.[8] Their book is, in fact, so dense with the research that it is a real challenge to read. Their intention was to apply social learning perspectives to criminal behavior, to argue in favor of considering the person in combination with the particular situation as a way of understanding crime. They succeed in showing that there has been a huge amount of research conducted on crime in the latter part of the twentieth century and that much of it points in the same direction. Along the way, they present a critique of what they call "mainstream sociological criminology," which they feel has lost its credibility for the explanation of crime because it leaves out too much of the accumulated research evidence and because it proposes to leave out the contribution of personality to crime. They are crusading against what they see as efforts "to deny, discount, and dismiss, the voluminous research on the relevance of personality to criminal behavior."[9]

Andrews and Bonta attribute the deficiencies of sociological criminology mainly to "theoreticism," which is the tendency of some social scientists to simply ignore evidence that does not fit a particular theory. We recommend that alert readers keep this issue of theoreticism always in the back of their minds when theories on the causes of crime are presented for their consideration. Theoreticism leads us to Dr. Lombroso's skull.

Andrews and Bonta assert that we can't know the cause of crime because of experimental design problems, but that we can know the correlates of crime and can know the effects of certain types of interventions with criminal offenders. From this research, we can infer cause. Their summary of the research leads to what they call "the big four": antisocial attitudes, antisocial associates, behavioral history, and personality. Their strategy is to choose for causal variables the strongest of the correlates. This strategy makes for the most empirically defensible theory. They rely on excellent summaries (called meta-analyses) of the research, some conducted by themselves and some by other notable researchers including Paul Gendreau, Bob Ross, and Mark Lipsey.[10] These summaries represent literally thousands of individual research studies. Andrews and Bonta conclude that the research as a whole supports reasonably well the following correlates of criminal behavior:

1. Antisocial/procriminal attitudes
2. Antisocial/procriminal associates and peers
3. Personality factors such as impulsivity, aggression, below average verbal intelligence, egocentrism, sensation seeking, and psychopathy
4. History of antisocial behavior evident from a young age
5. Family factors such as criminality, poor parenting, neglect, abuse, and low levels of affection
6. Low levels of education and employment

A history of antisocial behavior cannot be changed and so is called a *static risk factor*. Risk means that it is a correlate of criminal behavior. Static means that it cannot be changed. Andrews and Bonta suggest that our efforts to reduce crime at the individual level should be focused on *dynamic* risk factors, that is, risk factors that could be changed, such as antisocial attitudes and antisocial/procriminal associates and peers. Thus we reach the appealing shorthand formula for reducing criminal behavior: *antisocial attitudes and antisocial associates*. They argue that this conception of criminal behavior is more empirically derived than other concepts of crime causation and that it more clearly points to specific interventions that could reduce crime. It also corrects some commonly held misconceptions about the correlates of crime. They point out, for example, that low self esteem and personal distress are not on the list of empirically derived correlates of crime.

Andrews and Bonta argue for the application of the risk/needs principle in our efforts to reduce crime. This principle is that (1) criminal behavior can be predicted; (2) there are, as we saw above, two types of risk factors, dynamic and static; (3) there should be a match between offender risk and intensity of treatment, with the more intensive level of treatment for the highest risk offenders; (4) dynamic risk factors, also called "criminogenic needs," should be targeted for intervention, and this is what will reduce crime.

The immediate situation, or crime opportunity, antisocial attitudes, and antisocial associates are the key, or strongest, elements leading to criminal actions. In their continuing critique of "mainstream sociological criminology" Andrews and Bonta argue that "political economy, social structure, and culture are constants, distal background contextual conditions that do not account for variation in individual conduct within particular social arrangements."[11] Thus sociological factors are not considered in their analysis of the causes of crime.

Andrews and Bonta, along with the other authors of the meta-analyses, have made a valuable contribution to the understanding of crime. They have helped us to see how much research has been done and to what it does, and does not, point. They have made a rational empirical case for specific crime-reducing interventions. These are no small achievements. It would seem that at least some of those long, dark Canadian nights have been fruitful for the study of crime. But their constant diatribe against "mainstream sociological criminology" is delivered with such evangelical passion that it seems at times incongruent with their avowed commitment to rational empiricism. "Mainstream sociological criminology" is, in fact, the subject of part 4, which is next after our consideration of Lykken's low fear hypothesis.

No Fear, No Father

Kody Scott, also known as Sanyka Shakur, also known as "Monster," was a member of the Eight Tray Gangster Crips in south central Los Angeles. In 1995, he was serving a seven-year sentence in solitary confinement in a northern California prison. His autobiography, *Monster: The Autobiography of an L.A. Gang Member*, hardly required editing, because Monster is intelligent and unexpectedly well spoken, especially considering his lack of formal education. Kody became a member of the Eight Trays when he was 12 and shot his first victim that same night. He came to be known as Monster as a young teenager after an incident in which Kody beat a victim he was mugging to a bloody pulp because he tried to resist.

Kody's mother was a 21-year-old single mother of two living in Houston when she moved to Los Angeles and married an older man she had met while he was visiting Houston. The marriage was unstable and abusive, but Kody's mother had four more children before the marriage dissolved. Kody's real father was Dick Bass, a professional football player with the L.A. Rams, with whom Kody's mother had had a brief affair. Kody never knew his biological father. Kody's stepfather left the home when Kody was six years old.

Now the mother of six children, Kody's mother worked mostly at bar tending jobs. The family lived in a two-bedroom house in a lower middle class neighborhood. There were gangs in the area and an older brother was briefly involved in trouble with the law in the seventh grade. He was caught stealing a leather jacket and spent the night in a juvenile detention center. The experience stayed with him and he never joined a gang. But Kody was different. Here he is described by his own family members:

"He was like a demolition derby," his sister Kendis says, "reckless, wild, and intriguing." "He had no fear," says his older brother Kerwin. Kody built wooden ramps on the street and raced his bike at top speeds, jumping crates like a junior Evel Knievel. "No one else would do it, Kerwin says, "but he would."

The story of Kody Scott appears in Lykken's *The Antisocial Personalities*, a 1995 book on psychopathy.[12] Dr. Lykken, now a professor emeritus at the University of Minnesota, summarized Scott in this way: "A bright muscular adventurous boy with no fear and no father, a boy who might have become a professional athlete if his real father had been there to guide and inspire him, or a boxer or policeman or soldier, perhaps even an astronaut, but he became Monster instead, a classic example of primary psychopathy."[13]

No fear and no father! This eloquent phrase expresses the theoretical idea that a psychopath is the result of a combination of (1) biological dysfunction in the form of low levels of anxiety and fear and (2) inadequate parenting.

No Fear

Lykken first advanced his "low fear quotient" hypothesis in 1957.[14] The fundamental idea is that someone who is relatively fearless (or unanxious) will be harder to socialize than other people. Normal socialization depends on the punishment of antisocial behavior, and punishment works by the fearful inhibition of those impulses the next time that temptation presents itself. Someone who is relatively fearless will be harder to socialize in this way. However, a child with a low fear quotient whose parents succeed in instilling good values in him can grow up to be a socialized person who is valuable in stressful and dangerous situations. "I believe, in short, that the hero and the psychopath may be twigs on the same genetic branch" Lykken writes.[15]

Lykken's theory suggested three experimental predictions: when compared to normal subjects and when compared to criminals who are not psychopaths, the psychopathic subjects should (1) score lower on a general test of fearfulness; (2) in a conditioning experiment where the sound of a buzzer is followed by a painful electric shock, the psychopathic subjects should show weaker physiological signs of a fear reaction upon hearing the buzzer; and (3) in a situation where certain responses are punished by a painful shock, psychopaths should find it harder to learn to avoid the shock because of relatively less fear of it. Subsequent experiments confirmed these predictions. Lykken concludes that psychopathy "could result from the rearing by typical parents of a child who is normal in all respects save for a below average endowment of innate fearfulness,"[16] although these constitute a small group of psychopaths. He believes that the majority of psychopaths develop as the result of a combination of low fear and incompetent parenting.

No Father

Incompetent parenting is the broad category that Lykken identifies as a key element of psychopathy, but he is convinced that it is the absence of the father which is the major flaw: "fatherless rearing is the major proximate cause of delinquency and crime."[17] This is not to say that parenting by the mother is inconsequential. It certainly is not. Many normal citizens are raised by their mother alone. But the father may be especially crucial when the child is low in fear and anxiety by temperament. A boy growing up without a father is seven times more likely to engage in criminal behavior than a boy whose father is a competent parent.

The diagram below shows how Lykken attempts to account for the diversity observed among criminal offenders in terms of his theory, which he calls the "diathesis-developmental model of criminality."[18] (This diagram is a slightly simplified version of the one presented in Lykken's book.) He refers to it as his "armchair taxonomy" since it is not fully supported by empirical data. Even so, he believes that it accounts well for the known findings at present.

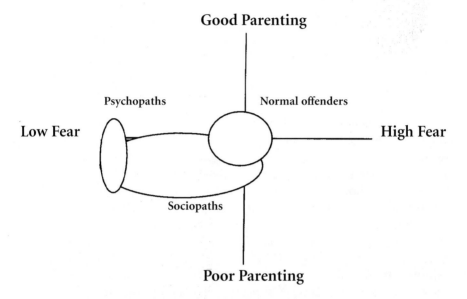

Diathesis — Developmental Model. (Adapted from David Lykken, *The Antisocial Personalities*, p. 42. Used with permission of the author and Lawrence Erlbaum Associates, Hillsdale, N.J.)

The horizontal axis represents the ease of socialization. Lykken's theory proposes that ease of socialization is basically determined by innate characteristics, particularly the degree of fear and anxiety; low fear and anxiety making a person very difficult to socialize. The vertical axis represents the competence of parenting. The parenting of an individual may be abusive or neglectful or simply incompetent. The total group of offenders is divided into those who have abnormal temperaments (psychopaths), those who were badly socialized (sociopaths), and those "normal" offenders who have neither abnormal temperaments nor inadequate parenting.[19]

Thus psychopaths are the most extreme group of offenders and are mostly the result of a temperament difficult to socialize combined with poor parenting, though some psychopaths are so extreme that even with basically competent parenting, they still resist socialization and become psychopathic. Sociopaths are criminal offenders who received such poor parenting that they did not become adequately socialized. They are less extreme in their temperament than are psychopaths. Normal offenders include victims of circumstance, and some career and white collar criminals who have neither abnormal temperaments nor incompetent parenting but chose crime as a rational economic decision. Also included among normal offenders are "dyssocial" offenders, whom Lykken describes as some juvenile offenders who are normal in terms of temperament and parenting but who identify with a deviant subculture, such as an inner city gang, and are not yet socialized, though they often become socialized later, with age and experience, after the turbulence of adolescence.

It can be seen from the diagram that Lykken proposes that the largest group of offenders are sociopaths, "persons of broadly normal temperament who have failed to acquire the attributes of socialization, not because of innate peculiarities in themselves, but because of a failure of the usual socializing agents, primarily their parents."[20] Psychopaths are a smaller and more extreme group of offenders. Kody Scott, the example cited above, is one of these. Normal offenders are a smaller group in which choice or rational decision making plays a larger role in the behavior. Thus Lykken is deterministic in his views and would place only a small group of "normal offenders" on the "choice" end of our continuum.

Criminal behavior is learned behavior. Whether it is the result of defects in certain individuals, which affect their learning processes, or whether criminal behavior is learned via normal learning processes, such as observation and imitation, is open to debate. It appears likely that some criminal offenders are explained by individual abnormality and others groups of criminal offenders are explained by normal learning in antisocial environments. Social learning theories overlap psychology and sociology and some of these theories, such as Edwin Sutherland's differential association and Ronald Akers' elaboration of it, are discussed in part 4.

Part Four

Sociological Explanations for Crime

The social environment is the cultivation medium of criminality; the criminal is the microbe, an element which only becomes important when it finds the medium which causes it to ferment; every society has the criminals that it deserves.

— J.A.E. Lacassagne[1]

10

The History of
Sociology and Crime

Moral Statistics

The French scientist A.M. Guerry and the Belgian mathematician Adolphe Quetelet were the leaders of a development in criminology that flourished between the 1830s and the 1880s in Europe. Their point of view became known as the cartographic school because of their study of geographical variables and their use of maps in studying the causes of crime. They were the forerunners of the Chicago school of criminology which was very productive in the 1920s and 1930s in the U.S. Today this orientation to the causes of crime is called ecological criminology.

Criminologists of the cartographic school were concerned with the distribution of crimes in certain geographical areas. They studied general crime rates, juvenile delinquency, and professional criminals. They also pioneered the use of statistical techniques in understanding crime. They called their work "moral statistics," by which they meant the application of mathematics, especially the laws of probability, to the study of human behavior.

Guerry's principal work, *Essay on Moral Statistics*, was published in 1833 and was famous at the time.[1] Guerry compiled and analyzed crime data by region in France and showed the variations in per capita crime rates from region to region. He tested the commonly held belief that crime was associated with poverty and found that the wealthiest region in France had the highest property crime rate, though it did have only one-half the violent crime rate. He suggested that opportunity was a better explanation for property crimes than was poverty. He made extensive use of charts, tables, graphs, and maps in his work. He is considered by some to be the first scientific criminologist.

Quetelet composed *Treatise on Man and the Development of His Fac-*

ulties, published in 1835.[2] He demonstrated that geographical and demographic differences in crime rates were stable over long periods of time and concluded from this that some characteristic of the area or group of people must be responsible for its crime rate. Quetelet studied poverty and the crime rate in France, Belgium, and Holland, and produced results similar to Guerry. He concluded that the wealthiest regions had the highest property crime rates because there was more to steal in those regions and because the conspicuousness of wealth in those regions excited passions and provoked temptations to steal in those who are poor in those regions.[3]

Quetelet's study of the numerical consistency of crimes generated a wide discussion of free will versus determinism. Quetelet wrote that "society prepares the crime and the guilty is only the instrument by which it is accomplished."[4] This point of view became the basis for social theories of crime and was resurrected by McKay and Shaw of the Chicago school a hundred years later. Quetelet was the first to note the very significant gender gap in arrest rates. He was also an astronomer and meteorologist. In the world of mathematics, he is known as the father of statistics.

The research and theoretical discussion of moral statistics that was generated by the cartographic school did not lead to agreement about the causes of crime. Students of moral statistics proposed and argued over many causes of crime: the price of wheat, population density, poverty, temperature, humidity, climate, lack of education, geographic location, good times, bad times, and whenever the price of rye increased by half a penny.[5] The causes of crime were not discovered in any very convincing way, but what did emerge was a new way of thinking about crime and new techniques for analyzing the crime data. Moral statistics provided a transition from classical criminology, in which people choose right or wrong, to positivist criminology in which people are driven by variables outside of their control. Quetelet wrote, "The more progress physical sciences make, the more they tend to enter the domain of mathematics, which is a kind of center to which they all converge. We may even judge the degree of perfection to which a science has finally arrived by the facility with which it may be submitted to calculation."[6]

Thus spoke the patriarch of statistics. If our modern criminology were to be judged by this criterion, it would have to be considered an undeveloped science.

The Collective Sadness

Emile Durkheim, the descendant of a long line of rabbinical scholars, was born in a small French town on the German border in 1858. He was educated in Paris and became a professor of philosophy at the age of 24, teaching at secondary schools near Paris for several years. He studied in Germany with the famous scientist Wilhelm Wundt, who founded the first experimental laboratory in psychology and is generally considered the father of scientific psychology. In 1887, while at the University of Bordeaux, Durkheim taught the first course in sociology to be offered at a French university. In 1892, he was awarded the first doctorate in sociology to be given by the University of Paris. His dissertation, published in 1893, was called *The Division of Labor in Society* and became a classic in sociology. He followed this work with *The Rules of Sociological Method* in 1895 and *Suicide: A Study in Sociology* in 1897. All three are major works in social science.[7]

Durkheim was mainly interested in explaining the great political, economic, and social upheavals that had taken place in France since the French Revolution in 1789 and the industrialization of French society in the nineteenth century. He was influenced by Auguste Comte, who had persuasively argued that the methods of science can be applied to the study of society and that adopting a scientific attitude is the best way to organize society. Comte had coined the term *sociological* and his point of view was called *positivism*. Following Comte, Durkheim believed that an "individual is rather a product than an author of society" and argued in favor of the explanatory power of social forces as opposed to free will, or psychological or biological explanations.[8] In his three major books, he developed some very influential ideas.

Durkheim believed that individuals possessed unlimited desires and aspirations, and that it is society's function to regulate such appetites. According to him, appetites and desires were regulated through the "collective conscience" of society, meaning people were bound together and controlled by their common morals, values, and beliefs. However, if this mechanism, the collective conscience, was weakened significantly, anomie would occur. Anomie was a period of disruption and conflict in a society. An anomic state would unleash the nearly limitless appetites of individuals and could result in a variety of deviant behaviors.[9]

He proposed that there are two forms of society. The first is a primitive kind of society in which there is a high degree of social homogeneity and a low division of labor. There are shared values, "the collective conscience," and very little specialization. He referred to this primitive type of society as being in "a state of mechanical solidarity." In this society, laws repress individuals from deviating from the group norms or from threatening the collective conscience. A small amount of crime does still exist in such a society, but this small amount keeps the primitive society from becoming too pathologically controlled. Overcontrolled societies, Durkheim argued, are not healthy and lack the means for social innovation: "To make progress, individual originality must be able to express itself. In order that the originality of the idealist whose dreams transcend his century may find expression, it is necessary that the originality of the criminal, who is below the level of his time, must also be possible. One does not occur without the other."[10]

This is the origin of the idea that some level of crime is the price of freedom. Durkheim argued that since happiness is the goal of humanity, it is natural that a division of labor should develop since specialization results in the faster production of more goods, greater general prosperity, and more leisure time to enjoy it. Thus a second form of society will eventually appear, with a more sophisticated social structure in which there is much diversity, heterogeneity of values, and a high division of labor. He referred to this type of advanced society as being in a "state of organic solidarity." As a society moves from a state of mechanical solidarity to a state of organic solidarity, there will occur some degree of social alienation and lawlessness. While the modernization of a mechanical society is a natural and expected development, it can be rough going and there are periods of disruption and conflict. In particular, financial crisis, "unnatural" class and caste divisions, and worker alienation can occur. Durkheim was not the first to use the term anomie, but he made it prominent in social science. Anomie is normlessness, the sense of isolation and loss of identity that occurs when great social changes take place as the result of an increased division of labor. Anomie produces a kind of social emptiness, isolation, and meaninglessness which Durkheim called "the collective sadness." In his work on suicide, he developed the concept of anomie further and applied it as an explanation for the increasing suicide rate in Europe at that time. A popular idea, anomie came to be seen as the explanation for a variety of social maladies, one of which was crime.

Durkheim proposed the unusual idea that crime is normal in society and that it serves useful purposes. Crime proceeds from the very nature of society. A society exempt from crime is unthinkable because it would necessitate that all individuals hold exactly the same moral concepts, which is neither possible nor desirable. Without crime there would be no evolution in law. He pointed to the conviction and execution of Socrates as an example. Socrates, Durkheim argued, was convicted and sentenced in accordance with the laws of Athens at the time. Yet his crime, corrupting the youth of the city, was really the teaching of independent, nonconformist thought. Socrates' example eventually led to an evolution of the laws in the direction of greater freedom of thought and expression.[11]

Durkheim declared that crime is inevitable. Imagine a society that consisted only of saints and in which there were no crime as we call crime. Behavior which would seem trivial and noncriminal to us would be very noticeable and reprehensible within that context. Even in such a society of saints, deviant behavior would still occur, which would offend against the collective conscience, and which would call for punishment; for crime, as Durkheim asserted, is whatever a society is willing to punish. Crime is therefore an integral part of all societies. It is even "a factor in public health," and a society entirely without it would be abnormal and pathological; it would be overcontrolled. Social solidarity is enhanced by the criminal because his deviant behavior draws together the rest of society to oppose his acts. To Durkheim, "The criminal plays a definite role in social life."[12] However, when social cohesion breaks down, where social isolation is great, where social controls no longer exist, where anomie is widespread, then crime rises to a high rate.

Durkheim did not set out to explain crime so much as he intended to explain the socioeconomic turmoil that had occurred since the French Revolution. He chose to study suicide, not crime, as an example of his ideas about social forces and anomie. He was one of the first to make extensive use of statistical data to support his theories. He assumed that the crime rate could be explained in the same way as he had explained the suicide rate. Unfortunately, the crime rate in Europe was not rising at that time, as McDonald has shown. The data were available to demonstrate this, but were not used, leading McDonald to write, "These facts suggest to me, at least, that there was more interest in work that was wrong, but fitted in with accepted theory, than in work, however thorough, that was right but that did not."[13] This is the "theoreticism" of which the psychologists Andrews and Bonta complained, as we noted in part 3. A further problem with Durkheim's work on crime is that he argued that laws in primitive society are mainly repressive, whereas laws in advanced societies are mainly restitutive. But this does not seem to be true. It is quite possible to argue that primitive societies are less punitive and repressive than more advanced ones. Primitive cultures, for example, rarely, if ever, carry out a death sentence, whereas, the U.S., possibly the most sophisticated and complex society so far, has hundreds of persons on death row and very severe criminal penalties in comparison to other societies, penalties that are not mainly restitutive.

Durkheim's work is important in the history of criminology because of his use of statistical data as evidence for his concepts, for the stimulus to debate and research which his work provided, and because of his focus on social forces as the cause of crime. Though this is the dominant view now, it was radical at the time that Durkheim argued for it. The concept of anomie provides the basis for subcultural theories of delinquency and crime and led to the famous analysis of anomie by the American sociologist Robert Merton. Durkheim's work is the forerunner specifically of both strain and control theories of crime, which are discussed later in this section. Along with Auguste Comte and Max Weber, Emile Durkheim is one of the principal founders of the science of sociology and has been a strong voice in the debate about the causes of crime.

Bands of Sparrows

One of Durkheim's most determined opponents in this debate about crime was also a professor of philosophy in Paris, Gabriel Tarde. On the subject of sociology, Tarde and Durkheim disagreed vociferously and waged unrelenting warfare with each other over the explanation of social phenomena in general and the cause of crime in particular. Tarde was born in the south of France in 1843. He became a lawyer and then a magistrate in his small hometown of Sarlat. His experience as a magistrate had stimulated his interest in criminality and in judicial and penal reform. He made the observation that particular crimes seemed to spread in waves through society as if they were fashions or fads. He became increasingly interested in how this "fashion" characteristic of crime might be just one example of a more general attribute of the social world. He further developed this idea and outlined a research program for sociology. After serving as a provincial magistrate for 15 years, he was appointed director of criminal statistics at the Ministry of Justice, Paris, in 1894. His position afforded him the means to provide evidence for his ideas. He published many articles in the French *Philosophical Review* between 1880 and 1900 and also wrote several books. In 1900, he became professor of modern philosophy at the Collège de France. His major works are *Comparative Criminality* (1886), *The Laws of Imitation* (1890), and *Penal Philosophy* (1890).[14]

In *Comparative Criminality*, Tarde argued against Cesare Lombroso's theory that biological abnormality was the cause of crime. He presented arguments and statistical evidence similar to that of Charles Goring's famous rebuttal of Lombroso's theory, but Tarde's argument was not as widely known as Goring's. Since it was not translated into English until 1912, Tarde has never gotten the credit he deserved for his argument against Lombroso. Unlike Goring, Tarde went beyond his refutation of Lombroso and developed the thesis that the causes of crime are chiefly social. He asserted that by "accident of birth" some people grew up in environments that taught criminality and that this learning took place by imitation.

Tarde proposed a different way of looking at the social world. Instead of thinking in terms of individuals or groups of individuals, Tarde focused on the actions, ideas, and products that were used to classify individuals or groups. By studying how these features were differentially reproduced, that is, repeated, he suggested it was possible to infer certain predictable regularities or laws that appeared to order the social world. Tarde's basic argument was that human history could be usefully interpreted as a series of imitations that have survived a process of "counter-imitation," that is, rejection. The primary task of Tarde's proposed sociology was to identify the variables that seemed to influence whether a specific imitation would become successful, that is, be reproduced.

In *The Laws of Imitation*, Tarde further developed his ideas about social processes and the learning of criminal behavior. He believed that imitation is universal and central to the human condition. He suggested that society itself could be defined as imitation because societies could be described in terms of populations of individuals with common imitated traits who are prone to share these imitations.

Some of his basic principles, or laws of imitation, and their application to criminal behavior were that

(1) People imitate each other in proportion to how much close contact they have with each other. Therefore imitation is more frequent and behavior changes more rapidly in cities than in the country, which explains higher urban crime rates.

(2) The inferior person usually imitates the person perceived as being superior. By Tarde's historical analysis, crimes such as drunkenness and murder had begun with royalty and were later imitated by all social classes.

(3) Newer fashions displace the older ones. For example, murder by knifing had decreased while murder by shooting had increased.[15]

Tarde's theory is essentially a cognitive one, in which there is learning by association of ideas from which the behavior follows. This line of thought led eventually to Edwin Sutherland's famous theory about crime, which he called *differential association*. Tarde's point of view is also reminiscent of the psychologists Andrews and Bonta, who wrote that the dynamic risk factors for criminality as identified by modern research are antisocial attitudes and antisocial associates. Then, of course, the reader will recall Professor Bandura's bobo dolls and modeling, learning by imitation.

In Tarde's social philosophy, historical progress is the outcome of a conflict between the inventive and conservative (imitative) members of society. He did, however, maintain that the individual is the principal actor. Tarde's conception of crime causation is a compromise between the total free will of the classical school and the determinism of the positivist school. Though he emphasized moral responsibility, he believed that chance played a role in crime causation and that biological explanations accounted for only a very small group of criminals.

Tarde, no doubt influenced by his experiences as a magistrate, also wrote very thoughtfully on the subjects of the professional criminal, the treatment of the mentally ill by the courts, and the reform of the penal system. Tarde's published work totals over 5,000 pages, but his research program was nevertheless substantially eclipsed by Durkheim's structural theories. Tarde's theory was criticized as an oversimplification of social learning. He did not work on the explanation of the mental processes that are involved in learning. Even so, his work is important because it was the first attempt to explain crime as a normal learning process rather than as a psychological or biological abnormality.

Crime, Tarde believed, has social origins, and he summarized this point of view in 1890. A hundred and ten additional years of international research and scientific analysis in numerous disciplines on the subject of crime have not negated this poignant passage:

> The majority of murderers and notorious thieves began as children who have been abandoned, and the true seminary of crime must be sought for upon each public square or crossroad of our towns, whether they be small or large, in these flocks of pillaging street urchins, who, like bands of sparrows, associate together, at first for marauding, and then for theft, because of a lack of education and food in their homes.[16]

The Chicago School

In the early part of the 1900s, the United States experienced an explosion of growth in its cities. Industrialization and the migration of large numbers of people from rural to urban areas resulted in bulging metropolitan populations and wretched slums. These conditions produced a progressive movement in America that rejected the assumption that poor people were inferior people and focused instead on how poor environments created social problems of all kinds, including crime. The Progressives initiated an "age of reform" and worked for policies that controlled the greed of industry and rendered assistance to the poor. Among these reforms were changes in the judicial and correctional systems that enabled the government to address the needs and problems of criminal offenders. According to the Progressives, criminals were not born, they were created by their inadequate, harsh, and abnormal environments.[17]

This point of view was especially popular in Chicago, which had experienced rapid economic and industrial growth along with huge population increases and all of the concomitant social ills. In addition, the city happened to have the oldest sociology program in the U.S., established at the University of Chicago in 1892. According to Lilly, Cullen, and Ball, this combination made Chicago a "hotbed of criminological research" during the early decades of the twentieth century.[18]

Sociologists in Chicago were interested in exploring the urban laboratory that lay all around them. Their work was directed and shaped primarily by Robert Parks and Ernest Burgess, colleagues and collaborators at the University of Chicago, and by Clifford Shaw and Henry McKay, who were employed as researchers at Chicago's Institute for Juvenile Research. Parks was a newspaper reporter prior to his academic career and claimed to have spent more time "tramping about" in the cities of the world than any other living man.[19] He urged students and colleagues to go out into the neighborhoods of Chicago and study them systematically. He maintained that the city's growth and organization were not random, but were established through basic social processes that could be observed, described, and understood.

Influenced by Parks' premises, Ernest Burgess developed a city model that led to Shaw and McKay's theory of crime. Burgess argued that cities "grow radially in a series of concentric zones or rings." He described five zones in his model. Zone One was the central business district, or "loop" of the city. The next concentric zone is "in transition." The third ring is "working men's homes," the fourth is the residential zone, and the last or outer ring is the commuter zone. Competition is the mechanism that determines who lives in which zone. Commercial enterprises were situated in the loop and constantly pushed outward, putting pressure on the zone of transition, which was a particular cause of concern. It typically consisted of rows of tenement buildings next to aging industrial complexes. The residents of the transition zone could not afford to move into the more prosperous outer residential zones. Waves of immigrants without means moved directly into the transition zone. This resulted in extreme social disorganization in the transition zone, and this social disorganization, as Burgess proposed, led to many social problems, one of which is a high crime rate. His model is shown in the diagram at the top of page 180.[20]

Shaw and McKay wanted to submit Burgess' model to empirical testing. Their data analysis tended to support Burgess' hypothesis. Using juvenile court statistics, they showed that delinquency was inversely related to (1) the distance from the central business district and (2) the zone's affluence.[21] Juvenile delinquency flourished in the transition zone. Shaw

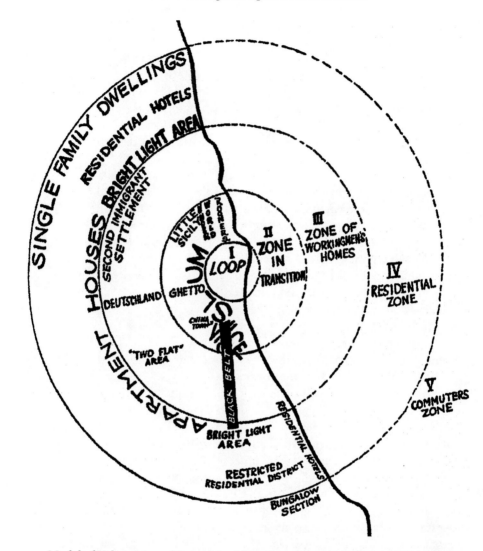

Model of Urban Areas. (Reproduced from Burgess, 1925/1967, p. 55. Copyright ©1925/1967 by the University of Chicago Press, Chicago, Ill. All rights reserved; used by permission.)

and McKay followed up their data analysis with interviews of delinquents. They developed life histories, which resulted in publications such as *The Jack Roller: A Delinquent Boy's Own Story, The Natural History of a Delinquent,* and *Brothers in Crime.* A good deal of this work was conducted during the Prohibition era in Chicago when Al Capone headed the Chicago mob, adding a special urgency and relevancy to the work. Shaw and McKay concluded that social disorganization and the resulting lack of control and absence of social bonding led to crime, but also that crime persisted because of the transmission of criminal values and traditions to young people, generation upon generation, within disorganized neighborhoods. They wrote that youths grew up in disorganized neighborhoods that sustained criminal traditions, which could be "transmitted down through successive generations of boys, much the same way that language and other social forms are transmitted."[22] This conclusion led eventually to Sutherland's influential theory of differential association. It also led Shaw and McKay to recommend programs that reformed entire neighborhoods rather than individual delinquents.

There have been generally been three criticisms of their theory: (1) Their study of neighborhoods failed to account for cultural factors within neighborhoods where delinquency rates have been shown to be markedly variable among different ethnic groups. (2) Their theory does not account for the existence of large groups of nondelinquents in the at-risk neighborhoods. (3) It has been argued that urban areas that are socially disorganized may attract delinquent individuals to them rather than creating them.[23] In addition, Ianni has argued that the transmission of criminal values may likely occur in a neighborhood as the result of common prison experiences rather than the influence of growing up in a particular neighborhood.[24] There is also the argument of differential law enforcement, that is, the police may be more likely and more willing to make arrests in disorganized areas than in other areas of a city.

The work of Shaw and McKay was painstaking and, to their credit, generated a large amount of research. They contended that criminal behavior is the result of the social conditions in which a child is reared, not the biological characteristics of his parents, and their theory of human ecology is a strong one today, though it is not without critics. Shaw and McKay also generated programs for improving neighborhoods, including the Chicago Area Project, a delinquency prevention program, which operated for decades and which many considered to be a successful intervention.[25] Shoemaker argues that social disorganization has proven to be a good starting point for understanding crime, but it inevitably leads to further analyses of why some boys living in disorganized neighborhoods engage in criminal behavior and others do not.[26] Nevertheless, Lilly, Cullen, and Ball conclude that the Chicago criminologists presented a formidable challenge, with impressive data, to the concept of crime as individual pathology, and their ecological criminology has stood the test of time. "They captured the truth that where people grow up and with whom they associate cannot be overlooked in the search for the origins of crime."[27]

The Swan Song of Differential Association

Edwin Sutherland was the most famous and popular criminologist of the twentieth century. He was born in a small town in Nebraska in 1883 and obtained his Ph.D. from the University of Chicago, linking him with the Chicago school of criminology. He wrote a classic textbook on criminology, which went through 11 editions from 1924 to 1992. After his death in 1950, periodic updated editions were written by Donald Cressey and David Luckenbill.[28] Sutherland responded in his second edition to a paper by Adler and Michael, written in 1933, which had severely criticized the state of criminology at that time.[29] Motivated by this critique, he proposed a general theory of crime, which he developed and revised until its final version in 1947.

Sutherland refined his theory eventually into a set of nine propositions, but he summarized his theory this way: "Criminal behavior is learned in association with those who define such behavior favorably," declared Professor Sutherland, "and in isolation from those who define it unfavorably, and a person in an appropriate situation engages in such criminal behavior if, and only if, the weight of the favorable definitions exceeds the weight of the unfavorable definitions."[30]

Sutherland was especially interested in career criminals and white collar criminals, subjects on which he produced excellent work. It was he who coined the term "white collar crime." He wanted to explain career criminals, but he later extended his theory as an explanation of all criminals. His nine propositions set off a flood of criminological research. His propositions were that

1. Criminal behavior is learned.
2. Criminal behavior is learned in interaction with others in a process of communication.
3. The principal part of the learning of criminal behavior occurs within intimate personal groups.
4. When criminal behavior is learned, the learning includes (a) techniques of committing the crime, which are sometimes very complicated, sometimes very simple; (b) the specific direction of motives, drives, rationalizations, and attitudes.
5. The specific nature of motives and drives is learned from definitions of the legal codes as favorable or unfavorable.
6. A person becomes delinquent because of an excess of definitions favorable to violations of law over definitions unfavorable to violation of law.
7. Differential association may vary in frequency, duration, priority, and intensity.

8. The process of learning criminal behavior by association with criminal and anticriminal patterns involves all of the mechanisms that are involved in any other learning.
9. While criminal behavior is an expression of general needs and values, it is not explained by those general needs and values since noncriminal behavior is an expression of the same needs and values.[31]

Sutherland's theory was a further development of Gabriel Tarde's laws of imitation and was significantly influenced by the symbolic interactionism of George Mead. Mead had been on the faculty at the University of Chicago while Sutherland was a student there. He had argued that individuals, through a process of social interaction, derive personal meanings from their particular experiences and that these personal meanings determine subsequent behavior. Sutherland applied this thinking to criminal behavior, asserting that criminals learned favorable meanings for criminal behavior in association with others.

The criminologist Leon Radzinowicz complained that it was only because of Sutherland's prestige and popularity that the theory received so much attention.[32] Sutherland's idea was simply the equivalent of saying that if one associates with Baptists, one is likely to become a Baptist, or if one associates with Democrats, one is likely to become a Democrat. We might also say that if one hangs out with criminologists, instead of becoming a criminal, one is likely to become a criminologist. Others argued that this was an unfair assessment and that differential association received attention because it was an improvement over previous theories of crime. It was a development along the way towards learning theories of criminal behavior, which, by the way, are back in favor today. Differential association placed sociological explanations at the forefront of criminology. According to Vold and Bernard, the assumption that criminal behavior is normal learned behavior had a "massive impact on criminology."[33] It highlighted, wrote Donald Shoemaker, the importance of the group context for criminal activity.[34] It anticipated later learning theory perspectives, including Andrews and Bonta, and their colleague Paul Gendreau, who report on massive amounts of research in the last part of the twentieth century demonstrating that assessments of antisocial attitudes and antisocial associates distinguish between offenders and nonoffenders with an excellent degree of accuracy. It is no surprise that they write, "We are favorably disposed to differential association theory."[35]

But there were too many questions left unresolved by Sutherland's propositions. What is the process of acquiring criminal attitudes? What about long-term maintenance of the attitudes? What about the fact that attitudes often do not explain behavior? Why do associations arise? What explains people who grow up in high crime areas and do not assimilate criminal attitudes? What explains the origin of crime, the first criminal act? — since for differential association to explain criminal behavior, such behavior must already exist. How do you measure favorable and unfavorable definitions of criminal behavior? The problem of measurement was one of paramount importance for a scientific validation of Sutherland's concepts.

Ronald Akers and Robert Burgess reformulated Sutherland's principles to include updated research in social learning theory and addressed some of the deficiencies in Sutherland's ideas.[36] They combined differential association with learning theories, such as B.F. Skinner's operant conditioning and Albert Bandura's modeling and imitation, discussed in part 3. Akers and Burgess called their theory *differential association* reinforcement theory. For example, they revised Sutherland's first principle, "criminal behavior is learned," to "criminal behavior is learned according to the principles of operant conditioning."[37] Their fundamental proposal was that differential association explains the origin of criminal behavior but that reinforcement by the environment explains its persistence. They in turn were criticized for circular reasoning: a behavior occurs because it is reinforced and it is reinforced because it occurs. They were also criticized for a lack of research evidence specifically related to criminal behavior. Still, this theory remains an important one in sociological criminology because it integrates two powerful and well researched theories.

There was an article published after his death that Sutherland had titled the "the swan song of differential association."[38] He reported that he had had doubts from the beginning about the soundness of this theory and he acknowledged that it was not an adequate explanation of crime. "Differential association as a sufficient explanation of criminal behavior is invalid."[39] Earlier, he had called his theory "an hypothesis which might quickly be murdered or commit suicide."[40] It did not do so quickly, but it did not pass the test of survival either, except as a worthy precursor and a stimulus for further investigation. Nevertheless, Sutherland has many achievements to his credit. Vold, Bernard, and Snipes have reported that Sutherland's theory, more than any other, was responsible for the decline of the view that crime was the result of psychological and biological abnormality and for "the rise of the view that crime is the result of environmental influences acting on biologically and psychologically normal individuals."[41] Jones writes that "Sutherland was the most popular criminologist of the twentieth century and the most popular American criminologist of all time."[42]

Self doubt is a valuable characteristic in pursuit of the causes of crime.

For example, compare the modesty of Dr. Sutherland's swan song with the hubris of Dr. Lombroso's skull.

Anomie

What do you suppose would be the odds that a boy, born in 1910 of immigrant parents, and growing up in a slum in south Philadelphia, would become an Ivy League sociologist of international renown? What set of variables would have this erstwhile gang member winning a fellowship to Harvard Graduate School instead of a prison sentence in a Pennsylvania penitentiary? What modern social scientist, armed with the mathematics of probability, would have predicted that this boy, who haunted the public library in his run-down neighborhood during the roaring twenties, would eventually propose one of the most influential theories of the causes of crime since the Roman philosopher Seneca in the first century A.D.?

Robert K. Merton, unlike most of the teenagers that he grew up with, was a successful student in high school, and received a scholarship to Temple University. He worked hard in college and eventually won a fellowship to Harvard Graduate School, where he matriculated in 1931. There he became interested in sociology, worked with Talcott Parsons and George Homans, and read Emile Durkheim's work on anomie. According to Morton Hunt, after reading Durkheim's theory, "Merton assigned himself the task of discovering what produces anomie."[43] In an article first published in 1938, Merton proposed the first "strain theory" of the causes of crime.[44] He later made some revisions to his ideas in an article in 1949 and in his book *Social Theory and Social Structure*.[45] A strain theory is the idea that certain social pressures, or strains, in society drive individuals to engage in various deviant behaviors, one of these deviant behaviors being crime. Merton argued that certain "phases" of the social structure produced pressures toward nonconformity. He opposed the idea that nonconformity was the result of biological drives breaking through social control, as Durkheim had believed, but instead argued that the social structure itself could produce pressures toward deviance. This could happen when the legitimate means to attaining accepted social goals are blocked. Since understanding deviant behavior as strong biological drives breaking through social controls could be thought of as a variation of the doctrine of original sin, Merton said that he wanted to replace it with a "doctrine of socially derived sin."[46]

Merton began by stating that there are two basic elements of social structure. The first element consists of culturally assigned goals and aspirations. These are the things that all individual members of the society want and expect out of life, including success, money, security, material things, recognition, etc. The second element of the social structure defines the acceptable ways of obtaining or achieving the goals and aspirations set by society, such as obeying laws and societal norms, seeking an education, cooperating with others, and hard work. In order for society to maintain stability, there must be a balance between goals and means to achieve them. According to Merton, there is a proper balance when individuals feel that they can achieve culturally sanctioned goals through conventional means, that is, through "the acceptable modes of achieving these goals."[47] In this balanced state of things, individuals receive internal satisfaction by playing by the rules and external satisfaction by achieving goals and realizing aspirations. When the cultural goals and the institutionalized means of achieving them are well balanced, there is a high degree of social stability.

However, when there is a gap between culturally accepted aspirations and the legitimate means of achieving them, this social condition produces a state of anomie, that state of confusion, lawlessness, and collective sadness described by Durkheim. This situation generates deviant behavior. As Merton states it, "the social order we have described necessarily produces this strain toward dissolution."[48] There are five possible reactions to this anomic situation. The first is *conformity*. Individuals decide to continue to accept the socially desirable goals and stick to legitimate means for obtaining them. The second possible reaction Merton calls *innovation*. By innovation he means that illegitimate or illegal means are adopted for attaining socially accepted goals. The category of innovation includes antisocial behavior. Here is, according to Merton, the cause of crime, for when legitimate means to culturally valued goals are blocked, illegitimate methods of obtaining those goals are adopted or invented. Individuals are motivated to seek out their goals by whatever means necessary, or as Merton puts it, there is "a strain towards innovational practices."[49] Lack of opportunity for conventional success leads to crime.

A third possible reaction is *ritualism,* in which individuals choose to follow the legitimate means even without being rewarded by achieving their goals and aspirations. Some individuals are simply going through the motions. A fourth reaction is *retreatism,* in which individuals reject both the goals and the means and essentially drop out of the culture. Finally, there is *rebellion,* in which both conventional goals and the means of achieving them are rejected and a new social order is sought, one with new goals and new means.

Merton provided this summary table of his theory:

(The "+" means acceptance, the "−" means rejection, and the "±" means rejection and substitution of new goals and means.)

Anomie: Goals and Means[50]

	Mode of Adjustment	Culture Goals	Institutionalized Means
I.	Conformity	+	+
II.	Innovation	+	−
III.	Ritualism	−	+
IV.	Retreatism	−	−
V.	Rebellion	±	±

Merton's paper presented some very fruitful ideas. According to David Jones, after Merton's publication, "There ensued a surge of analytic criminology."[51] Eventually, Merton applied Durkheim's theory to what he saw and heard in America just before, during, and after World War II. Merton's strain theory seemed ideal for investigating and explaining what was happening in the U.S. during the 1960s. By 1964, about 25 years after it was first published, Merton's article was called by sociologist Marshall Clinard "possibly the most quoted single paper in modern sociology."[52]

Since Merton had argued that anomie affected the lower socioeconomic classes disproportionately and permanently, his theory was effective in motivating social change. Programs of affirmative action and equal opportunity can be linked to Merton's influence and to those who followed up on his work, including Richard Cloward and Lloyd Ohlin. Cloward and Ohlin made a meaningful extension of Merton's theory by arguing that access to *illegitimate* opportunities is just as important in determining criminal behavior as is access to *legitimate* opportunities: "[W]e can think of individuals as being located in two opportunity structures—one legitimate, the other illegitimate. Given limited access to success goals by legitimate means, the nature of the delinquent response that may result will vary according to the availability of various illegitimate means." They referred to this idea as "differential opportunity."[53]

There followed other variations of strain theory. Albert Cohen in a 1955 book argued that lower class boys are expected to achieve according to middle class standards and that, since they are unprepared to do so, they experience frustration and lowered self esteem when judged by "the middle class measuring rod." Their failures lead them, according to Cohen, to develop a subculture that inverts middle class values and leads to criminal activities.[54] Walter Miller disagreed with Cohen and asserted that lower class boys are responding to their environment and its values and are not inverting middle class values out of frustration. Instead their values are naturally in conflict with middle class values.[55] There are other variations as well, but one particularly appealing idea is the routine activities approach of Lawrence Cohen and Marcus Felson. Cohen and Felson propose that a crime occurs when three factors converge. The three factors are (1) likely offenders, (2) suitable targets, and (3) absence of capable guardians. This approach has been found useful in explaining crime rates under varying conditions. It also has the capability of explaining how changes in legal behavior can increase illegal behavior. For example, more women entering the work force can mean no one at home (absence of capable guardian) and lead to an increase in burglaries.[56] This approach is simply stated and testable, and it can result in practical measures for reducing crime. But it shares a significant deficiency with Merton's original theory: how does a likely offender become a likely offender?

President Johnson's War on Poverty was heavily influenced by strain theory. However, specific programs that were initiated often failed to reduce crime and delinquency, such as the well studied Mobilization for Youth program, which intended to improve opportunity for lower class delinquents but failed to reduce crime among them.[57] A criticism of Merton's theory is that it does not specify how social conditions (such as anomie) become individual behaviors. It also does not show what causes people in a state of anomie, or experiencing strain, to become criminals instead of becoming conformists, ritualists, retreatists, or rebels. After all the intriguing theoretical speculation and social analysis, one is still left with the essential question, "How does this individual person become a criminal?" One might also ask, "How did Robert Merton, a child of the slum, become a criminologist?"

11

A Sampling of Theories

What follows is a sampling of sociological theories about crime. The samples are chosen to be representative rather than comprehensive. Not every theoretical idea that may be considered of some importance to the field is included. The selections are based on their impact on our thinking about crime, their historical importance, and the degree to which they represented a particular way of thinking about the causes of crime. The purpose of this sampling is not to provide a complete catalogue of theories but rather to inform the reader about different theoretical approaches and to inspire him to look further into this important and perplexing subject.

Labeling Theory: The Case of Robert H.

I worked in the mental health unit of the state's maximum security prison for three years. We had 144 beds, which were usually full, sometimes overflowing. Some of the inmates that we housed there were severely mentally ill, but others were simply seeking refuge from a prison situation they could not manage and were displaying symptoms in order to stay in the mental health facility where it was safer. During a part of this time, I was taking a graduate sociology course at the state university, which was located in sight of the prison. I made my way back and forth between the ivory tower and the dungeon. I thought that this was an ideal situation because I could study the causes of crime while working with criminals at the same time.

Working our way through the theories of crime, my class eventually reached labeling theory as an explanation for crime. Edwin Lemert, writing in 1951, had proposed that deviant behavior, including criminal behavior, could be considered to be of two types: *primary* deviant behavior or *secondary* deviant behavior. Primary deviant behavior is the first or original deviant behavior. But, Lemert argued, there is a reciprocal relationship between a person's deviant behavior and society's reaction to that behavior. If the deviant behavior is severe or is often repeated, then the social reaction to this behavior will increase in severity until a point is reached at which "a stigmatizing of the deviant occurs in the form of name calling, labeling, or stereotyping."[1] The person engaging in deviant behavior may then adopt the role which the labeling has assigned him. His continued deviant behavior then would be, in Lemert's view, *secondary* deviance; that is, the deviant behavior in which he now engages is his response to the stigmatizing and penalizing that his first, or primary, deviant behavior elicited. One might think here of the adolescent's outraged response, when accused of some transgression, "If that's what you think I am, then that's what I might as well be."

Lemert's concept of secondary deviance, of labeling as a cause of deviant behavior, had both precursors and followers. Frank Tannebaum wrote in 1938 that "the process of making a criminal is a process of tagging, defining, identifying, segregating, describing, emphasizing, making conscious and unconscious; it becomes a way of stimulating, suggesting, emphasizing, and evoking the very traits that are complained of. The person becomes the thing he is described as being."[2] It is a self fulfilling prophecy. Charles Cooley, in 1964, coined the term "the looking glass self" to describe this point of view.[3] Eventually the labeling perspective came to be called *social reaction theory*.

Howard Becker wrote an influential book which he called *The Outsiders*, first published in 1963 and revised in 1973. In this book, he argued that "[t]he deviant is one to whom the label has been successfully applied; deviant behavior is behavior that people so label." He believed that deviance was created by social rule enforcers who acted with bias towards lower class, relatively powerless offenders. He emphasized the study of the process by which some people are labeled deviant while others, who may have engaged in the same behavior, are not so labeled.[4]

Social reaction theory is an interesting and provocative perspective to take in explaining the conditions of our society. For example, the importance of labeling effects in psychiatric admissions and in employment situations has been competently demonstrated.[5] But, as an explanation for crime, it is less than compelling. First of all, it does not explain primary deviance, that is, the crimes that call forth the labeling in the first place. It fails to appreciate that labeling can have positive, beneficial effects as well as negative, damaging ones. And, once again, we have the limiting circumstance of a theory intended to explain social behavior on a broad scale being used to explain crime, as if to say, "Oh, by the way, this could explain crime, too." The research is not very strong in support of labeling as an explanation for crime. The criminologist Sue Reid reports in a summary in 1994 that "the research raises interesting questions but provides few answers."[6]

I went to my class on the causes of crime every Tuesday evening. On weekdays, I struggled with my disturbed inmates. To be sure, they were not a typical cross section of prisoners, since they were either mentally ill or, as we used to say, "inadequate personalities." I couldn't help but think of the case of Robert H. when labeling theory came up in our class discussions or in course reading. Robert H. was in prison for killing a man who had sexually abused him. Robert was a 35-year-old black man who was developmentally disabled and who had also been diagnosed as schizophrenic. He had a history of alcoholism. He wore thick glasses because he did not see very well. He was partially deaf and needed a hearing aid. He was a homosexual. He was HIV+ and had gonorrhea. He was diabetic. He was impulsive and unpredictable, he could be violent at times, and he was in prison for life. We could all agree that Robert was a handicapped person and that he could be "labeled" *ad nauseam*. None of the labels were false, except possibly the schizophrenic one, the one that justified the medication. What label brought Robert H. to prison? He probably would have *benefited* from being labeled earlier in his life. As it was, his conditions were ignored until he committed a serious crime. His various illnesses did not stop other inmates from seeking sexual favors from him constantly. Usually, a cup of coffee or a cigarette was sufficient. He told me once that what he wanted most was to be with another man who really cared about him. He never seemed to lose hope of finding such a relationship. We developed a ritual greeting between us for when I made my morning rounds. Robert would call out, "Hey, you got a cigarette, Mr. Burkhead?" I would answer, "No way, Roberto, I ain't goin' for that." It was the same as saying, "Good morning, how are things going for you today?" Robert would smile and chuckle. I always thought that labeling theory as an explanation for crime paled in significance at the door to Robert's cell.

Conflict Criminology

The group of theories that are called collectively *conflict criminology* arise from the idea that crime is the result of conflict between competing social groups, usually the powerful and the powerless, or the established and the disenfranchised, or the wealthy and the poor. The conflict perspective is that values, norms, and laws create conflict between social groups and that this conflict is the cause of crime, or at least, one of the causes of crime. Conflict criminologists focus on social structure and how social structure both creates and influences crime. Conflict analysis predicts that, within any society, there will be an inverse relationship between official crime rates and political power. Susan Walklate proposes that this category of theories could be understood as concern with "the criminality of the state" rather than the criminality of the individual.[7] Within the group of conflict theories may be found a number of variations, which refer to themselves as radical criminology, socialist criminology, new criminology, and critical criminology. Karl Marx is a good starting point:

> [T]he history of all hitherto existing society is the history of class struggles. Freeman and slave, patrician and plebian, lord and serf, guild-master and journeyman, in a word, oppressor and oppressed, stood in constant opposition to one another, carried on an uninterrupted, now hidden, now open fight, a fight that each time ended either in a revolutionary reconstitution of society at large, or in the common ruin of the contending classes.[8]

Thus did Marx open his grand theory on the progress of human civilization, a theory that exerted enormous influence in the world. With the collapse of the old USSR and the decline of communism worldwide in the last decades of the twentieth century it may seem irrelevant, perhaps even false, to seriously discuss "the Marxian perspective." Reports of its demise may be premature, however, as the world's largest nation, with its prestige ever growing, is still a communist one. It may also be reasonably argued that communism as practiced in the USSR was a very corrupt version of Marxism, and the jury is still out on the value of a purer strain of communism. But our discussion is about crime.

Marxist thought is a progenitor of conflict criminology, even though Marx, like Darwin and Freud, had little to say about crime. He, like them, did not set out to explain crime and presented no in-depth treatment of its causes. But some of his adherents did employ a Marxist perspective to analyze the causes of crime. One aspect of Marx's analysis is sometimes called the *primitive rebellion thesis.*[9] Marx thought that the individual who was relatively poor and powerless would struggle against the prevailing social and economic conditions. This struggle might include breaking the laws, which mainly represented the interests of the ruling classes. He also observed that there were people in industrialized societies who were unemployed or underemployed, and who became discouraged and demoralized. This group of people he called the *lumpenproletariat.* The creation of this group of people, who were especially vulnerable to addictive and criminal behavior, was a consequence of capitalism.[10]

In another brief passage in which he discusses crime, Marx suggests an additional basis for a Marxist criminology:

> A philosopher produces ideas, a poet poems, a clergyman sermons, a pro-
> fessor compendia and so on. A criminal produces crimes.... The criminal
> produces not only crime but also criminal law, and with this also the pro-
> fessor who gives lectures on criminal law and in addition to this the
> inevitable compendium in which this same professor throws his lectures
> onto the general market.... The criminal moreover produces the whole of
> the police and of criminal justice, constables, judges, hangmen, juries,
> etc.; and all these different lines of businesses, which form equally many
> categories of the social division of labor, develop different capacities of
> the human spirit, create new needs and new ways of satisfying them.[11]

David Jones reports that "the last quarter of the 19th century was replete with a number of Marxist thinkers who expounded their views on the causes of crime."[12] In general, their view was that crime was a natural and inevitable by-product of a capitalist society, that it was a kind of rebellion against oppression, and that it could even be used to contribute to the perpetuation of a capitalist social structure, as suggested in the passage above. One of the most influential of these social scientists with a Marxist perspective was the Dutch criminologist Willem Bonger.

Bonger published his doctoral dissertation in law, presented at the University of Amsterdam, in 1905 and it was subsequently published in English in 1916 as *Criminality and Economic Conditions*.[13] In this book, he tried to prove that it was economic and social conditions rather than hereditary or racial characteristics that accounted for the greater incidence of criminality among the lower classes. He gathered data from European cities to demonstrate that the poor classes were disproportionately involved in crime. Bonger was a sharp critic of capitalistic society, which he thought made people selfish and materialistic and led them to "unlimited egoism," which set an atmosphere for crime. He studied primitive people, who displayed more altruism and less crime in their communities than did modern societies. He proposed that the pressures of a capitalistic society were responsible for the differences between primitive societies and our own.

He published *An Introduction to Criminology* in 1932, considered by some to be a classic in criminology, and he went on to publish *Race and Crime* in 1939, in which he endeavored to show that economic deprivation, not heredity, was the cause of high crime rates among minority groups.[14] In his writings, he argued against Lombroso, admired Darwin, and ridiculed Freud's psychoanalytic theory.

Bonger argued that definitions of morality varied and the source of prevailing definitions at any given time could be found in the interests of the powerful. He wrote that a crime is "an immoral act" that is "harmful to the interests of a group of persons united by the same interests."[15] He believed that crime could be almost eliminated by a redistribution of wealth and political power.

He was a champion of blacks, Jews, and homosexuals when it was unpopular and dangerous to be so. As World War II approached, he worked to help Jewish refugees escape the Germans and was named in public by the Nazis as "an arch enemy." As the Germans approached the Dutch border, he wrote to his son, "I don't see any future for myself and I cannot bow to this scum which will now overmaster us."[16] An intellectual opponent of free will and a hard determinist, Bonger committed suicide in 1940, an act that he had previously written was the only one in which the human will plays a role. Thus he chose to express his humanity by exercising the small amount of free will that he believed he possessed.

In 1938, the famous criminologist Thorsten Sellin published *Culture, Conflict, and Crime*, a book that had a large influence in criminology at the time.[17] Sellin argued that people act according to "conduct norms," which are behavioral expectations supported by the social group to which the person belongs. Conflicts may occur between different cultures and between subgroups within a single culture. He defined "primary cultural conflicts" as those occurring between two different cultures and "secondary cultural conflicts" as those occurring within a single culture when it evolves into several subcultures, each having its own conduct norms. The law represents the conduct norms of the dominant culture.

Sellin also proposed that "culture conflict may be regarded as sometimes personalized, or mental, and sometimes as occurring entirely in an impersonal way solely as a conflict of group codes."[18] He offered an example that is often quoted in the criminological literature. He reported the case of a Sicilian father in New Jersey who killed a 16-year-old boy who had seduced his young daughter. From the father's point of view, he was defending his family honor in the traditional way and he was very surprised at his arrest for murder. Within his Sicilian culture, he had acted in accordance with conduct norms; but in the American culture, he had committed a serious crime. There was no "mental conflict" in this example, since the father believed without doubt that he had acted correctly. The conflict was between the conduct norms of the two cultures. This culture conflict was, according to Sellin, a source of crime. Crime is a social definition and is relative to the norms of the group that is defining it. He also encouraged criminologists to study all types of deviant behavior, irrespective of whether the behavior is illegal or not.

George Vold published in 1958 the first edition of *Theoretical Criminology*, a very useful work which, with updates by Bernard and Snipes, has been through five editions (so far).[19] Vold proposed a conflict theory but applied it to interest groups within a single culture. These were not necessarily different cultures or different evolved subcultures, but simply groups of people, such as management and labor, with competing and conflicting interests that might result in violent and illegal acts. He also argued that conflict was not abnormal but a fundamental, normal aspect of social life. Social order was achieved when the various competing groups were in a more or less stable equilibrium, "balanced forces in opposition." Vold studied white collar crime, organized crime, and labor/management conflicts, including conflicts between different unions, as examples of competing and conflicting groups. He believed that democracy progressed as a series of compromises among the groups, and that the criminal law at any given time was the result of this process of compromise. He recognized that his theory did not explain all crime, only some crime, and he cautioned that his theory "should not be stretched too far."[20] Unfortunately, it is one of the lessons from the history of criminology that interesting and promising theories are often "stretched too far" in pursuit of the causes of crime.

The year after Vold first published *Theoretical Criminology*, Ralf Dahrendorf completed *Class and Class Conflict in Industrialized Society*.[21] He believed that the struggle between the bourgeoisie and the proletariat as expounded by Marx was too simplistic a view. He argued that conflict between groups was a natural and expected part of society and that the inequality that resulted from capitalism was not the cause of this conflict. He thought that not all inequality could be eliminated and that there would always be powerful social groups who sought to enforce cultural norms.

As the United States moved into the turbulent decade of the 1960s, social conflict theory became ever more prominent in the explanation of crime. That decade included the civil rights movement, antiwar protest, the proliferation of a drug subculture, and challenges to conventional sexual mores, all of which involved illegal activities that were nevertheless considered legitimate by large portions of the population. Austin Turk completed his graduate studies during this tumultuous decade and, in 1969, published *Criminality and Legal Order*.[22] In this book, he offered a detailed account, within a conflict perspective, of what he called a "theory of criminalization." Criminalization is the process of "assigning criminal status to individuals" and it is a measure of the overt conflict between two groups. Turk set out the conditions under which "authorities" and "subjects" would likely come into conflict and the conditions under which criminalization would likely occur. He reasoned that conflict between authorities and subjects was most likely to occur when organization was high and sophistication was low. By sophistication, he meant the knowledge and skills that enabled group members to obtain their objectives without resorting to overt coercion.

When conflict does occur, there are three factors that influence the process of criminalization. The first factor is the meaning to the authorities of the prohibited acts or acts. The more serious the authorities are about the actions of the subjects, the more likely it is that criminalization will occur. The second factor is the relative power of the authorities and the subjects. If the difference is large, criminalization is more likely to occur. The third factor is how realistic are the moves made, or actions taken, by the authorities and by the subjects during the conflict. A realistic move is one likely to result in eventual success. Unrealistic moves made by either group makes criminalization more likely to occur.[23]

Turk offered considerable detail concerning the factors in his theory. He relied on logic and astute social commentary for his argument, and not on empirical data, though he did made specific suggestions for testing his theory. The reviews are mixed. Pelfrey describes Turk as "one of the most eloquent and steadfast of the contemporary conflict theorists."[24] But others report that "[f]ew aspects of conflict theory have withstood empirical testing, even using the least rigorous methodological techniques."[25]

Richard Quinney, write Lilly, Cullen, and Ball, is the most prolific and most controversial of the conflict theorists.[26] Quinney proposed his theory of "the social reality of crime" in 1970.[27] By the social reality of crime, he meant that individuals and groups with political power are able to decide what is criminal and what is not, disguising their own self interest as being for the common good. The views of the powerful are often accepted as legitimate by people with less power in the society. He considered American society to be a criminogenic social system, and the "politicality of crime" was central to his views. He meant by the "politicality of crime" that criminal behavior was not the result of inadequate socialization or personality disorder but was deliberate action taken against something, action for bringing about social change and in opposition to inequality. His position differed from other theorists, not so much in his analysis or in his conclusions, but in the underlying philosophy. Quinney rejected positivism and its approach to the study of crime altogether and adopted the view that there is no objective reality apart from the observer, that reality and its meanings are social constructions, ever changing and developing, and that crime should be studied and understood in this context. Whatever physical reality may be, there is no objective cause of crime to be found.

Quinney, however, eventually turned to a stricter Marxist point of view in the two volumes *Criminal Justice in America* and *Critique of the Legal Order*, published in 1974.[28] In these works, he repudiated both positivism and the phenomenology that he had embraced in *The Social Reality of Crime*. He returned to a Marxist analysis and to Marx's view that society is not only to be understood but also to be changed. Quinney concluded that "[o]nly with the collapse of capitalist society and the creation of a new society based on socialist principles, will there be a solution to the crime problem."[29]

In his 1977 book *Class, State, and Crime*, Quinney further developed his Marxist approach, placing special emphasis on the Marxist idea that a capitalist society produces a surplus population, the *lumpenproletariat* as Marx had called it, and that providing for and controlling this population is a major problem of capitalism.[30] Quinney wrote that crimes by working class people are nearly always a means of survival in a society that does not provide for their welfare. He begins this book with the declaration that an understanding of crime must start with "the historical development and operation of capitalist society" and concludes that "the only lasting solution to the crisis of capitalism is socialism."[31]

As his next evolution, in the second edition of *Class, State, and Crime*, published in 1980, Quinney turned to a concern with the religious implications of socialism, quoting the theology of Paul Tillich and the Biblical prophets. Lilly, Cullen, and Ball point out that this last version of Quinney's thought is often left out of the discussion of the causes of crime as if as if it were "either embarrassing or irrelevant."[32] In this work, Quinney argued for a "prophetic" understanding of reality. He wrote that "justice is more than a normative idea; it is charged with the transcendent power of the infinite and the eternal, with the essence of divine revelation."[33] He repudiated the Marxist idea that religion is the opiate of the masses. Even though he presents a crime typology and discusses at length "the understanding of crime," Quinney's real subject is social justice and always has been, just like Marx and Bonger. Considering his passionate concern with social justice, rather than a scientific search for the causes of crime, which he rejected early on, Quinney's progression of thought is very understandable and not at all surprising. Quinney's last development certainly ought to be included in the discussion.

Law, Order, and Power was published by William Chambliss and Robert Seidman in 1971.[34] Chambliss and Seidman produced a detailed analysis of the functioning of the criminal justice system. Chambliss had previously published a study in which he traced the laws of vagrancy from the fourteenth century in England through to the United States in the 1960s.[35] He concluded that the laws were originally created and changed over time for the benefit of powerful interest groups. In *Law, Order, and Power*, Chambliss and Seidman studied the legislative process, the appellate court process, and law enforcement agencies. They concluded that each of these parts of the system operates in the interests of power groups and reflects the public good only when that coincides with their interests. In a later work, Chambliss focused on the economy and how it affects the criminal justice system. He wrote, "Criminality is not something that people have or don't have; crime is not something that some people do and others don't do. Crime is a matter of who can pin the label on whom, and underlying this sociopolitical process is the structure of the social relations determined by the political economy."[36] This point of view was more explicitly Marxist than his earlier conflict analysis in *Law, Order, and Power*, and also showed the influence of labeling theory.

There are other voices in the development of conflict criminology, including Herman and Julia Schwendinger, who argued that criminologists should study all violations of human rights, and Stephen Spitzer, who illustrated how a capitalistic society handles its deviant population.[37] Not all conflict criminologists are Marxists, but a large amount of the literature on social conflict theory and criticism of it is concerned with its Marxist versions. This criminology has been criticized for being too deterministic, for not producing testable hypotheses, for focusing too much on economics, and for assuming that the criminal law is always in the interests of the wealthy classes. Ronald Akers, in a review of this work, concluded that "however much I disagree with Marxist criminology, I believe we should continue to hear about it and respond to it."[38]

But there is widespread agreement that the work of Taylor, Walton, and Young in *The New Criminology* ushered in a fresh era in criminology. To that work and its proliferation we will next turn our attention.

Critical Criminology

It is possible to debate what particular ideas should properly be called critical criminology. Sometimes the words new, critical, and radical are used as if they were interchangeable, but some authors complain that this results in a superficial examination of critical explanations for crime. Marvin Wolfgang offers the distinction that true Marxist criminology is proactive in character whereas critical criminology is reactive. He means that Marxist criminology aims to overthrow the ruling class and completely change the social structure whereas critical criminology maintains its ties with the prevailing political system no matter how much it criticizes that system for failing to provide social justice.[39] Lynch and Stretsky write that radical criminology looks at how forms of inequality, oppression, and conflict affect crime and law, especially how inequalities in class, race, and gender affect (1) participation in crime, (2) how crime is defined and (3) the making and enforcement of laws.[40] Walklate suggests that "critical criminology seeks to explore the ways in which the variables of class, race, and gender are played out in the criminal justice system."[41]

Central to this perspective was the publication in 1973 of *The New Criminology* by the British criminologists Ian Taylor, Paul Walton, and Jock Young.[42] There were, of course, precursors to the critical perspective, including those discussed in our previous sections on criminology. Taylor, Walton, and Young presented a detailed critique of "traditional criminology." They argued that the study of crime and deviance had become compartmentalized and isolated from the study of social organizations and social processes that are the proper subjects of sociology. They proposed seven tenets for an alternative theory of social deviance which would be more integrated and complete than previous theories. They claimed that the formal requirements this theory must be able to include and integrate are:

1. A Political Economy of Crime

The wider origins of the deviant act must be, and can only be, understood in terms of the rapidly changing political and economic contingencies of an advanced industrialized society.

2. A Social Psychology of Crime

The study and analysis of the factors (experiences, events, and structural developments) that precipitate the deviant act, which influence the individual to "choose the deviant road," must be included.

3. Social Dynamics Surrounding the Actual Acts

The explanation of the degrees to which the acts of men are the result of rational choice or the result of factors beyond choice must be included.

4. A Social Psychology of Social Reaction

An explanation of the immediate reaction of the social audience to the deviant act and of the contingencies and conditions that are crucial to the decision to act against the deviant must be included.

5. A Political Economy of Social Reaction

An explanation of the dynamics of periodic movements to control the amount and level of deviant behavior and to newly criminalize some behaviors and to decriminalize other behaviors must be included.

6. The Outcome of the Social Reaction on the Individual's Further Action

An explanation of the ways in which deviants respond to the social reaction that their primary deviance has elicited must be included.

7. The Scope of the Theoretical Analysis Must Be Whole

All of these factors must not only be included but must be integrated and must be explicated with all of their complexity and interrelatedness in order to achieve "a fully social theory of deviance."[43]

Taylor, Walton, and Young argued in opposition to that "analytical individualism" against which Durkheim had also rebelled. Crime was a "social fact," which could not be reduced to the individual level of analysis. They wrote, "The substantive history of twentieth century criminology is, by and large, the history of the empirical emasculation of theories (like those of Marx and Durkheim) which attempted to deal with the whole society, and a history therefore of the depoliticization of criminological issues."[44]

They argued in favor of a more encompassing perspective in examining rates of criminal offending. They predicted higher rates of crime would accompany greater inequality among social groups, that is, groups defined by social variables such as income, race, and gender. They also challenged empiricism as the sole provider of the truth and proposed instead that human knowledge is a group of competing ideologies. They emphasized the relative importance of social over individual factors in the explanation of crime and were passionately interested in social change: "[T]he causes of crime must be intimately bound up with the form assumed by the social arrangements of the time. Crime is ever and always that behavior seen to be problematic within the framework of those social arrangements: for crime to be abolished then, those social arrangements themselves must also be subject to fundamental social change."[45]

The "new" criminologists treated crime, deviance, and dissent as if they were all the same thing. But antiwar protest, civil rights marches, nose rings, draft evasion, gang rape, drug addiction, alternative rock, homicide, and insider trading are not essentially the same acts driven by the same processes and are not all equally the proper subjects of criminology. It is possible to greet with enthusiasm attempts to explain crime within the context of the whole society, as Taylor, Walton, and Young propose, without agreeing with them that crime is an entirely political subject. Their passion for social justice may have emerged more from the observation of the inequality of punishment for crime in our society. This is a very valuable topic for scrutiny, but a different subject than the causes of crime.

Lilly, Cullen, and Ball write that the heir apparent of critical criminology is "left realism."[46] Left realists responded to some of the criticisms of critical criminology by calling for a realistic victimology and emphasizing the origin and impact of crime on working class people, who not only have higher crime rates than the upper classes but also have higher rates of crime victimization. Left realists are interested in the class and political power dimensions of crime causation and in gender issues. They focused on crimes such as rape, domestic violence, and child abuse. Left realism, wrote Young, "takes seriously the complaints of women," a perspective that leads us to our next subject, feminist criminology.[47]

Feminist Criminology

In chapter 3 we discussed the problems of gender and crime, expressed by the question "Why is criminal man a man and not a woman?" We discussed the gender ratio problem: Why are male crime rates so high as compared to female crime rates? We also discussed the generalizability problem: Can explanations for male criminality be generalized to explain female criminality as well? We discussed the early history of studying female crime, beginning with Lombroso's *The Female Offender* and including Hagan's power control theory. We also discussed the contributions made to the debate by Freda Adler's *Sisters in Crime* and Rita Simon's *Women in Crime*. Most of the responses to the problem of gender and crime have not been from a feminist perspective, of course. In fact, some sociologists argued that Simon and Adler had not produced feminist theories of crime either. Some writers took it a step further and argued that feminist criminology is an oxymoron, a contradiction in terms, since the search for the causes of crime is about men and not about women. While there is certainly some justification for this point of view, it may unwittingly serve to perpetuate one of the central problems that feminists work to overcome, namely the exclusion of women's voices from the debate. In this section, we will mention responses to the question of gender and crime that are from a feminist perspective.

The entrance of feminist criminologists into the debate about crime and criminality has led to a deeper and more equitable examination of questions about gender and crime. The contributions of the feminist criminologists in analyzing the omissions and distortions of traditional criminology; their studies of women as victims, or survivors, of crime; and the identification of discrimination in the criminal justice system have resulted in important corrections in our thinking about the causes of crime.

There is, for example, the observation of the "stag effect" in criminology. As explained by Jessie Bernard, writing in 1964, the academic discipline of criminology attracted male scholars who wanted to study outlaw men, hoping that some of the romance and mystery of these rogue males might rub off.[48] At last, we had a theory about why men become criminologists instead of becoming criminals. This is a problem for strict determinists, who should be able to explain why a person becomes a criminal and why a person becomes a criminologist with equal facility. If Bernard is right about why men become criminologists, why do women become criminologists? Alas, we are left with same problem of generalizability that we have always had. Bernard may have had her tongue firmly pressed against her cheek, but it was certainly true that criminology was about male crime, male violence, male victimization, and male deviance. Women's issues, as offenders, as victims, and as criminologists, were "ignored, minimized, and trivialized."[49]

Chesney-Lind and Faith report that now, due to decades of advocacy by feminists, "excellent work exists on the problem of women's victimization — especially in the areas of sexual assault, sexual harassment, sexual abuse, and wife battery."[50] Also there eventually emerged more detailed and systemic analyses of traditional criminology such as Carol Smart's *Women and Criminology: A Feminist Critique*, published in 1976, in which she argued that, up until that time, theorizing about women and crime had been done with the assumption of the inferiority of women and their subordination to men in every facet of social life. According to Sue Titus Reid, her feminist criminology "challenges and struggles to overturn white male, capitalist domination and privilege not only in criminology and the criminal justice system, but in all our institutions."[51] This set the stage for other radical analyses of gender and crime in the following years. Critical criminologists looked at women as victims, and as offenders, in terms of conflicts within the social and economic structure.

There are, however, many feminist perspectives, and so there are a variety of feminist criminologies. Liberal feminists work within traditional criminology to promote women's issues, including particularly addressing disparities in the sentencing and treatment of female offenders and in job discrimination within criminology and the criminal justice system. For example, Chesney-Lind and Faith recount the astounding story that when Supreme Court Justice Sandra Day O'Connor graduated from Stanford Law School in 1952 in the top ten percent of her class, the only job that she was offered was that of a legal secretary.[52] The fact that this story today seems so astonishing is evidence of the successful work of the feminists. Their assumption is that bias against women is the result of ignorance, apathy, and poor scientific practice, but that there is nothing wrong with a scientific approach to these problems within the existing social and economic structure.

Radical feminists argue that social problems, including crime, are the result of the systemic and deliberate oppression of women by men. Patriarchy, as discussed by Kate Millet for example, is a central concept to their analysis of gender and crime.[53] Patriarchy is a social system that establishes the dominance of men over women by creating and maintaining "core gender identities" that work to the advantage of men and keep women in a subordinate position. Radical feminists concentrated on studies of women as victims, especially of sexual crimes, and on female offenders who were abused. The prominence today of rape crisis centers and child abuse prevention agencies is largely the result of the efforts of radical feminists. Marxist feminists extended this point of view to the assertion that men exert their control over women by their exclusive ownership of the means of production.

Socialist feminists focus on the combination of economic and gender factors. Messerschimdt, for example, argues that "[g]ender and class shape one's possibilities.... Criminality is related, then, to the interaction of patriarchy and capitalism and the structural possibilities this interaction creates."[54] He believes that the interactions of gender and class create positions of power and powerlessness and that this structure is reflected in the crime rates of men and women; that is, women commit crimes of powerlessness, such as prostitution, petty theft, and small scale fraud.

Postmodern feminists are one strand of an intellectual tradition called postmodernism that includes a wide variety of critiques of "modernity." Modernity refers to ways of thinking and building knowledge that became prominent during the period of Western history that began with the Enlightenment. Postmodernists oppose the assumption that scientific positivism is the only route to objective truth, and they seek to make all forms of thinking legitimate views of reality. They believe that "truth is an opinion that benefits some and not others" and that knowledge is an expression of privilege by those who have power.[55] They believe that modernism in general, and science in particular, has resulted, not in liberation, but in expanded oppression. Postmodernists attempt to "deconstruct" knowledge by placing emphasis not merely on the content but also on the audience to whom it is directed, the purpose of the assertions, the identity of the author, and the assumptions on which it is based. They study language through "discourse analysis," focusing on the values and assumptions that are implied in the language and the social position of the person who is speaking.[56] Postmodern criminologists reject the belief in the scientific model of thinking as the only path to a complete understanding of crime, and they study how official language is used in the criminal justice system to perpetuate the domination of the powerful over the relatively powerless. Postmodern feminists extend this point of view to the ways in which language is used to oppress women, both as victims and as offenders, and they seek to give voice to participants in the criminal justice system whose realities are often not understood or even heard. Postmodernist authors are often hard to read and, since they reject positivism as the only route to truth, they do not generate empirical research; indeed, scientific work could be seen as antithetical to their position. Consequently, their impact on criminology has not been large, though they have produced provocative critiques of criminology itself, for example, Alison Young's "Feminism and the Body of Criminology."[57]

Finally, multicultural feminists study the ways in which race, class, and gender interact with each other to produce criminal behavior. They propose to correct the over reliance of feminism on the experiences of white middle class women and to include the experiences of minority women of diverse cultural backgrounds. Ritchie's study of battered black women, for instance, has shown the suffering of African American women in abusive relationships and why they feel that they cannot escape from them. For them, involvement in crime is more a matter of "gender entrapment" than gender liberation.[58]

Chesney-Lind and Faith report that "[r]esearch consistently shows that victimization is at the heart of much of girls' and women's lawbreaking, and that this pattern of gender entrapment, rather than gender liberation, best explains women's involvement in crime."[59] This conclusion is probably true, but the same could be said of male offenders. The only point of contention between the two conclusions would be a more precise understanding of the word "much."

The contributions of feminist criminology to victimology and to equal treatment have been large and transforming, and are here to stay. The continuing challenge for feminist criminology in the search for the causes of crime is "to theorize gender," as Chesney-Lind and Faith have proposed.[60] They mean by this to begin thinking about the links between women's victimization, discrimination against women, and women's offending within the context of patriarchy. Or, as Walklate puts it, the task is to improve our understanding of "what underpins the circumstances in which gender matters more than any other variable and those circumstances in which it does not."[61]

The Culture of Poverty

The early nineteenth century "moral statisticians" Quetelet and Guerry, whom we discussed in chapter 10, were very interested in studying the relationship between poverty and the crime rate. The subject of social class and crime is therefore one of the oldest in criminology. There have been hundreds of studies on this relationship and, according to Vold, Bernard, and Snipes, these studies "often have given complicated and apparently contradictory results."[62]

Some of the issues involved in the study of crime and social class were discussed in the section on the Chicago School in chapter 10. McKay and Shaw also were concerned with the question of poverty and crime. Some of the problems involved in researching crime and social class include the problem of defining poverty, or the lower class, in a consistent and meaningful way and the problem of comparing studies that have used different definitions of poverty or social class. Another problem is that of distinguishing economic inequality from that of poverty. There is also the problem of two contradictory results about crime and the economy: some studies show that when economic conditions are bad, crime increases, but there are also studies that show the opposite: when the economy is good, crime increases.[63]

The *ecological fallacy* is another problem in the study of crime and social class. A consistent finding in criminology is that the crime rate does vary by location, by geography, an observation that is the foundation of ecological criminology. Crime rates are higher in low income communities than in high income communities. This finding comes from comparing aggregate crime rates with aggregate economic data, such as average family income in a particular neighborhood. However, it is false to announce causal links at the individual level from such statistical comparisons, and doing so, or implying such, is known as the *ecological fallacy*. At the individual level, there could be different reasons for this finding. For example, one possibility is that, in low income neighborhoods, both low income and high income persons commit more crimes. Another possibility is that high income individuals in low income neighborhoods are responsible for most of the crime. It is also possible that personal income is important, but only in low income neighborhoods. Finally, it is possible that nonresident criminals may choose low income areas as the scene for their crimes. A comparison of aggregate crime rates with aggregate income data would not rule out any of these possibilities. Therefore we must study individuals in order to explain individual crimes. This does not mean that the observation that crime rates are higher in low income areas is not important; it only means that we have not explained individual crime with this observation alone.

Yet another problem is that much of the research on social class and crime is conducted on the subject of juvenile delinquency rather than adult crime. As we shall see in the section called "Life Course Criminology," explanations of juvenile delinquency may not be the same as explanations of adult crime. Three major examples of subcultural explanations of lower class delinquency and crime are Cohen's middle class measuring rod, Miller's lower class values explanation, and Cloward and Ohlin's differential opportunity. These theories were discussed in chapter 10. These basic ideas also relate to social class and crime.

Albert Cohen's basic idea, first presented in 1955, was that delinquency is related to failure in school and that the lower class boy is evaluated in school by middle class values. When he fails, his feelings of low self esteem and rejection result in dropping out of school, which makes him vulnerable to the influence of gangs and the antisocial behavior in which they engage. The relationship between school performance and delinquency is one of the most consistently found relationships in the recent literature and lends some support to Cohen's ideas. However, we are once again left with that familiar and vexing problem of determining cause and effect from correlational data. There may be another factor, a "lurking third variable," which accounts for both poor school performance and delinquency, such as low self control or poor parenting or IQ or antisocial attitudes or learning disorders, among others.[64]

Walter Miller argued in 1958 that female dominated households resulted in the emergence of street corner male adolescent groups in lower class neighborhoods. These groups behaved according to a set of lower class values, which Miller catalogued and described as trouble, toughness, smartness, excitement, fate, and autonomy. Miller proposed that gang members in lower class neighborhoods are not nonconformists, but rather they are conforming to lower class values. However, this theory offers no explanation for middle class delinquency.[65]

Cloward and Ohlin, writing in 1960, proposed that juvenile delinquency was the result of blocked economic opportunity. They called their theory *differential opportunity*, by which they meant both the opportunity to succeed through conventional means and the opportunity to commit illegal acts. Low opportunity to succeed through legal means combined with high opportunity to commit illegal acts determines the existence of high delinquency in a particular area and the characteristics of the neighborhood determine the specific nature of the delinquency. Differential opportunity was a combination of Sutherland's differential association and

Merton's strain theory. Subsequent research did not support the theory of differential opportunity.[66]

What then are the major findings that relate social class and crime? Charles Tittle and his colleagues produced a major review of the research in 1978 and then, in 1990, Tittle and Meier conducted a review of the research since 1978. They avoided the ecological fallacy by looking at individual data. They concluded from both studies that class is a poor predictor of criminality.[67] Several other major research reviews have shown the same results.[68] Finally, Dunaway, Cullen, Burton, and Evans conducted a study, published in 2000, titled "The Myth of Social Class and Crime Revisited: An Examination of Class and Adult Criminality." They addressed some of the major problems in establishing a link between class and crime, including limited measures of social class, limited measures of crime, and the failure to study systematically the effect of social class on crime in the adult general population. They used self reported data from 555 adults in a large Midwestern city and analyzed it to assess effects of a wide range of class measures on crime measures. The overall results showed that regardless of how class or crimes were measured, social class exerted little direct influence on adult criminality in the general population. However, consistent with research findings from non–self reported studies, social class was related to criminal involvement for nonwhites.[69] Several other studies found that job history and education were moderate predictors of delinquency and that they were better predictors than social class.[70]

Nevertheless, this body of research led to numerous crime prevention programs, beginning in the 1930s with the Chicago Area Project, assisted by Shaw. The thrust of these programs has been to improve the communities where high crime rates existed, thereby reducing crime. As Ralph Taylor wrote in an article on ecological criminology in 2001, "If you want to reduce delinquency in a locale, you need to change the locale, to shift it from being socially disorganized to be being socially effective," a point of view also expressed by the "broken window" theory of James Q. Wilson, discussed in the section "Life Course Criminology."[71] There have been mixed results on the effectiveness of these crime prevention programs. There remains the possibility that improving the community, making it socially effective, fixing the broken window so to speak, may only succeed in displacing crime to another location, not actually reducing it, but merely changing its venue.

In spite of its weak showing so far, social class will probably continue to be a variable of interest because, as Shoemaker contends, "the desire to focus attention on social class values and life styles is quite strong, particularly among sociologists."[72] At the same time, Andrews and Bonta think

that the link between social class and crime is a major example of theoreticism and may turn out to be "one of the intellectual scandals of science."[73] In any event, however the debate about social class may go, there
is still room for the important work of the ecological criminologists who,
as Taylor writes, address the question of why crime rates (and victimization rates) are higher in some places than in others.[74]

Delinquency and Drift

David Matza first published *Delinquency and Drift* in 1964.[75] He criticized previous theories of delinquency for positing constraint and
differentiation. By constraint, he meant that earlier theories were too deterministic, making the delinquent's behavior entirely dependent on factors
beyond his control, leaving no room for decision making and choice. By
differentiation, he meant conceiving of juvenile delinquents as different
from normal adolescents in some fundamental way. Therefore the task of
criminologists was to specify the ways in which the juvenile delinquent
was basically different. Often this difference was supposed to be allegiance
to a nonconventional, antisocial value system. Matza argued that this
conception of juvenile delinquents as constrained by factors beyond their
control and committed to a criminal value system resulted in the over-
prediction of delinquent behavior. It failed to account for the fact that
most delinquents live very conventional lives with only occasional violations and that they "age out," that is, anywhere from 60 to 85 percent of
juvenile delinquents desist from delinquent behavior in their twenties and
do not become adult criminals. We will address this issue again when we
reach the section on life course criminology, but, if this older image of juvenile delinquents as constrained and committed is correct, why is there so
little juvenile crime and why do so many of them stop?

Matza proposed an "alternative image" of juvenile delinquents who
he described as "drifters." He did admit that there are some juvenile delinquents who are constrained and committed, but said that they are a relatively small group. The usual juvenile delinquent, according to Matza,
exists transiently "in a limbo between convention and crime, responding
in turn to the demands of each, flirting now with one, now the other, but
postponing commitment, evading decision. Thus he drifts between criminal and conventional action."[76] This drifting occurred whenever there was
a "loosening of social control." Matza asserted that social controls were
loosened by inadequate or nonexistent parental supervision and by "a sense
of irresponsibility." This sense of irresponsibility was engendered by using
what he and Gresham Sykes termed "techniques of neutralization."[77] These

techniques of neutralization are rationalizations that are employed by the juvenile offender to absolve himself of responsibility for his antisocial actions. These techniques of neutralization include (1) a *denial of responsibility*, attributing his actions to factors beyond his control, such as poverty or bad parents; (2) a *denial of injury*, claiming that no one was really injured by his actions; (3) a *denial of a victim*, claiming that the victim deserved it because he was a bad person; (4) *condemnation of the condemners*, viewing authority figures as hypocrites or as antisocial themselves; (5) an *appeal to higher loyalties*, claiming that his allegiance to a peer group is more important than any other value and that this loyalty sometimes requires delinquent acts. Using these techniques, the juvenile delinquent is able to consider himself not responsible for his antisocial behavior. Matza emphasized that delinquents do not reject conventional values, but they are able to "neutralize" them, rendering themselves guiltless, and thus setting the stage for specific criminal actions. He also adds that these rationalizations are often reinforced by the juvenile courts when they consider the delinquents to be not responsible for their behavior.

For the juvenile delinquent, according to Matza, a sense of irresponsibility is the immediate condition of drift, but drift also has an underlying component, which is "a sense of injustice." The delinquent thinks that he has no control over his life and he wants to experience himself as the cause of some events. He feels "pushed around" by a system that is uncaring and hypocritical.

Thus is the stage set for the juvenile to engage in delinquent acts. There still remains, however, an unpredictability to delinquent behavior because the juvenile can still choose to respond or not to respond to opportunities for crime that come his way. Matza writes, "There is a missing element by which the possibility of delinquency is realized.... I wish to suggest that the missing element which provides the thrust or impetus by which the delinquent act is realized is will."[78]

The will to crime is influenced by *preparation* and *desperation*. Preparation means the learning through experience that an antisocial action can be successfully performed (children, for example, may not know this). It provides the will to repeat old infractions, because the delinquent knows that it can be done. Desperation may have many sources, but Matza writes that a common one is the "mood of fatalism" that results from the sense of injustice. The delinquent may feel that he has no control over his life, that the system is uncaring and unjust, and therefore it does not matter what he does. He can do anything. The mood may deepen into a fatalistic frame of mind and it can be sufficiently strong to activate the will to commit entirely new violations.

Delinquents drift into antisocial behavior with inadequate parental supervision and a sense of irresponsibility, underpinned by a sense of injustice, which provides the setting for antisocial acts to which the delinquent may or may not respond. Their will to repeat old violations may be activated by preparation and their will to commit new violations may be activated by desperation, but the actual incidence of a violation remains not entirely predictable because there is a choice to be made each time. Recalling our continuum of choice from chapter 1, drift theory falls midway between "chosen" and "determined."

Matza writes that his "alternative image" of the juvenile delinquent is consistent with "the canons of classical criminology" and that he has "attempted to utilize the classic conception of a will to crime in order to maintain the ineradicable element of choice and freedom inherent in the condition of delinquent drift."[79] He refers to his position as "soft determinism," a stance that is different from positivistic criminology because it proposes to search for causative factors ("directs the analyst," as Matza puts it), both individual and environmental, without making any assumptions about the essential nature of man. The "hard determinism" of positivism views persons as no more capable of choice than hydrochloric acid is capable of choosing what it will dissolve and what it will not. Matza quotes Schopenhauer's image of hard determinism: "[T]he whole course of a man's life, in all its incidents great and small, is as necessarily predetermined as the course of a clock."[80] According to hard determinism, human freedom is illusory. Soft determinism retains the "ineradicable element of choice," but it is also different from classical criminology because it recognizes that some actions are less free than others and that some persons are less free than others. "Man is neither as free as he feels nor as bound as he fears," writes Silvan Tomkins.[81] Human beings are a combination of choice and constraint and this combination can be empirically investigated. Matza urges that we study "the conditions that make delinquent drift possible and probable."

Soft determinism is an unfortunate turn of phrase since many people would not want their views described as soft and, perhaps, because it sounds vaguely like "soft on crime," a modern anathema. The soft deterministic point of view is sometimes called neoclassical, but that strikes me as an equally unfortunate choice of words, so academic and more readily associated with art, architecture, and music, rather than crime. I had thought of "counterclockwise criminology" in honor of Schopenhauer and other like minded writers, or maybe "free will criminology," but that sounds like a religious sect, maybe not so different from schools of criminology after all. I liked "choice criminology" (different from "rational choice," of course) until I realized it could be read as a pun. Perhaps we have enough criminologies as it is.

Matza declares that in the social sciences we have seen "the partial restoration of classical man implicit in the tentative victory of soft over hard determinism."[82] Our "partially restored" classical offender has the freedom to choose. We might then characterize our "partially restored" classical criminologist as an analyst who recognizes human freedom of choice and searches out its boundaries, who is alert to influential forces, and who has respect for data, a worthwhile agenda for a twenty-first century criminology.

Rational Choice

The idea that criminals calculate the costs and benefits of committing a crime, and then decide what to do, is a concept from the classical criminologists, like Beccaria, who posited free will. It also comes from Jeremy Bentham, whose argument for "the two sovereign masters" of human conduct, pleasure and pain, was discussed in chapter 2, and which is here expressed in the language of economics as "costs and benefits." Another link in this chain is the Nobel Prize–winning economist Gary Becker who wrote an influential essay, first published in a journal in 1968, in which he applied economic analysis to the problem of crime. He wrote that Beccaria and Bentham had both "explicitly applied an economic calculus" and that this approach had lost favor in the last hundred years, though he intended to resurrect and modernize it. He thought that a useful theory of criminal behavior could dispense with sociological and psychological explanations for crime and "simply extend the economist's usual analysis of choice."[83] He argued that, if crime is considered the same as any economic activity that causes external harm, or "social cost," and if fines are considered to be the primary form of punishment, then crime and punishment can be analyzed in the same way any other economic enterprise is analyzed. Optimal benefits can be calculated and can inform public policy. He advocated the increased use of fines as punishment, and he rightly pointed out that imprisonment as a punishment has significant costs to society as well as to the offender and that these costs belong in the equation of effective punishment.

Ronald Clarke and Derek Cornish also return to the classical roots of criminology, writing that "every act of crime involves some choice by the offender."[84] According to rational choice theory, Beccaria's "cool scrutineer," the voice of reason, is found in the criminal as well as in the criminologist. The rational choice perspective, as Clarke and Cornish prefer to call it, states as its first proposition that "[c]rimes are purposive and deliberate acts, committed with the intention of benefiting the offender."[85] They analyze criminal choices by dividing these choices into two broad groups: (1) *involvement*, which is the general decision to become involved in criminal activities, and (2) *events*, which are decisions to commit specific crimes. The decision to become involved in criminal activities can be understood in three stages: (1) *initiation*, the offender deciding if he is willing to commit crimes in order to get what he wants; (2) *habituation*, the offender deciding if he should continue to commit crimes; (3) *desistance*, the offender deciding if he should stop committing crimes.

Event decisions are actually sequences of decisions to commit a specific crime. To study how these event decisions are made, Cornish uses "crime scripts," which are step by step accounts of the decisions made and the situational variables that affect each decision.[86] Understanding the background of these criminal choices, how they are made, and how offenders go about the task of committing a crime is the subject matter of the rational choice perspective.

The goal of the rational choice perspective is crime prevention. Crime prevention, argue Clarke and Cornish, requires a crime specific focus because offender decision making is quite different for different types of crime. Motivated offenders consider ease of access to the target, the likelihood of being observed or caught, and the expected reward. Situational crime prevention must have a crime specific focus and should concentrate on (1) increasing the perceived effort required by crime, (2) increasing the perceived risks, (3) reducing the anticipated rewards, and (4) removing excuses for crime.[87] Gibbons writes that "[i]f many offenders, and predatory offenders in particular, weigh at least some of the potential risks against the gains they anticipate from law breaking, criminal acts may often be deterred by making them riskier or harder to carry out."[88]

Rational choice is a theory of both crime and criminality; it addresses both the acts and the actors. Clarke and Cornish also believe that their perspective allows for effective crime prevention while avoiding "the uncertainties and inconsistencies of treating distant psychological events and social processes as the 'causes' of crime. Given that each event is in turn caused by others, at what point in the infinitely regressive chain should one stop in the search for effective points of intervention?"[89] Clarke and Cornish believe that an effective point for intervention is the decision by the offender to commit a specific crime. The criminal is "an economic decision maker" and thinking about crime and criminals in this way, rather than in terms of deep seated personality dispositions or broad social and economic inequality, makes possible specific, practical, and relevant policy decisions.

A closely related theory is called the routine activity approach, a theory that was already mentioned as an example in chapter 1. This theory was first introduced in 1979 by Cohen and Felson.[90] They proposed that for crime to occur, three things must converge in time and space: (1) a motivated offender, (2) a suitable target, and (3) the absence of a capable guardian. A capable guardian might be the police, or it might be a friend or relative whose presence increases your safety, or it may be you yourself protecting your property.

Cohen and Felson argued that crime had previously been studied in terms of the motivated offender and that crime rates were thought to vary according to changes in the offender's motivation. They believed that the development of modern life had resulted in daily routine activities that increased the likelihood that offenders would be in contact with targets in the absence of guardians. For example, when people are at home, they act as guardians of their own property. However, modern life now requires that people, both men and women, are away from home more often and for more extended periods of time than was previously the case. Thus "routine activities" can increase the likelihood of crime and drive the crime rate up. Consequently, crime prevention can consist of changes in the availability of targets or in the increased presence of capable guardians, for example, community oriented policing, neighborhood watches, and target hardening, such as better locks and antitheft devices.

Cohen and Felson shifted the focus away from the criminal and his internal states and towards the availability of targets and the absence of guardians. The routine activity approach is a tool for understanding the relationship between crime and everyday life. Felson concludes that his approach "helps replace vague hypotheses about social disorganization and crime with something better."[91]

Clarke and Felson point out differences between the rational choice perspective and routine activity theory.[92] They argue that the major difference is that routine activity theory is a *macro* theory that points at changes at a societal level that would reduce crime opportunities. Rational choice perspective is a *micro* theory that works with how these opportunities are perceived, evaluated, and acted upon by individual offenders. Often, however, the two theories are discussed together, as the similarities are stronger than the differences.

Several criticisms have been made of the rational choice perspective, including that it does not provide an explanation of crime but instead addresses the management of crime; that it is really nothing new and is essentially merely an opportunity theory; that too little attention is played to motivational factors; that all crimes are not rational and that often criminals are far from rational; and that it ultimately makes so many exceptions to the pure rationality that is the central point of the theory that there is then little to set it apart from other theories.[93]

Clarke and Cornish reply that the motivational variables of traditional criminology are so unclear as to be "unrewarding to study" and that the crucial test of a theory should be its success in helping to develop useful policy. They also argue that "[t]he cardinal rule is to never dismiss a criminal act as wanton or senseless or irrational, but rather to seek to understand the purposes of the offender."[94] They suggest that even crimes of violence that appear senseless have their rewards. This view is reminiscent of Jefferson's claim that until we understand the pleasures of crime as well as the opportunities for crime, we will never have a complete picture of criminal behavior.[95]

There is, however, a slippery slope here. Clarke and Cornish state that they intend to exclude mentally ill offenders from the rational choice perspective, though they wish to include offenders whose actions appear irrational to others but are purposeful from the offender's point of view. But the paranoid schizophrenic who kills two police officers because he believes that they are "white devils" who are intent on killing him unless he kills them first is acting with purpose. His delusional system may be internally consistent and it makes sense to him. Is he therefore a rational criminal? The claim of Clarke and Cornish that their theory offers a framework for understanding every kind of crime is true only if you accept that whatever makes sense to the offender qualifies as rational.[96] Some crimes do not make sense even to the offender: "I don't know why I did that." The offender sometimes uses this statement because he wishes to conceal his real motive, but offenders are often very impulsive and it is sometimes true that they don't know. There are also offenders who are "economic decision makers" sometimes but are impulsively irrational, even self defeating, at other times. If we start making exceptions, where precisely do we stop?

Clarke and Cornish report, "We came to believe that crime cannot be understood without attempting to discover how offenders think about their behavior and how they make their choices."[97] This is, of course, the point of view of cognitive behavioral psychology (discussed in chapter 8), indicating that the rational choice perspective is vulnerable to the "nothing new" criticism in at least some areas.

This is not to say that rational choice is not a valuable contribution to the debate. It certainly explains some crime and it has resulted in some effective crime prevention policies, as Clarke and Cornish rightly point out, such as the elimination of robberies of bus drivers in U.S. cities by introducing the exact fare system. It has also returned the issue of choice to the debate, which is refreshing. Both the rational choice perspective and the routine activities approach belong to a group of loosely related criminological theories that are sometimes referred to as "right realism." Right realism means taking the crime rate as a real problem and focusing on individual differences and changes at the individual level to solve the problem. Its opposite number is "left realism," which also takes the crime rate as a real problem, but focuses more on general social and economic changes to solve the problem.[98] Right realism is also associated with conservative law-and-order political policies, though there is no necessary connection between any of the theories and political orientation. It is thus ironic that the rational choice perspective may have been understood to justify harsher penalties in our country when Beccaria's earnest agenda was to reason against severe punishment. His "cool scrutineer" would be appalled.

A General Theory of Crime

Social control theories are based on the assumption that most people would commit crimes if there were no forces or factors to prevent or inhibit them from doing so; that is, without some form of social control. Proceeding from this point of view, the important question for social control theorists, as criminologists have pointed out, is why most people do *not* commit crimes. Social control theories are often proposed as explanations of juvenile delinquency, since much of the research on them has been done with adolescent populations, but these theories can also be employed as explanations for adult crime.

Emile Durkheim, whose work was reviewed in chapter 10, was a progenitor of social control theory since he believed that crime and delinquency would occur unless social solidarity, or morality ("everything which forces man to take account of other men"), was developed and maintained.[99] Matza's drift theory, discussed in the previous section, is a social control theory because Matza argues that a "loosening of social bonds" is the basis of delinquency. Another example of an early social control theory is that of Travis Hirschi. Hirschi's 1969 social control theory was grounded in the social environment.[100] He argued that "attachment" prevented delinquency and proposed four factors that determined participation in antisocial activities: attachment to others, involvement in legitimate activities, commitment to a future career, and belief in the morality of law. He wrote that "the chain of causation is thus from attachment to parents, through concern for the approval of persons in positions of authority, to belief that the rules of society are binding on one's conduct."[101] The strength of these beliefs vary and when the attachment is weak, the belief is weak and leads to antisocial behavior. Subsequent research did not show strong support for Hirschi's theory. After a detailed summary and analysis, Kempf wrote that "the research reveals little about the viability of social control as a scientific theory."[102] Hirschi abandoned this theory himself, but later collaborated with Michael Gottfredson to produce a new social control theory.

In 1990, Gottfredson and Hirschi published *A General Theory of Crime*.[103] In this book, they presented a detailed critique of both theory and research into the causes of crime, and then offered a theory of crime consisting of a single factor, intended to explain all forms of crime and delinquency. The single factor they posited was low self control. This theory was different from previous social control theories because it proposed a single factor rather than multiple factors. (The reader may recall the discussion in chapter 1 on the issue of "the one and the many.")

Gottfredson and Hirschi argued that positivistic criminology had produced an image of the criminal offender that was inconsistent with its own research. While research had supported the conclusions that criminal tendencies can be observed early in life, that these tendencies are reasonably stable over the life course, and that the diversity of deviant and antisocial acts is "the only pattern that can be identified," positivistic criminologists nevertheless seemed committed to offenders who were driven to crime by such forces as unemployment, social status, subcultural conformity, biological inheritance, and mental conflict. Gottfredson and Hirschi argued that the image of the offender offered by classical criminology was closer to the strongest research findings, but that the classical criminologists did not account for the influence of family values and relationships on criminal offending. Children who displayed behavioral problems early in life grew into adolescents who became juvenile delinquents who grew into adult criminals in their early twenties and who then seemed to slow down in their thirties and forties. What is our best explanation of this picture? Low self control, answered Gottfredson and Hirschi.

Proposing to connect the acts and the actors by a careful examination of crimes, Gottfredson and Hirschi focused on ordinary, mundane crime, that is, the majority of crime, which they defined as "acts of force and fraud in pursuit of self interest." They derived the element of self control from an analysis of criminal acts themselves. Most crime, they concluded, is largely petty, typically not completed, requires little or no skill or planning, and is usually of no lasting or substantial benefit to the offender, though these crimes cause loss, pain, and suffering to the victim. This understanding of the nature of crime calls forth an offender who is impulsive, insensitive, physical, risk taking, and shortsighted. These characteristics of the criminal may be subsumed under a single concept and be understood as low self control.

Gottfredson and Hirschi believed that low self control explains many of the relationships between delinquency and other factors such as poor school performance, peer group selection, and unemployment. Low self control explains many major findings in criminological research, such as the observations that offenders are more frequently involved in noncriminal forms of deviance than are nonoffenders, that offenders are more likely than nonoffenders to use legal and illegal drugs, that offenders have higher accident, illness, and death rates than nonoffenders, and that crimes may be prevented by increasing the effort it takes to commit them.

Self control, argued Gottfredson and Hirschi, is formed in children by the age of eight and stays stable throughout the rest of life. Low self control can be identified in children well before the age of responsibility. Ineffective child rearing is the most important contributor to low self control. They argued that the tasks of successfully socializing children are four: caring, monitoring, recognizing deviance, and correcting. When parents are effective in these four tasks, the child learns to avoid actions that will result in long-term negative consequences. But, if the parenting is ineffective, the child does not learn this lesson and the result is low self control. According to self control theory, low self control *is* criminality. Andrews and Bonta point out the similarity between Gottfredson and Hirschi's proposal and the "tentative causal formula" of Sheldon and Eleanor Glueck from 1950: weak attachment of parent to child, poor parental supervision, poor conduct standards, and ineffective punishment methods.[104]

Low self control as an explanation for crime has been criticized as well as supported. Vold, Bernard, and Snipes write that "the primary advantage of the theory is also its chief point of vulnerability: its simplicity."[105] Low self control as a theory has been assailed for being too simplistic and for being tautological: What is the cause of crime? Low self control. What is low self control? Engaging in behavior that is criminal. Low self control as a theory has also been criticized for not explaining crime that *does* require self control, such as some white collar crime and some organized crime. Gottfredson and Hirschi proposed that differences in the opportunity to commit crimes accounted for the fact that some low self control persons have much higher rates of offending than do other persons with low self control. Some critics argue that Gottfredson and Hirschi have not clarified how this differential opportunity interacts with low self control to produce different rates of offending in persons with low self control.[106] Elliot Currie has pointed out what he calls "the fallacy of autonomy," that is, low self control theory ignores the external social forces that impinge on the family to produce ineffective parenting. The family is not autonomous in its ability to provide effective parenting.[107]

Empirical research has overall been favorable towards self control theory. Lilly, Cullen, and Ball report that "[s]tudies generally support the theory's conclusion that low self control is related to criminal involvement."[108] There is some contradictory evidence, however. For example, Longshore and Turner found a relation between low self control and crimes of fraud, but the relationship did not hold for crimes of force.[109]

Gottfredson and Hirschi write, "The fact that crime is by all odds the major predictor of crime is central to our theory."[110] Past criminal behavior is the best predictor of future criminal behavior and criminality *is* low self control, the individual-level cause of crime. Andrews and Bonta comment that proposing a single construct to explain crime was a brave and innovative choice by Gottfredson and Hirschi.[111] They considered it brave because the difficulty of assessing and measuring self control in a consistent and valid manner is a major, unresolved problem in psychology. It was innovative because it derived the single construct, low self control, from the nature of crime itself. It was also a brave choice because it would inevitably attract the critical scrutiny of multicausal theorists, some of whom called it "just another rehash of rational choice theory."[112] Self control theory, while certainly not above criticism, is one of the best conceived and best supported of our modern explanations for crime.

Life Course Criminology

Some criminologists are interested in how crime occurs within the context of an individual's life course. They intend to explain how criminal behavior is started and how it is continued over a lifetime. Glen Elder, one of the early proponents of life course studies, wrote that individual life histories could be understood in terms of trajectories, transitions, and turning points. A trajectory is a pathway, a long-term pattern of behavior, taken up early in life by an individual. For instance, completing school, obtaining a good job, getting married, having children, and planning for retirement is a common trajectory in our society. Embedded within this trajectory are specific transitions, such as completing college or getting married. Transitions may become turning points, which are changes in a person's trajectory or life course. A person's life course is a combination of choice, chance, and constraint. The constraints emphasized in life course criminology are often macrolevel events beyond personal control, such as depression, war, and natural disasters. In addition to an individual's personal attributes, both social history and social structure have an impact on an individual's trajectory, transitions, and turning points.[113] This life course perspective has been applied to the explanation of crime.

In the language of life course criminology, *participation* refers to whether or not a person has ever committed a crime. *Prevalence* is that fraction of people who have ever participated in crime. *Frequency* is the rate of criminal activity of those who engage in crime, the number of crimes committed over a period of time. *Onset* means the beginning of a criminal career and *desistance* means the end of a criminal career. *Duration* is the period of time between onset and desistance. Life course criminologists argue that separate causal models may be required to explain participation, prevalence, frequency, onset, duration, and desistance in the course of a criminal career. The reader will recall the discussion in chapter 1 of "the one and the many." Life course criminologists argue for "the many." Two of their main opponents are, not surprisingly, Gottfredson and Hirschi who, as discussed in the last section, argue for "the one." They argue that a single factor, a "criminal propensity," or underlying criminogenic factor, such as low self control, explains crime well enough. All persons, criminal and noncriminal, who are engaged in any activity, criminal or noncriminal, experience a reduction in their activity as they age. According to Gottfredson and Hirschi, no further explanation of age and crime is needed. The question of what type of research to conduct was also a part of this debate. The life course criminologists argued for longitudinal research, following the same group of people over a lengthy period of their lives. Gottfredson and Hirschi contended that cross-sectional research, comparing two different groups at a single point in time, was easier and less expensive and was sufficient for the explanation of crime. Life course criminology was also criticized for not offering anything new to criminology and some theorists argued that older, standard theories explained crime just as well without considering age.[114]

There was also a lively debate about "career criminals" and "criminal careers." A *career criminal* is a chronic offender who commits a high frequency of crimes over a long period of time. A *criminal career* has an onset, a duration, and a desistance, but the idea of a "criminal career" implies nothing about frequency or severity of crimes. Gottfredson and Hirschi argued that crime has none of the attributes normally associated with a "career" of any sort, such as, for example, delay of gratification for the sake of long-term goals, and therefore the concept of a "criminal career" was nonsensical. They also argued that there was no such thing as a "career criminal" because, in their view, all criminals are career criminals; that is, criminal propensity changes very little over the life course. Nevertheless, the concept of the "career criminal" caught the imagination of criminologists, policy makers, and criminal justice practitioners alike. Interest in these persistent, high rate offenders has not abated since the classic study of Wolfgang and his colleagues on chronic offenders, published in 1972, showing that a relatively small number of offenders committed a large portion of crime.[115]

The life course perspective includes within it a number of developmental theories of crime. We will consider two examples: that of Robert Sampson and John Laub, and that of Terrie Moffitt.

Sampson and Laub have presented a theory of crime that they call "an age graded theory of informal social control."[116] It is "age graded" because it offers explanations of both juvenile and adult criminal behavior and it involves "informal social control" because it emphasizes family and other personal relationships as opposed to formal, or institutional, social control, such as the courts and the police. The theory has three parts: the first professes to explain juvenile delinquency, the second explores transitions from juvenile delinquency to adult crime, and the third explains adult criminal behavior. Juvenile delinquency is explained by *family context factors*, such as neglectful and ineffective parenting, and *background structural factors*, such as low family income and criminality in the parents. In the transition from juvenile to adult, cumulative continuity explains the stability of criminal behavior into adulthood. *Cumulative continuity* means that engaging in criminal and delinquent behavior narrows one's choices by degrees; it "closes doors" for the juvenile, narrows his choices, thus increasing the likelihood of more delinquent behavior. But, in the transition from juvenile to adult, change is also common. Often juvenile delinquents do not become adult criminals and adult criminals stop committing crimes. Sampson and Laub argued that this is explained by the strength and quality of social ties or bonds that may be acquired as an adolescent or even as an adult. They refer to these ties as "social capital." Social capital investment in relationships with law abiding persons, particularly through marriage and employment, is, they argue, the best predictor of adult criminal behavior. (This explanation is reminiscent of Frank Watson, a notorious criminal and convict in the North Carolina prison system who reformed later in life, became a counselor, and wrote a book. In his frequent public talks, he was fond of saying that the keys to offender rehabilitation are "work and a woman." Thus he was apparently also a criminological theorist.)[117] Sampson and Laub believe that a juvenile delinquent is handicapped by his criminal past but not entirely doomed by it.

Sampson and Laub arrived at support for their theory by reanalyzing the data that had been compiled by Sheldon and Eleanor Glueck. The Gluecks' study is one of the most famous in the history of criminology. They began their work in the 1930s and collected extensive data on 500 delinquents and 500 nondelinquents. They matched the two groups on age, intelligence, ethnicity, and residence. They then compared the two groups to determine the factors most related to delinquency. In 1985, Laub located the original Glueck data and he and Sampson embarked on a reanalysis of this data. They found general support in the data for their theory of age graded informal social control.[118]

Terrie Moffitt writes that she began her theoretical work by attempting to reconcile two incongruous facts about antisocial behavior.[119] These two facts are that antisocial behavior shows remarkable continuity over age and also that its prevalence changes markedly with age, showing a dramatic peak during adolescence. She reasoned that these facts could be explained if there are two distinct groups of adolescents who engage in antisocial behavior. She called these two groups the *life course persistent* and the *adolescence limited*. The life course persistent group are essentially the same people we discussed in chapter 3, the psychopaths, the antisocial personality disorders. As far as engaging in antisocial behavior in their life course, they "come early and stay late." Moffitt proposes that the behavior of this group of individuals, the life course persistent group, are the result of the interaction of neuropsychological deficits and poor parenting. She believes that the cognitive deficits involved in producing antisocial behavior are those affecting verbal and "executive" skills, such as problem solving, and those affecting inattention and impulsivity. These deficits may have a variety of causes (many of these were reviewed in chapters 2 and 3) and they may, to a large extent, be compensated for, or overcome by, effective parenting. However, when these cognitive deficiencies are not corrected by early, effective parenting, antisocial behavior ensues from a young age. Moffitt writes, "Across the life course, these individuals exhibit changing manifestations of antisocial behavior: biting and hitting at age 4, shoplifting and truancy at age 10, selling drugs and stealing cars at age 16, robbery and rape at age 22, and fraud and child abuse at age 30"[120] The underlying criminal disposition remains the same across the life course, though the types of crimes may vary with different opportunities and different constraints at different stages of life. The life course persistent antisocial person fails to learn prosocial alternatives to antisocial behavior and therefore suffers cumulative consequences as well as contemporary, or immediate, consequences. He makes irrevocable decisions that close the doors to opportunities. Moffitt emphasizes the reciprocal interaction between the person and the environment, which creates a snowballing effect: "The child acts; the environment reacts; and the child reacts back in mutually interlocking evocative interaction."[121] His options for conventional behavior are narrowed cumulatively.

The antisocial behavior of the adolescent limited group occurs within that gap which nearly everyone experiences between biological maturity and social maturity. Experiencing this gap motivates some adolescents to imitate antisocial peers in search of independence, a feeling of power, and status within the peer group. They are motivated to test themselves. This imitative behavior is rewarded by its own consequences, excitement and short-term pleasure, until the adolescent ages out of the maturity gap. He desists from antisocial behavior because he finds other rewards through prosocial behavior and because he matures into accepting delay of gratification for the sake of long-term rewards. This adolescence limited antisocial behavior is not psychopathology in Moffitt's view, but is a normal part of the maturation process. While almost all adolescents commit some illegal acts, some adolescents do not engage in any antisocial or delinquent behavior. Moffitt proposes that for some adolescents there may not be any antisocial role models to imitate, or that some adolescents, due to late maturation or early entrance into adulthood, do not experience the maturity gap in the same way as most adolescents do.

The adolescent limited group is a much larger group than the life course persistent group, and the two groups combined account for the relatively high prevalence of crime during the adolescent years. Moffitt suggests longitudinal research to understand the etiology of life course persistent antisocial behavior, beginning in infancy, even prenatally, and following the same individuals to adulthood.

Moffitt's work with the Dunedin Multidisciplinary Health and Development Study, discussed in chapter 1, is an example of such research efforts. Another that is underway is the Project on Human Development in Chicago Neighborhoods, headed by Felton Earls, Robert Sampson, Stephen Raudenbush, and their colleagues. This project has been funded for $51 million so far and will be soon completed.[122] It was partly inspired by the "broken windows theory" of crime as discussed by James Q. Wilson in his influential book *Thinking About Crime*, first published in 1975. In this book, Wilson wrote, "Social psychologists and police officers tend to agree that if a window in a building is broken *and is left unrepaired*, all the rest of the windows will soon be broken."[123] The broken window is a sign that no one cares and such signs in a neighborhood, any neighborhood, "invite criminal invasion." Wilson suggested that "untended property" and other signs of apathy and neglect lead to cascading social disorganization in the community, including eventually all kinds of crime. It follows then that crime prevention includes signs of orderliness and caring in the neighborhood. There has not been presented scientific evidence to support this theory, and Wilson reported in an article in 2004, "I still to this day do not know if improving order will or will not reduce crime. People have not understood that this was a speculation," not a theory.[124]

The Chicago project researchers are looking at the flip side of the broken windows idea, which they call *collective efficacy*, a concept introduced in 1997 by Sampson, Raudenbush, and Earls.[125] Collective efficacy means the ability of the community to take action and maintain order in public spaces, to have cohesion, mutual trust, and shared expectations. Jeremy Travis, director of the National Institute of Justice, calls this concept "far and away the most important research insight in the last decade."[126] Francis T. Cullen, past president of the American Society of Criminology, said in an interview that "[i]t is perhaps the most important research undertaking ever embarked upon in the study of the development of criminal behavior."[127] (Perhaps so, but the history of criminology teaches humility in the pursuit of the causes of crime.)

The project researchers are looking at how the development of an individual and the development of a community interact and influence each other to affect the probability of delinquent behavior. They believe that the willingness of a community to act for the benefit of the whole community, and especially in the interest of the children, reduces crime. This research is expected to increase our knowledge of how early childhood experiences lead to delinquency and crime in the long run. The project is a worthy enterprise, though, perhaps, we already have more knowledge about the relationship between childhood and crime than we have used.

PART FIVE

Conclusion

The reason we say people have free will is because we cannot predict what they will do.

— Stephen Hawking[1]

On the contrary, every act of crime involves some choice by the offender.

— Ronald Clarke and Derek Cornish[2]

Man is neither as free as he feels nor as bound as he fears.

— Silvan Tomkins[3]

12

Lessons from the History of Criminology

Lessons Learned

Our brief tour through the history of criminology has given us a glimpse of several recurring problems that we may wish to make a greater effort to avoid in the future. Among these, are theoreticism and territorialism. *Theoreticism* means ignoring evidence that contradicts a favored theory. *Territorialism* means ignoring or discounting evidence and arguments that are outside of one's own narrow specialty or outside of one's own academic discipline. It may be argued that the two have a kind of reciprocal relationship at times, where one reinforces the other. Territorialism can contribute to theoreticism and vice versa. Our present state of knowledge about the causes of crime is not such that we can afford either one. Remember Professor Dixon's observation that "our desires attract supporting reasons like iron filings to a magnet"; our desire to be right can just as efficiently repel contradictory evidence, as if such data are alien invaders whose total destruction is mandatory if our civilization is to survive.[1] Territorialism is often a problem in criminology. Raine complains that researchers and theorists often "too closely guard their own turf," impeding our progress in understanding crime.[2]

We would do well to avoid the *fallacy of extension*, meaning the effort to account for crime by extending some grand general theory that was never intended to explain crime. This has been the case, with Darwin's theory of evolution, Freud's theory of psychoanalysis, and Marx's theory of class struggle, among others. These attempts at explaining crime by extension of a theory that was never intended to explain crime have not been successful or convincing; criminology does best with its own theories, which are intended to explain crime.

Our history shows that we have often been overly optimistic about the contribution that biology may make to the explanation of crime. I have symbolized this unwarranted enthusiasm as Dr. Lombroso's skull. Some crime is certainly explained by biology, such as the paranoid schizophrenic whose mental disorder compels him to protect himself from the CIA by killing its agents, who turn out to be his family members or innocent victims, before they kill him. But the amount of crime explained by brain disorder is small. There have always been tantalizing hints about biology and crime, as, for example, in the case of Phineas Gage, as we saw in chapter 7, or in the abnormalities so often found in the nervous systems of psychopaths, which we discussed in chapter 8. But initial enthusiasm for whatever was the latest biological explanation of crime usually receded as investigators encountered unexpected difficulties in explaining criminal behavior and began a slow inevitable retreat into multiple categories of offenders and multiple factors in the explanation of crime, as did Dr. Lombroso himself.

A number of biological factors have been associated with crime, particularly with violent offending. Heart rate and EEG abnormalities have been extensively studied. Crime has been associated with diet (refined carbohydrates high in the diets of criminals), lead (high levels in the body of criminals), cortisol (low levels in violent offenders), hypoglycemia (high in violent populations), and testosterone (high in violent offenders). Violent offenders are more likely to have experienced birth complications and to have had a head injury at some time in their lives. But, as Raine points out, many of these biological factors have strong social and environmental implications. For example, high levels of lead in a person are also associated with living in a socially disadvantaged home in an urban area with a high crime rate. Head injury may be the result of having adopted a violent lifestyle; thus the frequency of head injury may be a result, not a cause of violent behavior.[3]

Psychiatrist Daniel Amen used brain imaging techniques to study 50 murderers and 200 other violent offenders. All, without exception, showed reduced activity in the prefrontal cortex, overactivity in the anterior cingulate gyrus, and abnormalities in the left temporal lobe. "If you have a left temporal lobe problem, you have dark, awful, violent thoughts. If you have a cingulate gyrus problem as well, you get stuck on the bad thoughts. And if you have a prefrontal cortex problem, you can't supervise the bad thoughts you get stuck on."[4] But are the abnormalities causative? These brain malfunctions may also be the *result* of still other factors that turned the capacity for violence into reality. Associations have been made, but no causal relationship has been established.

These observations of associations between biological factors and crime have been reported since Dr. Lombroso's work in the nineteenth century, but taken as a whole, they have not helped us much in our search for the causes of crime. Professors Gottfredson and Hirschi write that the search for the biological causes of crime "has produced little in the way of meaningful or interpretable research. Instead, as we have seen, it has produced a series of 'findings' (e.g., physiognomy, feeblemindedness, XYY, inheritance of criminality) that survived only so long as was necessary to subject them to replication or to straightforward critical analysis."[5]

Raine argues forcefully and in detail that crime may be a biological disorder. Crime and illness is an old debate. To illustrate its antiquity, consider, for example, Shakespeare's *Macbeth*, one of the great tales of ruthless ambition, crime, and murder. Contained within the larger plot of the play is a small dialogue on crime as illness. It is in the form of two conversations with the court physician, a "doctor of physic."

Macbeth has committed terrible crimes in pursuit of his political ambition, a string of crimes commencing with the bloody murder of Duncan. Lady Macbeth has been an instigator, since she kindled the flame of ambition in him and then suggested the crimes. She was a co-conspirator and a willing accomplice to murder. But she suffers guilt and remorse, cannot sleep, engages in compulsive hand washing, talks out loud to herself. Her servant calls the doctor to assess and offer treatment for this strange behavior. The court physician observes Lady Macbeth, questions her servant, and finally concludes, "This disease is beyond my practice."[6]

In a later passage, the doctor is questioned by Macbeth regarding his assessment of Lady Macbeth:

> MACBETH: Canst thou not minister to a mind diseased,
> Pluck from the memory a rooted sorrow,
> Raze out the written troubles of the brain,
> And with some sweet oblivious antidote
> Cleanse the stuffed bosom of that perilous stuff
> Which weighs upon the heart?
>
> DOCTOR: Therein the patient
> Must minister to himself.
>
> MACBETH: Throw physic to the dogs; I'll none of it.[7]

In our present time, physicians would not, of course, make the same assessment as the Scottish doctor in Macbeth. Lady Macbeth would be a good candidate for Prozac, which probably would succeed in reducing her symptoms. Lord Macbeth would be pleased and not so quick to "throw physic to the dogs." He seeks treatment for himself as well and hopes for some "sweet oblivious antidote" to cure "a mind diseased." The doctor understands that Macbeth is seeking treatment for himself as well as for Lady Macbeth because he answers that "therein the patient must minister to *him*self." With this statement, he is rejecting the concept of crime as illness. The doctor states his own view: "Unnatural deeds do breed unnatural troubles / Infected minds to their deaf pillows will discharge their secrets." The doctor sees Lady Macbeth's "infected mind" as the result, not the cause, of her crimes. The play leaves Macbeth too without excuse, "the author of his proper woe."

Shakespeare is generally thought to have written this play in 1606 and so Macbeth's physician could be considered to be the deliverer of a seventeenth century view on crime as illness. It may seem inappropriate to juxtapose modern biology with a 400-year-old dramatic play. It may seem like an unscientific endeavor, and indeed it is, but a part of the debate centers on whether or not the question of crime is a scientific question at all. Unlike Macbeth, we would not "throw physic to the dogs"; medical science has helped us too much. Yet I do suspect, like Macbeth's physician, that "this disease is beyond my practice"; that is to say, that crime is not a mental illness. Science cannot fully account for the individual decision to commit or not to commit a crime. Therein the patient must minister to himself. It is an old debate and will, I believe, continue into a new century of criminology.

To Which Then Should We Incline?

As we have seen in our concise history of criminology, there are many candidates for the causes of crime. To which then should we incline? No subject has greater need of Beccaria's "cool scrutineer of human nature" than does the topic of crime. So far, all of the explanations for crime have left us with troublesome problems and unanswered questions. If this were not so, we would consider the mystery of crime to be solved and no one would have any further doubts about it. While none of the theories provide us with a sublime certainty, or even a robust confidence, some of the theories do leave us with fewer problems than do others. Routine activities theory is helpful because of its simplicity and its practicality, but also because it is multifaceted; it permits us to give equal consideration to the offender, the victim, and the social environment. The psychology of criminal conduct is impressive because of the immense amount of research that has been reviewed and evaluated in building its base and because it seems to go where the data direct it. Life course criminology is useful as well. Life course criminology posits different explanations for juvenile delinquency and chronic adult offending, which in Moffitt's view is a combination of early cognitive deficits, identifiable in childhood, and ineffective parenting.

Our best course is to hold with those points of view that offer us the greatest simplicity without superficiality, and which leave the fewest difficulties upon our hands. One of those is certainly the general theory of crime proposed by Gottfredson and Hirschi. This theory offers important attributes in its simplicity, practical applications, policy implications, appeal to common sense, and support from empirical testing. It accounts, as its originators argued, for many of the major research conclusions in criminology. Does it solve all of our problems? Most certainly not. Some of its difficulties were reviewed in the previous chapter and there will continue to be plenty of work to do to substantiate it or discredit it, as the case may be.

Self control theory is the work of Gottfredson and Hirschi, but self control as an explanation for crime is not new; in fact, it is very old, at least 3,000 years old. In the fourth chapter of Genesis, the son of Adam and Eve kills his brother. In this first crime story, Cain was "very wroth," full of wrath, and God, seeing this, says to him, "If thou doest well, shalt thou not be accepted? But if thou doest not well, sin lieth at the door. And unto thee shall be his desire, and thou shalt rule over him." Despite this warning from God, we are told that Cain "rose up against his brother Abel and slew him." And then God punished Cain for his crime. In another translation, God's warning to Cain is, "Why are you angry? Why is your face downcast? If you do what is right, will you not be accepted? But if you do not do what is right, sin is crouching at your door; it desires to have you, but you must master it." In other words, God warns Cain that he has the potential for criminal behavior and must exert his self control. In quoting scripture here, I only wish to remind the reader that self control as the principal factor in criminal behavior is not a new idea; it is an ancient one. It may be our oldest idea about crime. Perhaps we have had from the beginning more light than we have used.

Twenty-First Century Criminology

The twenty-first century may see exciting times in our search for the causes of crime. Adrian Raine, an expert on neurology and criminal behavior, hopes advances in brain imaging technology and DNA research will add significantly to our understanding of crime. The history of criminology suggests that he is overly optimistic on this point, but we will be pleased if it turns out to be so. We are likely to see more attempts at melding the findings of biology and sociology into the sort of biosocial criminology that theorists like Anthony Walsh have proposed.

The reader will recall that often the best use of science has been to disprove false theories. However, Bernard has argued that in criminology we have relied too much on falsification, that "no criminology theories have been falsified in 40 years," and that we have given too much prominence to theory. He asserts that a theory should be "a fleeting phenomenon," identifying the relevant variables and the order and organization among them. The results of empirical testing of the theory will lead to a revision of the theory to make it a more accurate representation of reality. He proposes to stop the competitive testing of theories and instead to focus on integration, by looking at theories in terms of their variables and how they are related. The question is really how much, or how little of crime, a specific variable explains. He calls for a shift from a falsification approach to theories in criminology to a risk factor approach to understanding crime.[8]

In an article in 1990, "Twenty Years of Testing Theories," Bernard argued that the lack of progress in explaining crime was "intimately connected to the lurking presence of values in criminological theories."[9] Values are not falsifiable and therefore no scientific progress could be made with such theories. But what if the study of crime cannot be separated from values? Bernard believed that it could be if theorists paid much closer attention to the formulation of the theories, but this is not an easy problem to solve and accounts for considerable debate (and publication) among criminologists. He argued that theories must be presented in such a form that they are falsifiable, that they could be subjected to empirical testing. (It is also difficult to test theories against each other when the definition of the dependent variable, crime, keeps changing.) However, in another article in 2001, he recommends abandoning falsification as the principal way of evaluating criminological theory. "The problem is that crime is such a complex phenomenon that virtually anything can influence it at least some of the time."[10] Therefore, any reasonable theory will be true at least some of the time. It is from this position that he proposes that a risk factor approach is a better representation of reality.

By a risk factor approach to understanding crime, Bernard means integrating the variables that have been shown to be related to crime, including both individual and situational variables. A risk factor approach is expressed as structured probabilities. This approach leaves room for choice and chance as well as constraint. It is like the risk factor approach in public health where, for example, we suggest risk factors and probabilities for heart attack and stroke. Still, the patient has choices to make and chance has a role as well. This approach also more clearly suggests specific policies and programs, which are aimed at reducing risk for criminal behavior. Andrews and Bonta have shown in their psychology of criminal conduct, how well this approach is supported by decades of research. Criminology in the coming years will be considerably influenced by the risk factor approach.

One of the important facts of criminology is the importance of problems in early childhood to later criminal behavior. Early identification and early intervention will be areas of intense interest and effort. We can look forward to the conclusion of the Dunedin Multidisciplinary Health and Development Study. This large scale, ongoing study has already produced some results important for life course criminology, one of our best theories. The study will continue to follow up with data collection through the life cycle of its subjects. It promises to increase significantly our understanding of juvenile offenders and especially our knowledge of how to differentiate those juvenile offenders who desist their antisocial behavior from those who become adult chronic offenders.

There is also the Project on Human Development in Chicago Neighborhoods. The researchers, Robert Sampson, Felton Earls and their colleagues, have carefully collected data about the relationships between crime and where a young person grows up. They propose that the most important influence on the development of criminal behavior is "collective efficacy," a term introduced by Sampson and his coworkers. They mean the ability of the community to maintain order in public spaces. Data collection is continuing and papers on the explanation of its results may be out this year. This study is fascinating and we can look forward to its results, their interpretation, and the ensuing debate. Perhaps, however, its central ideas are not so new. Consider, for example, the following excerpt from the Second Annual Report of the Board of Public Charities of North Carolina, Raleigh, N.C., 1871:

> There is but little doubt, and we believe the annals of crime will prove it, that nine out of ten cases of crime can be traced for their ultimate source to bad training or the utter neglect of training in early youth.... It needs only a visit to our penal and reformatory institutions to learn what a very large proportion of this criminal and vicious class are yet only youths, and inquiry will in almost every case give assurance that they came there from bad homes— or never had homes or ran away from home very early or either received bad training in such as they had, or were left without restraint to indulge their wayward propensities ... the children of vice and crime will be met from every place where there are neglected orphans— homeless children and ungodly homes that train for crime. Every village depot-every cross roads grog shop will pour out to the traveler's view and

annoyance that unrestrained and untutored crew of bad children who make night hideous with their yells and wild songs—who are experts in mischief and who are in training for the prison or the gallows....

...In our country the results of the war have cast thousands of children on society that have been bereft of one or both parents—the manumission of the slaves has thrown upon the state many with none to care for them. Is there not due these care, guardianship, education, and proper training?

Two Great Facts

The truth is ... that no community, whether town, city, or State, can, with impunity, ignore the sufferings or the vices of any portion of itself, any more than the healthy portions of a human body can with impunity neglect a part diseased; and also that—

So long as Anybody's child is neglected, Nobody's child is safe.[11]

These "Two Great Facts" from 1871 are not a far stretch from the "collective efficacy" proposed by Earls and his colleagues in 1997. If the history of criminology is predictive of its future, then we will conduct the same debates all over again in the twenty-first century. Can we separate our moral values and our scientific investigations? What is the dependent variable? What constitutes proof? Do we have free will? Is biology destiny? Is crime an illness? Is morality relative? Is criminology a science? Should we intervene with the children? No honest question should be evaded.

The debate will continue. The data collection will continue as well with its concomitant arguments: is the data "good" data or "bad" data? Is there an alternative explanation of the data? When is there enough data? What do the data really mean? But not everything that counts can be counted.

We have had 170 years of scientific research in criminology since Guerry's *Essay on Moral Statistics* in 1833 and it seems to have had little impact on public policy. This may be because the results of scientific investigations rarely outweigh the politics of the day. An especially clear example is the DARE program. The Drug Abuse Resistance Education program exists in about one-half of all school districts in the U.S., in all 50 states, and in 13 foreign countries in spite of considerable empirical evidence showing that the program is ineffective in preventing adolescent drug abuse. In my hometown, the police chief reported that he intended to keep the DARE program no matter what the research says because any opportunity that law enforcers have to be in school is worthwhile. In a review of the research on DARE programs, Gorman argued that the empirical evidence was unable to influence public policy because the program matched up so well with official government drug control policy and because it was easy to implement.[12] The program remains very popular in many places. Data alone does not often carry the day. At this writing, the North Carolina legislature is considering its budget for the coming year. Included are two proposals, one to decrease funding for Smart Start programs and another to increase construction spending for prisons. Criminological research could not have been considered in these proposals.

But it is also true that we have not influenced public policy because we have not made the case well enough, the case for a clear and convincing scientific explanation of the causes of crime. This is because we don't have one yet. It may be that it is not possible to have one. In this state of uncertainty, I propose that our theory making can be profitably informed by its own history. A historical perspective teaches us modesty, skepticism, respect for data, attention to context, and vigilance on issues of values. It also suggests a place at the table for choice, chance, and constraint. Our best course is to continue the work, the data collection and the debates, the theories and their revisions, the observations and their interpretations, until a better, more convincing scientific map of the causes of crime emerges. When we have done so, the explanation of crime may resemble some very old ideas.

Suggested Reading

Since the publication of Guerry's *Moral Statistics* in 1833, there has been over 170 years of theory and research on the causes of crime. There is now a vast ocean of criminological literature and it is possible for a sincere reader to drown in it. In conducting one's own search for the causes of crime, the best course to follow through this sea of articles and books is to rely on the bibliographic advice of respected scholars and scientists who have spent their careers investigating, reading, and writing about it, while at the same time remembering that this is fundamentally a moral enterprise, no matter how much they themselves may disavow that position. Below are some publications that I have found especially helpful on the journey. My particular bias is historical; that is, I have been especially interested in the history and progression of our thought about the causes of crime (and how we have repeated ourselves). I am not so much focused on what are the most recent proposals and speculations on the subject; time will tell their value. Therefore, the reader should not be surprised to see that some of my favorites are old rather than brand new and that most of them reflect an interest in the history of criminology.

For an overview, *Theoretical Criminology* by Vold, Bernard, and Snipes is the classic work. There is also *Explaining Criminals and Crime*, edited by Paternoster and Bachman, which includes major theories and approaches explained and updated by their original authors. *Understanding Criminology* by Susan Walklate is a short, yet useful, book which helps in organizing one's thinking about the causes of crime. *Criminological Theory: Context and Consequences* by Robert Lilly, Francis T. Cullen, and Richard A. Ball is very historically minded, lucidly describing theories about crime and the context in which they became prominent. For an overview of theories about juvenile delinquency, see Donald Shoemaker, *Theories of Delinquency*.

For history, I have been helped by *Classics of Criminology*, edited by Joseph Jacoby, and by *Pioneers of Criminology*, edited by Hermann Mannheim. Jacoby's book offers abbreviated versions of the best writing of the best criminologists and is good reading for the historically minded. The articles in Mannheim are uneven in quality but are filled with interesting information about criminologists as well as criminological theory. *The History of Criminology* by David Jones, though oddly organized to my way of thinking, abounds with useful and interesting historical facts. *Juvenile Offenders for a Thousand Years*, edited by Wiley Sanders, is a fascinating historical perspective on juvenile delinquency. *Inventing Criminology* by Piers Bierne is an example of the very best work in the history of criminology.

For biology, I have been helped by Sarnoff Mednick, especially *The Causes of Crime: New Biological Approaches*; Anthony Walsh's *Biosocial Criminology*; and Adrian Raine's *The Psychopathology of Crime*. Yaralian and Raine have published an update in the aforementioned *Explaining Criminals and Crime*.

For psychopathy, I recommend Millon, Simonsen, Birket-Smith, and Davis, *Psychopathy: Antisocial, Criminal, and Violent Behavior*. They are willing to present many sides of the issue. R.D. Hare's *Without Conscience*, written for a general popular audience, is easy to read and thought provoking. The classic work is Hervey Cleckley's *Mask of Sanity*. First published in 1941, it is still well worth reading if you have any interest in that group of people we have chosen to call psychopathic. For psychology, Don Andrews and James Bonta have reviewed and summarized a vast amount of research in *The Psychology of Criminal Conduct*. It is truly remarkable how much information is in this book.

For sociology, the literature is much larger and therefore selections are harder to make. I am partial to David Matza's *Delinquency and Drift*, not because his theory turned out to be the "right" one, but because he is so interesting and stimulating to read and because, admittedly, we share the same views about choice and causation. *Life Course Criminology*, edited by Alex Piquero and Paul Mazerolle, is a good introduction to that important subject. One of the best books that you can read about criminology, whether or not you agree with the specific theoretical proposal, is *A General Theory of Crime* by Michael Gottfredson and Travis Hirschi. *The New Criminology* by Ian Taylor, Paul Walton, and Jock Young is very important in the development of criminological thinking. Like *A General Theory of Crime*, it is well worth reading for its general critique of criminology.

Cesare Beccaria is only one of many candidates for the title "father of criminology," but his *Of Crimes and Punishments* is a great and eloquent work in the canon of criminology. For a general criminology text, I like Sue Titus Reid, *Crime and Criminology*.

I don't wish to slight any of the valuable works in the criminological literature, but if I give too much advice it will become progressively less helpful, so if you are interested in more bibliographic advice, a good procedure is to look at the bibliographies of the books already suggested, especially the ones that are overviews, see what these authors have relied upon themselves, and make further selections from there. I wish you a good journey.

Notes

Part One

1. Cesare Beccaria, *Of Crimes and Punishments*. Marsilio Publishers, New York, 1996, p. 112.
2. Edwin Sutherland and Donald Cressey, *The Principles of Criminology*, 7th ed. J.B. Lippincott and Company, Philadelphia, 1966, p. 20.
3. Quoted in David Jones, *History of Criminology*. Greenwood Press, New York, 1986, p. 101.
4. J. Robert Lilly, Francis T. Cullen, and Richard A. Ball, *Criminological Theory: Context and Consequence*, 2nd ed., Sage Publications, Thousand Oaks, 1995, p. 4.

Chapter 1

1. Michael Gottfredson and Travis Hirschi, *A General Theory of Crime*. Stanford University Press, Stanford, California, 1990, p. xv.
2. Adrian Raine, *The Psychopathology of Crime*. Academic Press, San Diego, 1993, p. 317.
3. Piers Bierne, *Inventing Criminology*. State University of New York Press, Albany, 1993, pp. 235–6.
4. Clarence R. Jeffrey, "The Historical Development of Criminology," in Hermann Mannheim, *Pioneers in Criminology*. Patterson Smith, Montclair, New Jersey, 1973, p. 459.
5. Edwin Sutherland and Donald Cressey. *The Principles of Criminology*, 7th ed. J.B. Lippincott and Company, Philadelphia, 1966, p. 3.
6. Sue Titus Reid, *Crime and Criminology*, 7th ed. Brown and Benchmark, Chicago, 1994, p. 4.
7. Cited in D.A. Andrews and James Bonta, *The Psychology of Criminal Conduct*. 1st ed. Anderson Publishing Company, Cincinnati, Ohio, 1994, p. 24.
8. Susan Walklate, *Understanding Criminol-ogy*. Open University Press, Philadelphia, 1998, p. 5.
9. *The American Heritage Dictionary*, 3rd ed. Houghton Mifflin Company, Boston, 1996.
10. Thorsten Sellin, "Culture Conflict and Crime," in Joseph Jacoby, ed., *Classics in Criminology*. Waveland Press, Prospect Heights, Illinois, 1994, p. 189.
11. Jeffrey, op. cit., p. 487.
12. Emile Durkheim, "The Normal and the Pathological," in Joseph Jacoby, ed., *Classics in Criminology*. Waveland Press, Prospect Heights, Illinois, 1994, p. 84.
13. Ibid., pp. 84–88.
14. Thorsten Sellin, *Culture Conflict and Crime*. Social Science Research Council, New York, 1938, pp. 63–70.
15. Francis A. Allen, "Raffaele Garofalo," in Hermann Mannhei, *Pioneers in Criminology*. Patterson Smith, Montclair, New Jersey, 1973, p. 321.
16. Gottfredson and Hirschi, op. cit., p. 15.
17. William Chambliss, "Toward a Political Economy of Crime," *Theory and Society* 2: 152–153, 1975.
18. Edwin Sutherland, "White Collar Criminality," *American Sociological Review*, 5, no.1: 2–10, 1940.
19. Raine, op. cit., p. 2.
20. William McCord and Joan McCord, *Origins of Crime*. Patterson Smith, Montclair, New Jersey, 1972, p. 196.
21. Jeffrey, op. cit., p. 487.
22. Andrews and Bonta, op. cit., p. 23.
23. James Q. Wilson and Richard J. Herrnstein, *Crime and Human Nature*. Simon and Schuster, New York, 1985, p. 14.
24. Samuel Yochelson and Stanton Samenow, *The Criminal Personality*, vol. II. Jason Aronson, New York, 1977, p. 4.
25. Jeffrey, op. cit., p. 464.
26. Gottfredson and Hirschi, op. cit., p. 3.
27. Andrews and Bonta, op. cit., p. 24.
28. Yochelson and Samenow, op. cit., p. 4.

241

29. See Sutherland and Cressey, op. cit., p. 20 and C.S. Widom and J.P. Newman, "Characteristics of Non-Institutionalized Psychopaths," in D.P. Farrington and J. Gunn, eds., *Aggression and Dangerousness*. Wiley, New York, 1985.

30. Herbert Spencer, *The Principles of Psychology*, vol. I, D. Appleton and Company, New York, 1872, p. 503.

31. Stephen Hawking, *A Brief History of Time*. Bantam Books, New York, 1998, p. 167.

32. Ibid., p. 186.

33. Sutherland and Cressey, op. cit., p. 20.

34. Sutherland and Cressey, op. cit., p. 74.

35. Bierne, op. cit., pp. 11–43.

36. J.M. Chaiken and M.R. Chaiken, "Crime Rates and the Active Criminal," in J.Q. Wilson, ed., *Crime and Public Policy*. Institute for Contemporary Studies, San Francisco, 1983.

37. Gottfredson and Hirschi, op. cit., p. 24.

38. Jeffrey, op. cit., p. 487.

Chapter 2

1. See Elio Monachesi, "Cesare Beccaria," in Hermann Mannheim, ed., *Pioneers in Criminology*. Patterson Smith, Montclair, New Jersey, 1973; David Jones, *History of Criminology*. Greenwood Press, New York, 1986; Piers Bierne, *Inventing Criminology*. State University of New York Press, Albany, 1993, Ch. 2; and Marvin Wolfgang, Introduction to Cesare Beccaria, *Of Crimes and Punishments*. Marsilio Publishers, New York, 1996.

2. Jones, op. cit., pp. 33–34.

3. Beccaria, op. cit., p. 9.

4. Edwin Sutherland and Donald Cressey, *The Principles of Criminology*, 7th ed. J.B. Lippincott and Company, Philadelphia, 1966, pp. 314–315.

5. Wolfgang, op. cit., pp. xi–xii.

6. Jones, op. cit., p. 5 and Bierne, op. cit., pp. 11–12.

7. Beccaria, op. cit., pp. 7–8.

8. Ibid., pp. 11–13.

9. Ibid., p. 119.

10. Graeme Newman, *Just and Painful: A Case for the Corporal Punishment of Prisoners*. Free Press, New York, 1983, p. 71.

11. Jones, op. cit., p. 6.

12. Ibid., p. 5.

13. Mario Cuomo, foreword to Cesare Beccaria, *Of Crimes and Punishments*. Marsilio Publishers, New York, 1996, p. vii.

14. Wolfgang, op. cit., p. x.

15. Gilbert Geis, "Jeremy Bentham," in Hermann Mannheim, ed., *Pioneers in Criminology*. Patterson Smith, Montclair, New Jersey, 1973.

16. Jones, op. cit., p. 40.

17. Jeremy Bentham, *The Principles of Morals and Legislation*. Prometheus Books, Amherst, New York, 1988, p. 1.

18. Geis, op. cit., p. 64.

19. Ibid., p. 51.

20. Ibid., p. 58.

21. Ibid., p. 67.

22. Jones, op. cit., p. 81.

23. Ibid., p. 82.

24. Ibid., p. 82.

25. Susan Walklate, *Understanding Criminology*. Open University Press, Philadelphia, 1998, pp. 16–32.

26. J. Robert Lilly, Francis T. Cullen, and Richard A. Ball, *Criminological Theory: Context and Consequences*, 2nd ed. Sage Publications, Thousand Oaks, 1995, pp. 19–21

27. Anthony Walsh, *Biosocial Criminology*. Anderson Publishing Company, Cincinnati, Ohio, 2002; Curt Bartol, *Criminal Behavior: A Psychosocial Approach*. Prentice Hall, Upper Saddle River, New Jersey, 1999.

Chapter 3

1. Michael Gottfredson and Travis Hirschi. *A General Theory of Crime*. Stanford University Press, Stanford California, 1990, p. 124.

2. Ibid; U.S. Department of Justice, *Uniform Crime Reports*, Washington, D.C., 1994–2002.

3. Charles Goring, *The English Convict*. 1913. Reprinted by Patterson Smith, Montclair New Jersey, 1972.

4. Piers Bierne, *Inventing Criminology*. State University of New York Press, Albany, 1993, pp. 84–86.

5. Terrie Moffitt, "Adolescence-Limited and Life Course Persistent Antisocial Behavior: A Developmental Taxonomy," in Alex Piquero and Paul Mazerole, eds., *Life Course Criminology*. Wadsworth, United States, 2001.

6. Gordon Trasler, "Aspects of Causality, Culture, and Crime." Paper presented at the Fourth International Seminar at the International Center of Sociological, Penal, and penitentiary Research and Studies, Messina, Italy, 1980.

7. Gottfredson and Hirschi, op. cit., pp. 124–144.

8. David Matza, *Delinquency and Drift*. Transaction Publishers, New Brunswick, 1992. Originally published in 1964.

9. Gottfredson and Hirschi, op. cit., pp. 124–144.

10. Gina Lombroso-Ferrero, "Criminal Man," in Joseph Jacoby, ed., *Classics of Criminology*.

Waveland Press, Inc., Prospect Heights, Illinois, 1994, pp. 130–131.

11. Marvin E. Wolfgang, "Cesare Lombroso," in Hermann Mannheim, ed., *Pioneers in Criminology*. Patterson Smith, Montclair, New Jersey, 1973.

12. Wolfgang, op. cit., pp. 255–256.

13. Lombroso-Ferrero, op. cit., p. 131.

14. Wolfgang, op. cit., p. 255.

15. W.I. Thomas, *Sex and Society*. Little Brown, Boston, 1907.

16. W.I. Thomas, *The Unadjusted Girl*. Harper and Row, New York, 1923.

17. Otto Pollak, *The Criminality of Women*. University of Pennsylvania Press, Philadelphia, 1950.

18. Susan Walklate, *Understanding Criminology*. Open University Press, Philadelphia, 1998, p. 74.

19. John Hagan, *Structural Criminology*. Rutgers University Press, New Brunswick, New Jersey, 1989.

20. Terrie Moffitt, Avshalom Caspi, Michael Rutter, and Phil A. Silva, *Sex Differences in Antisocial Behavior*. Cambridge University Press, Cambridge, 2001.

21. Freda Adler, *Sisters in Crime*. McGraw Hill, New York, 1975.

22. Rita Simon, *Women in Crime*. Lexington Books, Lexington, Mass., 1975.

23. Phyllis Coontz and Eric Sevigny, "Revisiting the Rise of the Violent Female Offender: Drugs and Violent Crime." University of Pittsburg, Graduate School of Public and International Affairs, February 2003.

24. M. Cain, "Towards Transgression: New Directions in Feminist Criminology," *International Journal of the Sociology of Law* 18: 1–18, 1990.

25. See, for example, Anthony Walsh, *Biosocial Criminology*. Anderson Publishing Company, Cincinnati, Ohio, 2002; and Michael Gottfredson and Travis Hirschi, *A General Theory of Crime*. Stanford University Press, Stanford California, 1990.

26. M. Rutter and H. Giller, *Juvenile Delinquency: Trends and Perspectives*. Guilford, New York, 1984.

27. J. Rushton, "Race and Crime: International Data for 1989–1990," *Psychological Reports* 76: 307–312, 1995.

28. Hans Eysenck and G. Gudjonsson, *The Causes and Cures of Criminality*. Plenum, New York, 1989.

29. U.S. Department of Justice, *Uniform Crime Reports*, 2002.

30. Walsh, op. cit., p. 175.

31. Adrian Raine, *The Psychopathology of Crime*. Academic Press, San Diego, 1993.

32. Michael J. Hindelang, "Variations in Sex-Age-Race Specific Incidence Rates of Offending," *American Sociological Review* 46: 461–74, 1981.

33. William Wilbanks, *The Myth of a Racist Criminal Justice System*. Brooks/Cole, Belmont, California, 1986.

34. Walsh, op. cit., p. 177 and Gottfredson and Hirschi, op. cit., p. 150.

35. H.H. Goddard, "Feeblemindedness," in Joseph Jacoby, ed., *Classics of Criminology*, Waveland Press, Inc., Prospect Heights, Illinois, 1994, p. 141.

36. R.D. Hare, "Psychopaths and Their Nature," in Theodore Millon, Erik Simonsen, Morten Birket-Smith, and Roger D. Davis, *Psychopathy*. The Guilford Press, New York, 1998, p. 206.

37. See James Q. Wilson and Richard J. Herrnstein, *Crime and Human Nature*. Simon and Schuster, New York, 1985, pp. 150–151.

38. See Edwin D. Driver, "Charles Buckman Goring," in Hermann Mannheim, ed., *Pioneers in Criminology*. Patterson Smith, Montclair, New Jersey, 1973.

39. H.H. Goddard. *Human Efficiency and Levels of Intelligence*. Princeton University Press, Princeton, 1920, pp 73–74.

40. H.H. Goddard, "Feeblemindedness" in Joseph Jacoby, ed., *Classics of Criminology*, Waveland Press, Inc., Prospect Heights, Illinois, 1994, p. 140–141.

41. Franz Alexander and William Healy, *The Roots of Crime*. New York, 1935.

42. L.D. Zelney, "Feeblemindedness and Criminal Conduct," *American Journal of Sociology* 38: 564–578, 1933.

43. Carl Murchison, *Criminal Intelligence*. Worcester, 1926.

44. Edwin H. Sutherland, "Mental Deficiency and Crime," in Kimball Young, ed., *Social Attitudes*. Henry Holt, New York, 1931.

45. Wilson and Herrnstein, op. cit., p. 153–4.

46. M. Wolfgang, R.F. Figlio, and T. Sellin, *Delinquency in a Birth Cohort*. University of Chicago Press, Chicago, 1972.

47. T. Hirschi and M. Hindelang, "Intelligence and Delinquency: a Revisionist View," *American Sociological Review* 42: 571–587, 1977.

48. Wilson and Herrnstein, op. cit., pp. 154–5.

49. David Farrington, "Early Predictors of Adolescent Aggression and Adult Violence," *Violence and Victims* 4: 79–100, 1989.

50. David Lykken, *The Antisocial Personalities*. Lawrence Erlbaum Associates, Hillsdale, New Jersey, 1995, p. 106.

51. D.A. Andrews and James Bonta, *The Psychology of Criminal Conduct*. Anderson Publishing Company, Cincinnati, Ohio, 1994, p. 133.

52. H.C. Quay. "Intelligence," in H.C. Quay,

ed., *Handbook of Juvenile Delinquency*, Wiley, New York, 1987, pp. 106–117.
53. Adrian Raine, *The Psychopathology of Crime*. Academic Press, San Diego, 1993, pp. 233–4.
54. Travis Hirschi. *Causes of Delinquency*. University of California Press, Berkeley, Calif., 1969, p. 111.
55. Wilson and Hernnstein, op. cit., p. 171.

Part Two

1. Cited in David Jones, *History of Criminology*. Greenwood Press, New York, 1986, p. 101.
2. Adrian Raine, *The Psychopathology of Crime*. Academic Press, San Diego, 1993, p. 304.

Chapter 4

1. Roger Cooter, "Phrenology and the British Alienists," in Andrew Scull, ed., *Madhouse, Mad-Doctors, and Madmen: The Social History of Psychiatry in the Victorian Era*. University of Pennsylvania Press, Philadelphia, 1981, p. 64.
2. Jones, op. cit., p. 136.
3. Ibid., p. 136. See also Pierre Schlag, "Commentary: Law and Phrenology," *Harvard Law Review* 110: 877, 1997.
4. Robert Carroll, "Phrenology," in Robert Carroll, ed., *The Skeptics Dictionary*. John Wiley and Sons, Hoboken, New Jersey, 2003.
5. Schlag, op. cit., p. 888.
6. See www. phrenology.org.
7. Antonio R. Damasio, *Descartes' Error: Emotion, Reason, and the Human Brain*. G.P. Putnam's Sons, New York, 1994, p. 14.
8. Schlag, op. cit.
9. Ibid., p. 887.
10. Raine, op. cit. pp. 314–16.
11. Robert Carroll, "Anthropometry," in Robert Carroll, ed., *The Skeptics Dictionary*, John Wiley and Sons, Hoboken, New Jersey, 2003.
12. Schlag, op. cit., p. 886.
13. Macneile Dixon, *The Human Situation*. Longmans, Green, and Company, New York, 1938, p. 17.
14. Cooter, op. cit., p. 80.
15. Schlag, op. cit.
16. Ibid., p. 885.
17. Ibid., p. 884.
18. Cited in Marvin E. Wolfgang, "Cesare Lombroso," in Hermann Mannheim, ed., *Pio-

neers in Criminology*. Patterson Smith, Montclair, New Jersey, 1973, p. 248.
19. Gina Lombroso-Ferrero, "Criminal Man," in Joseph Jacoby, ed., *Classics of Criminology*, Waveland Press, Inc., Prospect Heights, Illinois, 1994, pp. 116–7.
20. Wolfgang, op. cit., p. 248.
21. Lombroso-Ferrero, op. cit., p. 124.
22. Wolfgang, op. cit., p. 251.
23. Ibid., p. 247.
24. Havelock Ellis, *The Criminal*, 2nd ed. Charles Scribner's Sons, New York, 1895, chapter 1.
25. Wolfgang, op. cit., pp. 237–8.
26. Ibid., p. 257. See also Edwin Sutherland and Donald Cressey, *The Principles of Criminology*, 7th ed. J.B. Lippincott and Company, Philadelphia, 1966, p. 57.
27. Jones, op. cit., pp. 84–86; Wolfgang, op. cit., pp. 249–54.
28. Wolfgang, op. cit., p. 232.
29. Cesare Lombroso, *Crime: Its Causes and Remedies*. 1912. Reprinted by Patterson Smith, Montclair, New Jersey, 1968, pp. 72–3.
30. Sutherland and Cressey, op. cit., p. 129.
31. Jones, op. cit., p. 101.
32. Raine, op. cit., p. 79.
33. Ibid., p. 155.
34. See Edwin D. Driver, "Charles Buckman Goring," in Hermann Mannheim, ed., *Pioneers in Criminology*. Patterson Smith, Montclair, New Jersey, 1973; and Jones, op. cit., pp. 106–8.
35. Charles Goring, *The English Convict: A Statistical Study*. 1913. Reprinted by Patterson Smith, Montclair, New Jersey, 1972, pp. 200–1.
36. Driver, op. cit., p. 439; and Piers Bierne, *Inventing Criminology*. State University of New York Press, Albany, 1993, chapter 6.
37. Bierne, op. cit., p. 213.
38. Goring, op. cit., p. 212.
39. Cited in Jones, op. cit., p. 107.
40. E.A. Hooten, *Crime and the Man*. Harvard University Press, Cambridge, 1939, p. 130.
41. Ibid.; and E.A. Hooten, *The American Criminal: An Anthropological Study*. Harvard University Press, Cambridge, 1939.
42. Cited in Wilson and Herrnstein, op. cit., p. 78.
43. See Jones, op. cit., pp. 108–9; Wilson and Herrnstein, op. cit., pp. 76–81; and Sutherland and Cressey, op. cit., p. 129; R. Merton and M.F. Ashley-Montague, op. cit., p. 384–408.
44. See Jones, op. cit., pp. 110–123.
45. E.A. Hooten, "The American Criminal," in Joseph Jacoby, ed., *Classics of Criminology*. Waveland Press, Inc., Prospect Heights, Illinois, 1994, p. 155.
46. Ibid., p. 155.
47. Ibid., p. 158.

48. Jones, op. cit., p. 123.

49. Ellis, op. cit., chapter 2.

50. Jones, op. cit., p. 82.

51. Ibid., p. 138.

52. Ibid.

53. William H. Sheldon, *Varieties of Delinquent Youth*. Harper, New York, 1949, p. 572.

54. Wilson and Herrnstein, op. cit., p. 81.

55. Ibid., pp. 81–90.

56. Sheldon, op. cit.

57. Sheldon Glueck and Eleanor Glueck, *Unraveling Juvenile Delinquency*. Commonwealth Fund, New York, 1950.

58. T.C.N. Gibbens, *Psychiatric Studies of Borstal Lads*. Oxford University Press, London, 1963; Juan B. Cortes and Florence Gatti, *Delinquency and Crime*. Seminar Press, New York, 1972; E.M. Hartl, E.P. Monnelly, and R.D. Elderkin, *Physique and Delinquent Behavior: A Thirty Year Follow Up of William H. Sheldon's Varieties of Delinquent Youth*. Academic Press, New York, 1982.

59. Wilson and Herrnstein, op. cit., p. 90.

60. S.L. Washburn, "Review of W.H. Sheldon, Varieties of Delinquent Youth," *American Anthropologist* 53: 561–563, 1951.

61. Sutherland and Cressey, op. cit., p. 130.

62. Don C. Gibbons, *Delinquent Behavior*. Prentice Hall, Englewood Cliffs, 1970, pp. 75–76.

63. George Vold and Thomas Bernard, *Theoretical Criminology*, 3rd ed. Oxford University Press, New York, 1986, p. 65. This book is now in its fifth edition, which apparently does not repeat this conclusion.

64. Raine, op. cit., p. 202.

65. Donald Shoemaker, *Theories of Delinquency*. Oxford University Press, New York, 1996, p. 26.

66. Cited in Wilson and Herrnstein, op. cit., p. 79.

67. E.B. Reuter, "Review of E.A. Hooten, Crime and the Man," *American Journal of Sociology* 45: 123–6, 1939.

Chapter 5

1. Anthony Walsh, *Biosocial Criminology*. Anderson Publishing Company, Cincinnati, Ohio, 2002, p. 29.

2. Adrian Raine, *The Psychopathology of Crime*. Academic Press, San Diego, 1993, p. 79.

3. David Lykken, *The Antisocial Personalities*. Lawrence Erlbaum Associates, Hillsdale, New Jersey, 1995, p. 97.

4. Walsh, op. cit., chapter 1.

5. A.A. Sandberg, G.F. Koepf, T. Ishihara, and J.S. Hauschka, "An XYY Human Male," *Lancet* 2: 488–9, 1961.

6. P. Jacobs, M. Brunton, and M. Melville, "Aggressive Behavior, Mental Subnormality, and the XYY Male," *Nature* 208: 1351, 1965.

7. R.G. Fox. "The XYY Offender: a Modern Myth?" *Journal of Criminal Law, Criminology, and Political Science* 62: 59–73, 1971, p. 72.

8. H.A. Witkin, S.A. Mednick, F. Schulsinger, E. Bakkestrom, K.O. Christiansen, D.R. Goodenough, K. Hirschorn, C. Lundsteen, D.R. Owen, J. Phillip, D.B. Rubin, and M. Stocking, "Criminality, Aggression, and Intelligence among XYY and XXY Men," in S. A. Mednick and K.O. Christiansen, eds., *Biosocial Bases of Criminal Behavior*. Gardner Press, New York, 1977, pp. 165–188.

9. Raine, op. cit., p. 54.

10. J. Lange, *Crime As Destiny*. Unwin, London, 1929. Translated 1931. For a discussion of twin research, see also Raine, op. cit., Andrews and Bonta, op. cit., and Jones, op. cit.

11. Karl O. Christiansen, "A Preliminary Study of Criminality Among Twins," in S.A. Mednick and K.O. Christiansen, eds., *Biosocial Bases of Criminal Behavior*. Gardner Press, New York, 1977.

12. O.S. Dalgaard and E. Kringlen, "A Norwegian Twin Study of Criminality," *British Journal of Criminology* 16: 213–233, 1976.

13. Hans J. Eysenck, *Crime and Personality*, 2nd ed. Routledge and Kegan Paul, London, 1977.

14. Raine, op. cit., p. 55.

15. S.A. Mednick, W.H. Gabrielli, and B. Hutchings, "Genetic Influences in Criminal Convictions: Evidence from an Adoption Cohort," *Science* 224: 891–894, 1984.

16. Data from Mednick, Gabrielli, and Hutchings, op. cit., and also cited in Lykken, op. cit., p. 96.

17. C.R. Clonniger, S. Sigvardsson, M. Bohman, and A.L. Knorring, " Predisposition to Petty Criminality in Swedish Adoptees: Cross Fostering Analysis of Gene-Environmental Interaction," *Archives of General Psychiatry* 99: 1242–1247, 1982; and R.J. Cadoret, C.A. Cain, and R.R. Crowe, "Evidence for Gene-Environment Interaction in the Development of Adolescent Antisocial Behavior," *Behavior Genetics* 13: 301–310, 1983.

18. W.M. Grove, E.D. Eckert, L. Heston, T.J. Bouchard, N. Segal, and D.T. Lykken, "Heritability of Substance Abuse and Antisocial Behavior: A Study of Monozygotic Twins Reared Apart," *Biological Psychiatry* 27: 1293–1304, 1990.

19. Raine, op. cit., pp. 62–66.

20. G.D. Walters and T.W. White, "Heredity and Crime: Bad Genes or Bad Research," *Criminology* 27: 455–485, 1989.

21. Michael Gottfredson and Travis Hirschi, *A General Theory of Crime*. Stanford University Press, Stanford California, 1990, p. 60.
22. Raine, op. cit., p. 72.
23. Cited in Lykken, op. cit., p. 97.
24. Cited in Lykken, op. cit., p. 92.
25. Sutherland and Cressey, op. cit., p. 128.

Chapter 6

1. Charles Darwin, *On the Origin of Species*. John Murray, London, 1859.
2. Charles Darwin, *The Descent of Man and Selection in Relation to Sex*. 1871. Reprinted by IndyPublish.com, 2003.
3. Francis Darwin, *The Life and Letters of Charles Darwin*. University Press of the Pacific, 2001, letter to Asa Gray, May 22, 1860.
4. Cited in David Jones, *History of Criminology*. Greenwood Press, New York, 1986, p. 82.
5. Herbert Spencer, *First Principles*, originally published in 6 parts (1860–1862). Published as one volume, Williams and Norgate, London, 1862.
6. Francis Galton, *Hereditary Genius: An Inquiry into Its Laws and Consequences*. Macmillan, London, 1869.
7. E.O. Wilson, *Sociobiology: The New Synthesis*. Harvard University Press, Cambridge, Mass., 1975.
8. W.D. Hamilton. "The Genetic Evolution of Social Behavior," *Journal of Theoretical Biology* 7: 1–52, 1964; and Robert L. Trivers, "The Evolution of Reciprocal Altruism," *Quarterly Review of Biology* 46: 35–57, 1971.
9. Richard Dawkins, *The Selfish Gene*. Oxford University Press, Oxford, 1976.
10. J. Tooby and L. Comides, "The Psychological Foundations of Culture," in J.H. Barlow, L. Cosmides, and J. Tooby, eds., *The Adapted Mind: Evolutionary Psychology and the Generation of Culture*. Oxford University Press, Oxford, 1992.
11. Hilary Rose and Stephen Rose, eds., *Alas Poor Darwin! Arguments Against Evolutionary Psychology*. Harmony Books, 2000.
12. William R. Clark and Michael Grunstein, *Are We Hardwired? The Role of Genes in Human Behavior*. Oxford University Press, Oxford, 2000; David Buss, *The Evolution of Desire*. Basic Books, New York, 2003.
13. John Haught, *God After Darwin: A Theology of Evolution*. Westview Press, Boulder Colorado, 2001; Kenneth R. Miller, *Finding Darwin's God*. Harper Collins, New York, 2000.
14. Paul Ehrlich, *Human Natures: Genes, Cultures, and the Human Prospect*. Penguin Putnam, Inc., New York, 2002, p. 4.
15. Ibid.
16. Kim Sterelny, *Dawkins vs. Gould*. Totem Books, U.S.A., 2001.
17. Phillip E. Johnson, *Darwin on Trial*, 2nd ed. Intervarsity Press, Downers Grove, Illinois, 1993.
18. Cited in Macneile Dixon, *The Human Situation*. Longmans, Green, and Co., New York, 1938, p. 17.
19. M. Milinski and T.C. Bakker, "Female Sticklebacks Use Male Coloration in Male Choice and Hence Avoid Parasitized Males," *Nature* 344: 330–333, 1990.
20. Dixon, op. cit., p. 125.
21. Dawkins, op. cit.
22. John Maynard Smith, *Evolution and the Theory of Games*. Cambridge University Press, Cambridge, 1982.
23. See Adrian Raine, *The Psychopathology of Crime*. Academic Press, San Diego, 1993, pp. 31–37.
24. R. Thornhill and N.M. Thornhill, "Human Rape: The Strengths of the Evolutionary Perspective," in C. Crawford, M. Smith, and D. Krebs, eds., *Sociobiology and Psychology*. Erlbaum, Hillsdale, N.J., 1987.
25. Raine, op. cit., p. 42.
26. M. Daley and M. Wilson, *Homicide*. Aldine de Gruyter, New York, 1988.
27. Raine, op. cit., p. 44.

Chapter 7

1. See Antonio Damasio, *Descartes' Error: Emotion, Reason, and the Human Brain*. G.P. Putnam's Sons, New York, 1994, pp. 2–33; and Adrian Raine, *The Psychopathology of Crime*. Academic Press, San Diego, 1993, p. 109.
2. Cited in Damasio, op. cit., p. 8.
3. Damasio, op. cit., p. 22.
4. H. Damasio, T. Grabowski, R. Frank, A.M Galaburda, and A.R. Damasio, "The Return of Phineas Gage: The Skull of a Famous Patient Yields Clues About the Brain," *Science* 264: 1102–05, 1994.
5. Damasio, op. cit., p. 17.
6. Michael Gottfredson and Travis Hirschi, *A General Theory of Crime*. Stanford University Press, Stanford California, 1990, pp. 61–2.
7. Adrian Raine, *The Psychopathology of Crime*. Academic Press, San Diego, 1993, p. 317–8.
8. Raine, op. cit., p. 175.
9. Pauline Yaralian and Adrian Raine, "Biological Approaches to Crime," in Raymond Paternoster and Ronet Bachman, eds.,

Explaining Criminals and Crime. Roxbury Publishing Company, Los Angeles, 2001, p. 65.
10. Raine, op. cit., p. 116. See chapter 8 for discussion.
11. Yaralian and Raine, op. cit., pp. 64–66.
12. Raine, op. cit., pp. 122–4.
13. Cited in Raine, op. cit., pp. 86–89.
14. U.S. Department of Justice, Bureau of Justice Statistics, *Source Book of Criminal Justice Statistics,* 1998.
15. Raine, op. cit., pp. 98–9.
16. Lana Harrison and Joseph Gfroerer, "The Intersection of Drug Use and Criminal Behavior: Results from the National Household Survey on Drug Abuse," *Crime and Delinquency* 38: 423, October 1992.
17. See Yaralian and Raine, op cit., and Raine, op. cit.
18. D.O. Lewis, S.A. Shanok, and D.A. Balla, "Perinatal Difficulties, Head and Face Trauma, and Child Abuse in the Medical Histories of Seriously Delinquent Children," *American Journal of Psychiatry* 136: 419–423, 1979; and S.A. Mednick and E. Kandel, "Genetic and Perinatal Factors in Violence," in S.A. Mednick and T. Moffitt, eds., *Biological Contributions to Crime Causation.* Martinus Nijhoff, Dordrecht, Holland, 1988, pp. 121–134.
19. Daniel Amen, *Firestorms in the Brain.* MindworksPress.com, 1999.
20. Raine, op. cit., p. 155.

Part Three

1. Hervey Cleckley, *The Mask of Sanity.* 1941. Reprinted by Emily S. Cleckley, Publishers, Augusta, Georgia, 1988, p. 452.
2. Hans Eysenck, "Personality and Crime," in Theodore Millon, Erik Simonsen, Morten Birket-Smith, and Roger D. Davis, *Psychopathy: Antisocial, Criminal, and Violent Behavior.* The Guilford Press, New York, 1998, p. 46.

Chapter 8

1. David Lykken, *The Antisocial Personalities.* Lawrence Erlbaum Associates, Hillsdale, New Jersey, 1995, p. 31.
2. William McCord and Joan McCord, *The Origins of Crime.* 1959. Patterson Smith, Montclair, New Jersey, 1969, p. 198.
3. Robert Hare, *Without Conscience.* The Guilford Press, New York, 1993, p. xi.
4. *Oxford English Dictionary,* 10th ed. Oxford University Press, Oxford, 1999.
5. G.E. Partridge, "Current Conceptions of Psychopathic Personality," *American Journal of Psychiatry* 10: 53–99, 1930.
6. Cited in Theodore Millon, Erik Sorenson, and Morten Birket-Smith, "Historical Conceptions of Psychopathy in the United States and Europe," in Theodore Millon, Erik Sorenson, Morten Birket-Smith, and Roger Davis, eds., *Psychopathy: Antisocial, Criminal, and Violent Behavior.* The Guilford Press, New York, 1998, p. 11.
7. Hulsey Cason, "The Psychopath and the Psychopathic," *Journal of Criminal Psychopathology* 4: 522–7, 1943.
8. D. Curran and P. Mallinson, "Recent Progress in Psychiatry: Psychopathic Personality," *Journal of Mental Science* 90: 266–84, 1944.
9. American Psychiatric Association, *Diagnostic and Statistical Manual of Mental Disorders, Text Revision,* 4th ed. American Psychiatric Association, Washington, D.C., 2000, pp. 701–6.
10. Ibid., p. 706.
11. T.J. Harpur, R.D. Hare, and A.R. Hakistan, "Two Factor Conceptualization of Psychopathy: Construct Validity and Assessment Implications," *Psychological Assessment* 1: 6–17, 1989, p. 9.
12. See Adrian Raine, *The Psychopathology of Crime.* Academic Press, San Diego, 1993, and Robert Hare, *Without Conscience.* The Guilford Press, New York, 1993.
13. Robert W. White, *The Abnormal Personality,* 2nd ed. The Ronald Press Company, New York, 1956, pp. 9–11; Millon, Sorenson, and Birket-Smith, op. cit., p. 4.
14. Cited in White, op. cit., p. 9.
15. Cited in Hervey Cleckley. *The Mask of Sanity.* 1941. Reprinted by Emily S. Cleckley, Publishers, Augusta, Georgia, 1988, p. 226.
16. See White, op. cit., pp. 394–5.
17. Cited in Winfred Overholser, "Isaac Ray," in Hermann Mannheim, ed., *Pioneers in Criminology.* Patterson Smith, Montclair, New Jersey, 1973, p. 184.
18. Millon, Sorenson, and Birket-Smith, op. cit., p. 10.
19. White, op. cit., p. 395. Though written in 1956, this statement is perfectly appropriate in 2004.
20. See Samuel Yochelson and Stanton Samenow, *The Criminal Personality,* vol. I. Jason Aronson, New York, 1976, p. 80.
21. Franz Alexander and William Healy, *The Roots of Crime.* Alfred A. Knopf, New York, 1935.
22. Hervey Cleckley, *The Mask of Sanity.* 1941. Reprinted by Emily S. Cleckley, Publishers, Augusta, Georgia, 1988, p. 452.
23. Ibid., p. 368.

24. Corbett Thigpen and Hervey Cleckley, *The Three Faces of Eve*, revised edition. Arcata Graphics, Kingsport, Tennessee, 1992.

25. David Lykken, *The Antisocial Personalities*. Lawrence Erlbaum Associates, Hillsdale, New Jersey, 1995, p. 114.

26. Cleckley, op. cit., pp. 337–8.

27. Ibid., pp. 261–4.

28. Ibid., p. 189.

29. Ibid., p. 388.

30. Ibid., p. 391.

31. Ibid., p. 403.

32. Ibid., p. viii.

33. Ibid., p. 188.

34. Ibid., p. 419.

35. Ibid., p. 440.

36. Edward Sagarin, "In Search of Criminology Through Fiction," *Deviant Behavior* 21, no. 1: 81, 1980.

37. August Goll, *Criminal Types in Shakespeare*. Haskell House, New York, 1966, originally published in 1909 and translated from the Danish by Mrs. Charles Weeks; Victoria Time, *Shakespeare's Criminals*. Greenwood Press, Westport, Connecticut, 1999.

38. Lykken, op. cit., p. 114.

39. Cleckley, op. cit., pp. 317–8.

40. Karl Holzknecht and Norman McClure, eds., *Selected Plays of Shakespeare*, vol. 3. American Book Company, New York, 1937.

41. Holzknecht and McClure, op. cit., pp. 3–11.

42. Lykken, op. cit., p. 116.

43. Holzknecht and McClure, op. cit., p. 9.

44. Time, op. cit., p. 31.

45. Robert Hare, *Without Conscience*. The Guilford Press, New York, 1993.

46. Robert Hare, *The Hare Psychopathy Checklist–Revised*. Multi Health Systems, Toronto, 1991.

47. H. Johns and H.C. Quay, "The Effect of Social Reward on Verbal Conditioning in Psychopathic and Neurotic Military Offenders," *Journal of Consulting Psychology* 36: 217–220.

48. Hare, op. cit.

49. Lykken, op. cit., p. 154.

50. Ibid., p. 166.

51. Hare, op. cit., p. 77.

52. Hare, op. cit., p. 75.

53. Jack Henry Abbott, *In the Belly of the Beast: Letter from Prison*. Random House, New York, 1981.

54. Abbott, op. cit., p. 13.

55. Lykken, op. cit., p. 174.

56. Hare, op. cit., p. xii.

57. Ibid., p. 74 and 87.

58. Ibid., p. 174.

59. Ibid., p. 158.

60. Ibid., p. 22.

61. Ibid., p. 219.

62. Samuel Yochelson and Stanton Samenow, *The Criminal Personality*, vols. I (1976), II (1977), and III (1986). Jason Aronson, New York.

63. Stanton Samenow, *Inside the Criminal Mind*. Times Books, New York, 1984, p. xiii.

64. Ibid.

65. Yochelson and Samenow, op. cit., vol. I, pp. 252–255.

66. Ibid.

67. Samenow, op. cit., p. xiv.

68. Samenow and Yochelson, op. cit., pp. 44–54.

69. J. Reid Meloy, *The Psychopathic Mind: Origins, Dynamics, and Treatment*. Jason Aronson, North Vale New Jersey, 1988.

70. Ibid., p. 59.

71. Lykken, op. cit., p. 186.

72. Sigmund Freud, "The Ego and the Id," in *The Complete Psychological Works of Works of Sigmund Freud*, vol. 19. Hogarth, London, 1961, p. 52.

73. Franz Alexander and Hugo Staub, *The Criminal, the Judge, and the Public*. Macmillan, New York, 1931.

74. Edward Glover, *The Roots of Crime*. International Universities Press, New York, 1960, p. 302.

75. Meloy, op. cit., p. 309.

76. Ibid.

77. Ibid., p. xviii.

78. Ibid., p. 117.

79. Ibid., p. 123.

80. Ibid., p. 120.

81. Sigmund Freud, "Psycho-Analysis and the Ascertaining of Truth in Courts of Law," in *Collected Papers*, vol. 2. Hogarth, London, 1948, p. 21.

82. W.H.S. Jones, "Hippocrates," in *Loeb Classical Library*, vol. 1. Harvard University Press, Cambridge, Mass., 1984.

83. Israel Drapkin, *Crime and Punishment in the Ancient World*. Lexington Books, Lexington Mass., 1989, p. 242.

84. Cited in Theodore Millon, Erik Sorenson, and Morten Birket-Smith, "Historical Conceptions of Psychopathy in the United States and Europe," in Theodore Millon, Erik Sorenson, Morten Birket-Smith, and Roger Davis, eds., *Psychopathy: Antisocial, Criminal, and Violent Behavior*. The Guilford Press, New York, 1998, p. 3.

85. Theodore Millon and Roger Davis, "Ten Subtypes of Psychopathy," in Millon, Sorenson, Birket-Smith, and Davis, op. cit., p. 162.

86. Cited in Millon, Sorenson, and Birket-Smith, op. cit., p. 8.

87. Ibid., pp. 9–10.

88. Ibid., pp. 15–16.

89. E.I. Megargee and M.J. Bohn, *Classifying*

Criminal Offenders: A New System Based on the MMPI. Sage, Beverly Hills, Calif., 1979.

90. Herbert Quay, *Managing Adult Inmates: Classification for Housing and Program Assignments.* American Correctional Association, College Park, Maryland, 1984.

91. Theodore Millon and Roger Davis, "Ten Subtypes of Psychopathy," in Millon, Sorenson, Birket-Smith, and Davis, op. cit., pp. 161–170.

92. Hans Toch, "Psychopathy or Anti Social Personality in Forensic Settings," in Millon, Sorenson, Birket-Smith, and Davis, op. cit., pp. 144–158.

93. John Gunn, "Psychopathy: An Elusive Concept with Moral Overtones," in Millon, Sorenson, Birket-Smith, and Davis, op. cit., pp. 32–39. Blackburn is cited in Gunn.

94. See Samuel Yochelson and Stanton Samenow, *The Criminal Personality.* Op. cit.; and D.A. Andrews and James Bonta, *The Psychology of Criminal Conduct.* Anderson Publishing Company, Cincinnati, Ohio, 1994.

Chapter 9

1. A. Bandura, D. Ross, and S.A. Ross, "Transmission of Aggression Through Imitation of Aggressive Models," *Journal of Abnormal and Social Psychology* 63: 575–582, 1961. See also A. Bandura, *Aggression: A Social Learning Analysis.* Prentice Hall, New York, 1973.

2. See, for example, Eliot Aronson. *The Social Animal,* 5th ed. W.H. Freeman and Company, New York, 1988, p. 187.

3. J. Dollard, N.E. Miller, L.W. Doob, and O.H. Mowrer, *Frustration and Aggression.* Yale University Press, New Haven, Connecticut, 1939.

4. J.B. Watson and R. Raynor, "Conditioned Emotional Reactions," *Journal of Experimental Psychology* 3: 1–14, 1920.

5. Hans Eysenck, *Crime and Personality,* 1st ed. Houghton Mifflin Company, Boston, 1964.

6. I.P. Pavlov, *Conditioned Reflexes.* 1927. Reprinted by Dover, New York, 1960.

7. Eysenck, op. cit., chapter 6.

8. D.A. Andrews and James Bonta, *The Psychology of Criminal Conduct.* Anderson Publishing Company, Cincinnati, Ohio, 1994. A third edition was published in 2001.

9. Ibid., p. 20.

10. Ibid., pp. 187–193.

11. Ibid., p. 113.

12. David Lykken, *The Antisocial Personalities.* Lawrence Erlbaum Associates, Hillsdale, New Jersey, 1995, pp. 34–5.

13. Ibid., p. 35.

14. Ibid., p. 118.

15. Ibid., p. 118.

16. Ibid., p. 154.

17. Ibid., p. 212.

18. Ibid., p. 42.

19. Ibid., pp. 41–42.

20. Ibid., p. vii.

Part Four

1. Cited in Havelock Ellis, *The Criminal,* 2nd ed. Charles Scribner's Sons, New York, 1895, p. 24.

Chapter 10

1. See Piers Bierne, *Inventing Criminology.* State University of New York Press, Albany, 1993, pp. 111–141; David Jones, *History of Criminology.* Greenwood Press, New York, 1986, pp. 157–8, and Joseph Jacoby, ed., *Classics of Criminology.* Waveland Press, Prospect Heights, Illinois, 1994, pp. 21–26.

2. See Bierne, op. cit., pp. 65–110, and Jones, op. cit., p. 158.

3. See Bierne, op. cit., pp. 83–84.

4. David Jones, *History of Criminology.* Greenwood Press, New York, 1986, p. 158.

5. Ibid., pp. 158–159.

6. Adolphe Quetelet, *Instructions Populaires Sur le Calcul des Probabilités.* Tarlier, Brussels, 1828, p. 230.

7. Walter A. Lunden, "Emile Durkheim," in Hermann Mannheim, ed., *Pioneers in Criminology.* Patterson Smith, Montclair, New Jersey, 1973, pp. 385–399; Emile Durkheim, *The Division of Labor in Society.* Free Press, New York, 1986; Emile Durkheim, *The Rules of Sociological Method.* Macmillan, London, 1982; and Emile Durkheim, *Suicide: A Study in Sociology.* Free Press, New York, 1951.

8. Walter A. Lunden, op. cit., p. 390.

9. See George B. Vold, Thomas J. Bernard, and Jeffrey B. Snipes, *Theoretical Criminology,* 5th ed. Oxford University Press, New York, 2002, pp. 103–116.

10. Cited in Vold, Bernard, and Snipes, p. 106.

11. Emile Durkheim, "The Normal and the Pathological," in Joseph Jacoby, ed., *Classics of Criminology.* Waveland Press, Prospect Heights, Illinois, 1994, p. 87.

12. Ibid.

13. Lynn McDonald, "Theory and Evidence of Rising Crime in the Nineteenth Century," *British Journal of Criminology* 33: 404–420, Sept. 1982.

14. See Margaret S. Wilson Vine, "Gabriel Tarde," in Hermann Mannheim, ed., *Pioneers in Criminology*. Patterson Smith, Montclair, New Jersey, 1973, pp. 292–304; Jones, op. cit., 159–161; and Gabriel Tarde, *Penal Philosophy*. 1890. Reprinted by Patterson Smith, Montclair, New Jersey, 1968.

15. Vine, op. cit., p. 295.

16. Cited in Vine, op. cit., p. 293.

17. J. Robert Lilly, Francis T. Cullen, and Richard A. Ball, *Criminological Theory: Context and Consequences*, 2nd ed. Sage, Thousand Oaks, 1995, pp. 38–40.

18. Ibid, p. 40

19. Ibid.

20. E.W. Burgess, "The Growth of the City: An Introduction to a Research Project," in R.E. Park, E.W. Burgess and R.D. McKenzie, eds., *The City*. 1925. Reprinted by University of Chicago Press, Chicago, 1967, p. 55.

21. Lilly, Cullen, and Ball, op. cit., p. 43.

22. Ibid., p. 44.

23. Donald J. Shoemaker, *Theories of Delinquency*, 3rd ed. Oxford University Press, New York, 1996, p. 83.

24. Frances A. Ianni, *Black Mafia*. Simon and Schuster, New York, 1974.

25. Lilly, Cullen, and Ball, op. cit., p. 52.

26. Shoemaker, op. cit., p. 89.

27. Lilly, Cullen, and Ball, op. cit., p. 49.

28. Edwin Sutherland, Donald Cressey, and David Luckenbill. *Principles of Criminology*, 11th ed. General Hall, Dix Hills, New York, 1992.

29. Jerome Michael and Mortimer J. Adler, *Crime Law, and Social Science*. Harcourt Brace, New York, 1933.

30. Edwin H. Sutherland, *White Collar Crime*. Holt, Rhinehart, and Winston, New York, 1961, p. 234.

31. Edwin Sutherland and Donald Cressey. *The Principles of Criminology*, 7th ed. J.B. Lippincott Company, New York, 1966, pp. 81–82. This book is now in its eleventh edition.

32. Cited in Jones, op. cit., p. 171.

33. George B. Vold, Thomas J. Bernard, and Jeffrey B. Snipes, *Theoretical Criminology*, 5th ed. Oxford University Press, New York, 2002, p. 174.

34. Shoemaker, op. cit., p. 151.

35. D.A. Andrews and James Bonta, *The Psychology of Criminal Conduct*, 1st ed. Anderson Publishing Company, Cincinnati, Ohio, 1994, p. 104.

36. See Ronald Akers, "Social Learning Theory," in Raymond Paternoster and Ronet Bachman, eds., *Explaining Criminals and Crime*. Roxbury Publishing Company, Los Angeles, 2001, pp. 192–210.

37. Ibid., p. 193.

38. Albert K. Cohen, Alfred Lindesmith, and Karl Schuessler, *The Sutherland Papers*. Indiana University Press, Bloomington, 1956, p. 19.

39. Ibid.

40. Cited in Jones, op. cit., p. 169.

41. George B. Vold, Thomas J. Bernard, and Jeffrey B. Snipes, *Theoretical Criminology*, 5th ed. Oxford University Press, New York, 2002, p. 174.

42. Jones, op. cit., p. 172.

43. M.M. Hunt, "How Does It Come to Be So? A Profile of Robert K. Merton," *New Yorker*, January 28, 1961, pp. 39–64. Also see Randy Martin, Robert J. Mutchnick, and W. Timothy Austin, *Criminological Thought: Pioneers Past and Present*. Macmillan Publishing Company, New York, 1990.

44. Robert K. Merton, "Social Structure and Anomie," *American Sociological Review* 3: 672–682, 1938.

45. Robert K. Merton, *Social Theory and Social Structure*. The Free Press, New York, 1949.

46. Robert K. Merton, "Social Structure and Anomie," in Joseph Jacoby, ed., *Classics of Criminology*. Waveland Press, Prospect Heights, Illinois, 1994, p. 185, note 1.

47. Ibid., p. 178.

48. Ibid., p. 184.

49. Ibid., p. 182.

50. Ibid., p. 181.

51. Jones, op. cit., p. 190.

52. Marshall Clinard, *Anomie and Deviant Behavior*. The Free Press of Glencoe, New York, 1964, p. 10.

53. Richard A. Cloward and Lloyd E. Ohlin, "*Delinquency and Opportunity*," in Joseph Jacoby, ed., *Classics of Criminology*. Waveland Press, Prospect Heights, Illinois, 1994, p. 240.

54. Albert K. Cohen, *Delinquent Boys: The Culture of the Gang*. Free Press, New York, 1955.

55. Walter Miller, "Lower Class Culture as a Generating Milieu of Gang Delinquency," *Journal of Social Issues*. 14: 5–19, 1958.

56. L.E. Cohen and M. Felson, "Social Change and Crime Rate Trends: A Routine Activity Approach," *American Sociological Review* 44: 588–608, 1979.

57. Lamar T. Empey, *American Delinquency*, 2nd ed. Dorsey, Homewood, Illinois, 1982.

Chapter 11

1. Edwin Lemert, "Primary and Secondary Deviation," in Joseph Jacoby, ed., *Classics of Criminology*. Waveland Press, Prospect Heights, Illinois, 1994, p. 262.

2. Frank Tannebaum, "The Dramatization of Evil," in Joseph Jacoby, ed., *Classics of*

Criminology. Waveland Press, Prospect Heights, Illinois, 1994, p. 259.

3. Charles Horton Cooley, *Human Nature and the Social Order*. 1902. Reprinted by Schoken, New York, 1964.

4. Howard Becker, *The Outsiders*. 1963. Reprinted by Free Press, New York, 1973, p. 9.

5. Sue Titus Reid, *Crime and Criminology*, 7th ed. Brown and Benchmark, Chicago, 1994, pp. 259–260.

6. Ibid., p. 260.

7. Susan Walklate, *Understanding Criminology*. Open University Press, Philadelphia, 1998, p. 16.

8. Karl Marx, "Class Conflict and Law," in Joseph Jacoby, ed., *Classics of Criminology*. Waveland Press, Prospect Heights, Illinois, 1994, p. 89.

9. George B. Vold, Thomas J. Bernard, and Jeffrey B. Snipes, *Theoretical Criminology*, 5th ed. Oxford University Press, New York, 2002, p. 252.

10. Ibid.

11. Cited in David Jones, *History of Criminology*. Greenwood Press, New York, 1986, p. 188.

12. Jones, op. cit., p. 189.

13. Willem Bonger, *Criminality and Economic Conditions*. Little Brown, Boston, 1916. Reprinted by Agathon, New York, 1969.

14. Willem Bonger, *An Introduction to Criminology*. 1932. Methuen, London, 1935; and Willem Bonger, *Race and Crime*. 1939. Reprinted by Patterson Smith, Montclair, N.J., 1969.

15. Willem Bonger, *Criminality and Economic Conditions*, p. 379.

16. Cited in J.M. van Bemmelen, "Willem Adriaan Bonger," in Hermann Mannheim, ed., *Pioneers in Criminology*. Patterson Smith, Montclair, New Jersey, 1973, p. 455.

17. Thorsten Sellin, *Culture Conflict and Crime*. Social Science Research Council, New York, 1938.

18. Thorsten Sellin, "Culture Conflict and Crime" in Joseph Jacoby, ed., *Classics of Criminology*. Waveland Press, Prospect Heights, Illinois, 1994, p. 190.

19. George B. Vold, Thomas J. Bernard, and Jeffrey B. Snipes, *Theoretical Criminology*, 5th ed. Oxford University Press, New York, 2002.

20. Cited in Jones, op. cit., p. 193.

21. Ralf Dahrendorf, *Class and Class Conflict in Industrial Society*. Stanford University Press, Palo Alto, Calif. 1958.

22. Austin Turk, *Criminality and Legal Order*. Rand McNally, Chicago, 1969.

23. See Vold, Bernard, and Snipes, op. cit., p. 231; and J. Robert Lilly, Francis T. Cullen, and Richard A. Ball, *Criminological Theory: Context and Consequences*, 2nd ed. Sage, Thousand Oaks, 1995, pp. 142–149.

24. William V. Pelfrey, *The Evolution of Criminology*. Anderson, Cincinnati, Ohio, 1980, pp. 64, 68.

25. Jones, op. cit., p. 196.

26. Lilly, Cullen, and Ball, op. cit., p. 156.

27. Richard Quinney, *The Social Reality of Crime*. Little Brown, Boston, 1970.

28. Richard Quinney, *Criminal Justice in America*. Little Brown, Boston, 1974; and Richard Quinney, *Critique of the Legal Order*. Little Brown, Boston, 1974.

29. Richard Quinney, *Critique of the Legal Order*, p. 16.

30. Richard Quinney, *Class, State, and Crime*. McKay, New York, 1977.

31. Richard Quinney, "Class, State, and Crime," in Joseph Jacoby, ed. *Classics of Criminology*. Waveland Press, Prospect Heights, Illinois, 1994, pp. 106, 111.

32. Lilly, Cullen, and Ball, op. cit., p. 164.

33. Richard Quinney, *Class, State, and Crime*, 2nd ed., McKay, New York, 1980, pp. 30–31.

34. William J. Chambliss and R.T. Seidman, *Law, Order, and Power*. Addison Wesley, Reading, Mass., 1971.

35. William J. Chambliss, "The Law of Vagrancy," in Joseph Jacoby, ed., *Classics of Criminology*. Waveland Press, Prospect Heights, Illinois, 1994, pp. 287–293.

36. Cited in Susan Walklate, *Understanding Criminology*. Open University Press, Philadelphia, 1998, p. 27.

37. See Jones, op. cit., p. 201.

38. Ronald L. Akers, "Theory and Ideology in Marxist Criminology: Comments on Turk, Quinney, Toby, and Klockers," *Criminology* 16: 528, 543, September 1979.

39. Cited in Jones, op. cit., p. 200.

40. Michael J. Lynch and Paul B. Stretsky, "Radical Criminology," in Raymond Paternoster and Ronet Bachman, eds., *Explaining Criminals and Crime*. Roxbury Publishing Company, Los Angeles, 2001, p. 267.

41. Walklate, op. cit., p. 31.

42. Ian Taylor, Paul Walton, and Jock Young, *The New Criminology*. 1973. Routledge and Kegan Paul, Boston, 1979.

43. Taylor, Walton, and Young, op. cit., p. 270–278.

44. Ibid., p. 278.

45. Ibid., p. 282.

46. Lilly, Cullen, and Ball, op. cit., p. 195.

47. Jock Young, "The Failure of Criminology: The Need for a Radical Realism," in J. Young and R. Matthews, eds., *Confronting Crime*. Sage, London, 1986, p. 24.

48. Cited in Meda Chesney-Lind and Karlene Faith, "What About Feminism? Engendering Theory Making in Criminology," in

Raymond Paternoster and Ronet Bachman, eds., *Explaining Criminals and Crime*. Roxbury Publishing Company, Los Angeles, 2001, p. 287.

49. Ibid.

50. Ibid.

51. Cited in Sue Titus Reid, *Crime and Criminology*, 7th ed. Brown and Benchmark, Chicago, 1994, pp. 215–216.

52. Chesney-Lind and Faith, op. cit., p. 291.

53. Kate Millet, *Sexual Politics*. Doubleday, New York, 1970.

54. James Messerschimdt, *Capitalism, Patriarchy, and Crime: Towards Socialist Feminist Criminology*. Rowman and Littlefield, Totowa, N.J., 1986, p. 41.

55. Nancy A. Wonders, "Post Modern Feminist Criminology and Social Justice," in Bruce A. Arrigo, ed., *Social Justice, Criminal Justice*. West Wadsworth, Belmont, Calif., 1998, pp. 111–128.

56. Vold, Bernard, and Snipes, pp. 259–264.

57. Alison Young, "Feminism and the Body of Criminology," in D.P. Farrington and S. Walklate, eds., *Offenders and Victims: Theory and Policy*. British Society of Criminology and Institute for the Study and Treatment of Delinquency, London, 1992. See also Walklate, op. cit., pp. 77–78.

58. Beth Ritchie, *Compelled to Crime: The Gender Entrapment of Battered Black Women*. Routledge, New York, 1996.

59. Chesney-Lind and Faith, op. cit., p. 299.

60. Ibid., p. 290.

61. Walklate, op. cit., p. 90.

62. Vold, Bernard, and Snipes, op. cit., p. 85.

63. Ibid., pp. 86–87.

64. Albert K. Cohen, *Delinquent Boys: The Culture of the Gang*. Free Press, New York, 1955.

65. Walter Miller, "Lower Class Culture as a Generating Milieu of Gang Delinquency," *Journal of Social Issues* 14: 5–19, 1958.

66. Richard A. Cloward and Lloyd E. Ohlin, "*Delinquency and Opportunity*," in Joseph Jacoby, ed., *Classics of Criminology*. Waveland Press, Prospect Heights, Illinois, 1994.

67. C.R. Tittle, W.J. Villimez, and D.A. Smith, "The Myth of Social Class and Criminality: An Empirical Assessment of the Empirical Evidence," *American Sociological Review* 43: 643–656, 1978; C.R. Tittle and R.F. Meier, "Specifying the SES/Delinquency Relationship," *Criminology* 28: 271–299, 1991.

68. D.A. Andrews and James Bonta, *The Psychology of Criminal Conduct*. 1st ed. Anderson Publishing Company, Cincinnati, Ohio, 1994, pp. 53–57. A third edition was published in 2001.

69. R. Gregory Dunaway, Francis T. Cullen,

Velmer S. Burton, and T. David Evans, "The Myth of Social Class and Crime Revisited: An Examination of Class and Adult Criminality," *Criminology* 38: 589–632, 2000.

70. See Andrews and Bonta, op. cit., pp. 55–57.

71. Ralph Taylor, "The Ecology of Crime, Fear, and Delinquency," in Raymond Paternoster and Ronet Bachman, eds., *Explaining Criminals and Crime*. Roxbury Publishing Company, Los Angeles, 2001, p. 135.

72. Donald J. Shoemaker, *Theories of Delinquency*, 3rd ed. Oxford University Press, New York, 1996, p. 128.

73. Andrews and Bonta, op. cit., p. 57.

74. Taylor, op. cit., p. 125.

75. David Matza, *Delinquency and Drift*. 1964.Transaction Publishers, New Brunswick, 1992.

76. Ibid., p. 28.

77. Gresham M. Sykes and David Matza, "Techniques of Neutralization: A Theory of Delinquency," *American Journal of Sociology* 22: 664–670, 1957.

78. Matza, op. cit., p. 181.

79. Ibid., preface.

80. Cited in Matza, ibid., p. 6.

81. Silvan S. Tomkins, *Affect, Imagery, and Consciousness: The Positive Affects*, vol. 1, Springer, New York, 1962, pp. 108–109.

82. Ibid., p. 13.

83. Gary S. Becker, "Crime and Punishment: An Economic Approach," in Gary S. Becker and William M. Landes, eds., *Essays in the Economics of Crime and Punishment*. Columbia University Press, New York, 1974, pp. 1–54.

84. Ronald V. Clarke and Derek B. Cornish, "Rational Choice," in Raymond Paternoster and Ronet Bachman, eds., *Explaining Criminals and Crime*. Roxbury Publishing Company, Los Angeles, 2001, p. 34.

85. Ibid., p. 24.

86. Ibid., p. 31.

87. Ibid., p. 37.

88. Don C. Gibbons, *Talking About Crime and Criminals*. Prentice Hall, Englewood Cliffs, N.J., 1994, p. 124.

89. Ronald V. Clarke, "Situational Crime Prevention: Theory and Practice," *British Journal of Criminology* 20, no. 2: 138, 1980.

90. L.E. Cohen and M. Felson, "Social Change and Crime Trends: A Routine Activities Approach," *American Sociological Review* 44: 588–608, 1979.

91. Marcus Felson, "The Routine Activity Approach," in Raymond Paternoster and Ronet Bachman, eds., *Explaining Criminals and Crime*. Roxbury Publishing Company, Los Angeles, 2001, p. 46.

92. Ronald V. Clarke and Marcus Felson, "Routine Activity and Rational Choice," in R. V. Clarke and M. Felson, eds., *Advances in Criminological Theory*, vol. 5. Transaction, New Brunswick, 1993.

93. Clarke and Cornish, op. cit., pp. 37–40.

94. Ibid., p. 25.

95. Cited in Walklate, op. cit., p. 87.

96. Clarke and Cornish, op. cit., pp. 25–26.

97. Ibid., p. 40.

98. See Walklate, op. cit., pp. 34–70.

99. Emile Durkheim, *The Division of Labor in Society*. Free Press, Glencoe, Ill., 1933, p. 398.

100. Travis Hirschi, *Causes of Delinquency*. University of California Press, Berkeley, 1969, p. 200.

101. Ibid., p. 200.

102. Kimberly Kempf, "The New Empirical Status of Hirschi's Control Theory," in Freda Adler and William S. Laufer, eds., *New Directions in Criminological Theory: Advances in Criminological Theory*, vol. 4. Transaction New Brunswick, New Jersey, 1993, p. 173.

103. Michael R. Gottfredson and Travis Hirschi, *A General Theory of Crime*. Stanford University Press, Stanford, California, 1990.

104. Andrews and Bonta, op. cit., p. 88.

105. Vold, Bernard, and Snipes, op. cit., p. 194.

106. Hugh Barlow, "Explaining Crimes and Analogous Acts, or the Unrestrained Will Grab at Pleasure Whenever They Can," *Journal of Criminal Law and Criminology* 82, no. 1: 229–242, 1991.

107. Elliott Currie, *Confronting Crime: An American Challenge*. Pantheon, New York, 1985, p. 185.

108. Lilly, Cullen, and Ball, op. cit., p. 103.

109. Douglas Longshore and Susan Turner, "Self Control and Criminal Opportunity," *Criminal Justice and Behavior* 25, no. 1: 81–98, 1998.

110. Gottfredson and Hirschi, op. cit., p. 232.

111. Andrews and Bonta, op. cit., p. 87.

112. Gottfredson and Hirschi, op. cit., p. 274.

113. Glen H. Elder, Jr., "Time, Human Agency, and Social Change," in Alex Piquero and Paul Mazerolle, eds., *Life Course Criminology*. Wadsworth, United States, 2001.

114. See, for example, Michael Gottfredson and Travis Hirschi, "The True Value of Lambda Would Appear to Be Zero: An Essay on Career Criminals, Criminal Careers, Selective Incapacitation, Cohort Studies and Related Topics," in Alex Piquero and Paul Mazerolle, eds., *Life Course Criminology*. Wadsworth, United States, 2001, pp. 67–86.

115. M. Wolfgang, R.F. Figlio, and T. Sellin, *Delinquency in a Birth Cohort*. University of Chicago Press, Chicago, 1972.

116. See John H. Laub, Robert J. Sampson, and Leana C. Allen, "Explaining Crime over the Life Course: Toward a Theory of Age Graded Informal Social Control," in Raymond Paternoster and Ronet Bachman, eds., *Explaining Criminals and Crime*. Roxbury Publishing Company, Los Angeles, 2001, pp. 97–112

117. Frank Watson, *Been There and Back*. J.F. Blair, Winston Salem, N.C., 1976.

118. Laub, Sampson, and Allen, op. cit.

119. Terrie Moffitt, "Adolescent Limited and Life Course Persistent Antisocial Behavior: A Developmental Taxonomy," in Alex Piquero and Paul Mazerolle, eds., *Life Course Criminology*. Wadsworth, United States, 2001, pp. 91–145.

120. Ibid., p. 100.

121. Caspi et al., cited in Moffitt, op. cit., p. 107.

122. Dan Hurley, "On Crime as Science (a Neighbor at a Time)," *The New York Times*, January 6, 2004.

123. James Q. Wilson, *Thinking About Crime*. 1975. Vintage Books, New York, 1985, p. 78.

124. Hurley, op. cit.

125. Robert J. Sampson, Stephen W. Raudenbush, and Felton Earls, "Neighborhoods and Violent Crimes: A Multilevel Study of Collective Efficacy," *Science* 277: 918–924, 1997.

126. Hurley, op. cit., p. 1.

127. Ibid.

Part Five

1. Stephen Hawking, *A Brief History of Time*. Bantam Books, New York, 1998, p. 167.

2. Ronald Clarke and Derek Cornish, "Rational Choice," in Raymond Paternoster and Ronet Bachman, eds., *Explaining Criminals and Crime*. Roxbury Publishing Company, Los Angeles, 2001, p. 34.

3. Silvan Tomkins, *Affect, Imagery, and Consciousness: The Positive Affects*, vol. 1. Springer, New York, 1962, p. 108.

Chapter 12

1. Macneile Dixon, *The Human Situation*. Longmans, Green, and Company, New York, 1938, p. 17.

2. Adrian Raine, *The Psychopathology of Crime.* Academic Press, San Diego, 1993, p. 317.

3. Raine, op. cit.

4. Daniel Amen, *Firestorms in the Brain.* Mind Works Press, Newport Beach, California, 1999. Quotations from Harriet Barovick, "Bad to the Bone," *Time Magazine,* December 27, 1999.

5. Michael Gottfredson and Travis Hirschi, *A General Theory of Crime.* Stanford University Press, Stanford California, 1990, pp. 61–62.

6. William Shakespeare, *Macbeth,* V, ii, 66.

7. William Shakespeare, *Macbeth,* V, iv, 40–47.

8. Thomas Bernard, "Theoretical Development in Criminology" in Raymond Paternoster and Ronet Bachman, eds., *Explaining Crime and Criminals.* Roxbury Publishing Company, Los Angeles, California, 2001.

9. Thomas Bernard, "Twenty Years of Testing Theories," *Journal of Research in Crime and Delinquency* 27: 325–347, 1990.

10. Thomas Bernard, "Theoretical Development in Criminology," p. 340.

11. Wiley Sanders, ed., *A Thousand Years of Juvenile Offenders.* University of North Carolina Press, Chapel Hill, N.C., 1970.

12. D.M. Gorman, "The Irrelevance of Evidence in the Development of the School Based Drug Presentation Policy," *Evaluation Review* 22, no. 1: 118–146, 1998.

References

Abbott, Jack Henry. *In the Belly of the Beast: Letters from Prison*. Random House, New York, 1981.

Adler, Freda. *Sisters in Crime*. McGraw Hill, New York, 1975.

Akers, Ronald L. "Social Learning Theory." In Raymond Paternoster and Ronet Bachman, eds., *Explaining Criminals and Crime*. Roxbury Publishing Company, Los Angeles, 2001.

_____. "Theory and Ideology in Marxist Criminology: Comments on Turk, Quinney, Toby, and Klockers." *Criminology* 16: 528, 543, September 1979.

Alexander, Franz, and Hugo Staub. *The Criminal, the Judge, and the Public*. Macmillan, New York, 1931.

Alexander, Franz, and William Healy. *The Roots of Crime*. New York, 1935.

Allen, Francis A. "Raffaele Garofalo." In Hermann Mannheim, *Pioneers in Criminology*. Patterson Smith, Montclair, New Jersey, 1973.

Amen, Daniel. *Firestorms in the Brain*. Mind-works Press, 1999.

American Psychiatric Association. *Diagnostic and Statistical Manual of Mental Disorders, Text Revision*. 4th ed. American Psychiatric Association, Washington, D. C., 2000.

Andrews, D.A., and James Bonta. *The Psychology of Criminal Conduct*. 1st ed. Anderson Publishing Company, Cincinnati, Ohio, 1994.

Aronson, Eliot. *The Social Animal*. 5th ed. W. H. Freeman and Company, New York, 1988.

Bandura, A. *Aggression: A Social Learning Analysis*. Prentice Hall, New York, 1973.

Bandura, A., D. Ross, and S.A. Ross. "Transmission of Aggression Through Imitation of Aggressive Models." *Journal of Abnormal and Social Psychology* 63: 575–582, 1961.

Barlow, Hugh. "Explaining Crimes and Analogous Acts, or the Unrestrained Will Grab at Pleasure Whenever They Can." *Journal of Criminal Law and Criminology* 82, no. 1: 229–242, 1991.

Bartol, Curt. *Criminal Behavior: A Psychosocial Approach*. Prentice Hall, Upper Saddle River, New Jersey, 1999.

Beccaria, Cesare. *Of Crimes and Punishments*. Marsilio Publishers, New York, 1996.

Becker, Gary S. "Crime and Punishment: An Economic Approach." In Gary S. Becker and William M. Landes, eds., *Essays in the Economics of Crime and Punishment*. Columbia University Press, New York, 1974.

Becker, Howard. *The Outsiders*. 1963. Reprinted by Free Press, New York, 1973.

Bentham, Jeremy. *The Principles of Morals and Legislation*. Prometheus Books, Amherst, New York, 1988.

Bernard, Thomas. "Theoretical Development in Criminology." In Raymond Paternoster and Ronet Bachman, eds., *Explaining Crime and Criminals*. Roxbury Publishing Company, Los Angeles, California, 2001.

_____. "Twenty Years of Testing Theories." *Journal of Research in Crime and Delinquency* 27: 325–347, 1990.

Bierne, Piers. *Inventing Criminology.* State University of New York Press, Albany, 1993.

Bonger, Willem. *Criminality and Economic Conditions.* 1916. Reprinted by Agathon, New York, 1969.

_____. *An Introduction to Criminology.* 1932. Methuen, London, 1935.

_____. *Race and Crime.* 1939 Reprinted by Patterson Smith, Montclair, N.J., 1969.

Burgess, E.W. "The Growth of the City: An Introduction to a Research Project." In R.E. Park, E.W. Burgess and R.D. McKenzie, eds., *The City.* 1925. University of Chicago Press, Chicago, 1967, p. 55.

Buss, David. *The Evolution of Desire.* Basic Books, New York, 2003.

Cadoret, R.J., C.A. Cain, and R.R. Crowe. "Evidence for Gene-Environment Interaction in the Development of Adolescent Antisocial Behavior." *Behavior Genetics* 13: 301–310, 1983.

Cain, M. "Towards Transgression: New Directions in Feminist Criminology." *International Journal of the Sociology of Law* 18: 1–18, 1990.

Carroll, Robert. "Anthropometry." In Robert Carroll, ed., *The Skeptics Dictionary.* John Wiley and Sons, Hoboken New Jersey, 2003.

_____. "Phrenology." In Robert Carroll, ed., *The Skeptics Dictionary.* John Wiley and Sons, Hoboken, New Jersey, 2003.

Cason, Hulsey. "The Psychopath and the Psychopathic." *Journal of Criminal Psychopathology* 4: 522–7, 1943.

Caspi, A., G.H. Elder, and D.J. Bem. "Moving Against the World: Life Course Patterns of Explosive Children." *Developmental Psychology* 23: 308–313, 1987.

Chaiken, J.M., and M.R. Chaiken. "Crime Rates and the Active Criminal." In J.Q. Wilson, ed., *Crime and Public Policy.* Institute for Contemporary Studies, San Francisco, 1983.

Chambliss, William J. "The Law of Vagrancy." In Joseph Jacoby, ed., *Classics of Criminology.* Waveland Press, Prospect Heights, Illinois, 1994.

_____. "Toward a Political Economy of Crime." *Theory and Society* 2: 152–153, 1975.

Chambliss, William J., and R.T. Seidman. *Law, Order, and Power.* Addison Wesley, Reading, Mass., 1971.

Chesney-Lind, Meda, and Karlene Faith. "What About Feminism? Engendering Theory Making in Criminology." In Raymond Paternoster and Ronet Bachman, eds., *Explaining Criminals and Crime.* Roxbury Publishing Company, Los Angeles, 2001.

Christiansen, Karl O. "A Preliminary Study of Criminality Among Twins." In S.A. Mednick and K.O. Christiansen, eds., *Biosocial Bases of Criminal Behavior.* Gardner Press, New York, 1977.

Clark, William R., and Michael Grunstein. *Are We Hardwired? The Role of Genes in Human Behavior.* Oxford University Press, Oxford, 2000.

Clarke, Ronald V. "Situational Crime Prevention: Theory and Practice." *British Journal of Criminology* 20, no. 2: 138, 1980.

Clarke, Ronald V., and Derek B. Cornish. "Rational Choice." In Raymond Paternoster and Ronet Bachman, eds., *Explaining Criminals and Crime.* Roxbury Publishing Company, Los Angeles, 2001.

Clarke, Ronald V., and Marcus Felson. "Routine Activity and Rational Choice." In R.V. Clarke and M. Felson eds., *Advances in Criminological Theory.* vol. 5. Transaction, New Brunswick, 1993.

Cleckley, Hervey. *The Mask of Sanity.* 1941. Reprinted by Emily S. Cleckley, Publishers, Augusta, Georgia, 1988.

Clinard, Marshall. *Anomie and Deviant Behavior.* The Free Press of Glencoe, New York, 1964.

Clonniger, C.R., S. Sigvardsson, M. Bohman, and A.L Knorring. "Predisposition to

Petty Criminality in Swedish Adoptees: Cross Fostering Analysis of Gene-Environmental Interaction." *Archives of General Psychiatry* 99: 1242–1247, 1982.

Cloward, Richard A., and Lloyd E. Ohlin. "Delinquency and Opportunity." In Joseph Jacoby, ed., *Classics of Criminology*. Waveland Press, Prospect Heights, Illinois, 1994.

Cohen, Albert K. *Delinquent Boys: The Culture of the Gang*. Free Press, New York, 1955.

Cohen, Albert K., Alfred Lindesmith, and Karl Schuessler. *The Sutherland Papers*. Indiana University Press, Bloomington, 1956.

Cohen, L.E., and M. Felson. "Social Change and Crime Rate Trends: A Routine Activity Approach." *American Sociological Review* 44: 588–608, 1979.

Cooley, Charles Horton. *Human Nature and the Social Order*. 1902. Reprinted by Schoken, New York, 1964.

Coontz, Phyllis, and Eric Sevigny. "Revisiting the Rise of the Violent Female Offender: Drugs and Violent Crime." University of Pittsburg, Graduate School of Public and International Affairs, February 2003.

Cooter, Roger. "Phrenology and the British Alienists." In Andrew Scull, ed., *Madhouse, Mad-Doctors, and Madmen: The Social History of Psychiatry in the Victorian Era*. University of Pennsylvania Press, Philadelphia, 1981.

Cortes, Juan B., and Florence Galtti. *Delinquency and Crime*. Seminar Press, New York, 1972.

Cuomo, Mario. Foreword to Cesare Beccaria, *Of Crimes and Punishments*. Marsilio Publishers, New York, 1996.

Curran, D., and P. Mallinson. "Recent Progress in Psychiatry: Psychopathic Personality." *Journal of Mental Science* 90: 266–84, 1944.

Currie, Elliott. *Confronting Crime: An American Challenge*. Pantheon, New York, 1985.

Dahrendorf, Ralf. *Class and Class Conflict in Industrial Society*. Stanford University Press, Palo Alto, Calif., 1958.

Daley, M., and M. Wilson. *Homicide*. Aldine de Gruyter, New York, 1988.

Dalgaard, O.S., and E. Kringlen. "A Norwegian Twin Study of Criminality." *British Journal of Criminology* 16: 213–233, 1976.

Damasio, Antonio R. *Descartes' Error: Emotion, Reason, and the Human Brain*. G.P. Putnam's Sons, New York, 1994.

Damasio, H., T. Grabowski, R. Frank, A.M Galaburda, and A.R. Damasio. "The Return of Phineas Gage: The Skull of a Famous Patient Yields Clues About the Brain." *Science* 264: 1102–05, 1994.

Darwin, Charles. *The Descent of Man and Selection in Relation to Sex*. 1871. Reprinted by IndyPublish.com, 2003.

_____. *On the Origin of the Species*. John Murray, London, 1859.

Darwin, Francis. *The Life and Letters of Charles Darwin*. University Press of the Pacific, 2001.

Dawkins, Richard. *The Selfish Gene*. Oxford University Press, Oxford, 1976.

Dixon, Macneile. *The Human Situation*. Longmans, Green, and Company, New York, 1938.

Dollard, J., N.E. Miller, L.W. Doob, and O.H. Mowrer. *Frustration and Aggression*. Yale University Press, New Haven, Connecticut, 1939.

Drapkin, Israel. *Crime and Punishment in the Ancient World*. Lexington Books, Lexington Mass., 1989.

Driver, Edwin D. "Charles Buckman Goring." In Hermann Mannheim, ed., *Pioneers in Criminology*. Patterson Smith, Montclair, New Jersey, 1973.

Dunaway, R. Gregory, Francis T. Cullen, Velmer S. Burton, and T. David Evans. "The Myth of Social Class and Crime Revisited: An Examination of Class and Adult Criminality." *Criminology* 38: 589–632, 2000.

Durkheim, Emile. *The Division of Labor in Society*. Free Press, Glencoe, Ill., 1986.

_____. "The Normal and the Pathological." In Joseph Jacoby, ed., *Classics in Criminology*. Waveland Press, Prospect Heights, Illinois, 1994.

_____. *The Rules of Sociological Method*. Macmillan, London, 1982.

_____. *Suicide: A Study in Sociology*. Free Press, New York, 1951.

Ehrlich, Paul. *Human Natures: Genes, Cultures, and the Human Prospect*. Penguin Putnam, New York, 2002.

Elder, Glen H., Jr. "Time, Human Agency, and Social Change." In Alex Piquero and Paul Mazerolle, eds., *Life Course Criminology*. Wadsworth, United States, 2001.

Ellis, Havelock. *The Criminal*. 2nd ed. Charles Scribner's Sons, New York, 1895.

Empey, Lamar T. *American Delinquency*. 2nd ed. Dorsey, Homewood, Illinois, 1982.

Eysenck, Hans J. *Crime and Personality*. 1st ed. Houghton Mifflin Company, Boston, 1964.

_____. *Crime and Personality*. 2nd ed. Routledge and Kegan Paul, London, 1977.

Eysenck, Hans, and G. Gudjonsson. *The Causes and Cures of Criminality*. Plenum, New York, 1989.

Farrington, David. "Early Predictors of Adolescent Aggression and Adult Violence." *Violence and Victims* 4: 79–100, 1989.

Felson, Marcus. "The Routine Activity Approach." In Raymond Paternoster and Ronet Bachman, eds., *Explaining Criminals and Crime*. Roxbury Publishing Company, Los Angeles, 2001.

Fox, R.G. "The XYY Offender: A Modern Myth?" *Journal of Criminal Law, Criminology, and Political Science* 62: 59–73, 1971.

Freud, Sigmund. "The Ego and the Id." In *The Complete Psychological Works of Works of Sigmund Freud*. Vol. 19. Hogarth, London, 1961.

_____. "Psycho-Analysis and the Ascertaining of Truth in Courts of Law." In *Collected Papers*. Vol. 2. Hogarth, London, 1948.

Galton, Francis. *Hereditary Genius: An Inquiry into Its Laws and Consequences*. Macmillan, London, 1869.

Geis, Gilbert. "Jeremy Bentham." In Hermann Mannheim, ed., *Pioneers in Criminology*. Patterson Smith, Montclair, New Jersey, 1973.

Gibbens, T.C.N. *Psychiatric Studies of Borstal Lads*. Oxford University Press, London, 1963.

Gibbons, Don C. *Delinquent Behavior*. Prentice Hall, Englewood Cliffs, N.J., 1970.

_____. *Talking About Crime and Criminals*. Prentice Hall, Englewood Cliffs, N.J., 1994.

Glover, Edward. *The Roots of Crime*. International Universities Press, New York, 1960.

Glueck, Sheldon, and Eleanor Glueck. *Unraveling Juvenile Delinquency*. Commonwealth Fund, New York, 1950.

Goddard, H.H. "Feeblemindedness." In Joseph Jacoby, ed., *Classics of Criminology*. Waveland Press, Prospect Heights, Illinois, 1994.

_____. *Human Efficiency and Levels of Intelligence*. Princeton University Press, Princeton, 1920.

Goll, August. *Criminal Types in Shakespeare*. Haskell House, New York, 1966.

Goring, Charles. *The English Convict: A Statistical Study*. 1913. Reprinted by Patterson Smith, Montclair, New Jersey, 1972.

Gorman, D.M. "The Irrelevance of Evidence in the Development of the School Based Drug Presentation Policy." *Evaluation Review* 22, no. 1: 118–146, 1998.

Gottfredson, Michael, and Travis Hirschi. *A General Theory of Crime*. Stanford University Press, Stanford, California, 1990.

_____. "The True Value of Lambda Would Appear to Be Zero: An Essay on Career Criminals, Criminal Careers, Selective Incapacitation, Cohort Studies and Related Topics." In Alex Piquero and Paul Mazerolle, eds., *Life Course Criminology*. Wadsworth, United States, 2001.

Grove, W.M., E.D. Eckert, L. Heston, T.J Bouchard, N. Segal, and D.T. Lykken. "Heritability of Substance Abuse and Antisocial Behavior: A Study of Monozygotic Twins Reared Apart." *Biological Psychiatry* 27: 1293–1304, 1990.

Gunn, John. "Psychopathy: An Elusive Concept with Moral Overtones." In Millon, Theodore, Erik Simonsen, Morten Birket-Smith, and Roger D. Davis. *Psychopathy: Antisocial, Criminal, and Violent Behavior.* The Guilford Press, New York, 1998.

Hagan, John. *Structural Criminology.* Rutgers University Press, New Brunswick, New Jersey, 1989.

Hamilton, W.D. "The Genetic Evolution of Social Behavior." *Journal of Theoretical Biology* 7: 1–52, 1964.

Hare, R.D. *The Hare Psychopathy Checklist Revised.* Multi Health Systems, Toronto, 1991.

_____. "Psychopaths and Their Nature." In Theodore Millon, Erik Simonsen, Morten Birket-Smith, and Roger D. Davis, *Psychopathy.* The Guilford Press, New York, 1998.

_____. *Without Conscience.* The Guilford Press, New York, 1993.

Harpur, T.J., R.D. Hare, and A.R. Hakistan. "Two Factor Conceptualization of Psychopathy: Construct Validity and Assessment Implications." *Psychological Assessment* 1: 6–17, 1989.

Harrison, Lana, and Joseph Gfroerer. "The Intersection of Drug Use and Criminal Behavior: Results from the National Household Survey on Drug Abuse." *Crime and Delinquency* 38: 423, October 1992.

Hartl, E.M., E.P. Monnelly, and R.D. Elderkin. *Physique and Delinquent Behavior: A Thirty Year Follow Up of William H. Sheldon's Varieties of Delinquent Youth.* Academic Press, New York, 1982.

Haught, John. *God After Darwin: A Theology of Evolution.* Westview Press, Boulder Colorado, 2001.

Hawking, Stephen. *A Brief History of Time.* Bantam Books, New York, 1998.

Hindelang, Michael J. "Variations in Sex-Age-Race Specific Incidence Rates of Offending." *American Sociological Review* 46: 461–74, 1981.

Hirschi, Travis. *Causes of Delinquency.* University of California Press, Berkeley, Calif., 1969.

Hirschi, T., and M. Hindelang "Intelligence and Delinquency: a Revisionist View." *American Sociological Review* 42: 571–587, 1977.

Holzknecht, Karl, and Norman McClure, eds. *Selected Plays of Shakespeare.* Vol. 3 American Book Company, New York, 1937.

Hooten, E.A. "The American Criminal." In Joseph Jacoby, ed., *Classics of Criminology.* Waveland Press, Prospect Heights, Illinois, 1994.

_____. *The American Criminal: An Anthropological Study.* Harvard University Press, Cambridge, 1939.

_____. *Crime and the Man.* Harvard University Press, Cambridge, 1939.

Hunt, M.M. "How Does It Come to Be So? A Profile of Robert K. Merton." *New Yorker,* January 28, 1961.

Hurley, Dan. "On Crime as Science (a Neighbor at a Time)." *The New York Times,* January 6, 2004.

Ianni, Frances A. *Black Mafia.* Simon and Schuster, New York, 1974.

Jacobs, P., M. Brunton, and M. Melville. "Aggressive Behavior, Mental Subnormality, and the XYY Male." *Nature* 208: 1351, 1965.

Jacoby, Joseph, ed. *Classics in Criminology.* Waveland Press, Prospect Heights, Illinois, 1994.

Jeffrey, Clarence R. "The Historical Development of Criminology." In Hermann Mannheim, *Pioneers in Criminology.* Patterson Smith, Montclair, New Jersey, 1973.

Johns, J.H., and H.C. Quay. "The Effect of Social Reward on Verbal Conditioning in Psychopathic and Neurotic Military Offenders." *Journal of Consulting Psychology* 36: 217–220, 1962.

Johnson, Phillip E. *Darwin on Trial*. 2nd ed. Intervarsity Press, Downers Grove, Illinois, 1993.

Jones, David. *History of Criminology*. Greenwood Press, New York, 1986.

Jones, W.H.S. "Hippocrates." In *Loeb Classical Library*. Vol. 1. Harvard University Press, Cambridge, Mass., 1984.

Kempf, Kimberly. "The New Empirical Status of Hirschi's Control Theory." In Freda Adler and William S. Laufer, eds., *New Directions in Criminological Theory: Advances in Criminological Theory*. Vol. 4. Transaction New Brunswick, New Jersey, 1993.

Lange, J. *Crime as Destiny*. Unwin, London, 1929.

Laub, John H., Robert J. Sampson, and Leana C. Allen. "Explaining Crime Over the Life Course: Toward a Theory of Age Graded Informal Social Control." In Raymond Paternoster and Ronet Bachman, eds., *Explaining Criminals and Crime*, Roxbury Publishing Company, Los Angeles, 2001, pp. 97–112.

Lemert, Edwin. "Primary and Secondary Deviation." In Joseph Jacoby, ed., *Classics of Criminology*. Waveland Press, Prospect Heights, Illinois, 1994.

Lewis, D.O., S.A. Shanok, and D.A. Balla. "Perinatal Difficulties, Head and Face Trauma, and Child Abuse in the Medical Histories of Seriously Delinquent Children." *American Journal of Psychiatry* 136: 419–423, 1979.

Lilly, J. Robert, Francis T. Cullen, and Richard A. Ball. *Criminological Theory: Context and Consequences*. 2nd ed. Sage Publications, Thousand Oaks, 1995.

Lombroso, Cesare. *Crime: Its Causes and Remedies*. 1912. Reprinted by Patterson Smith, Montclair, New Jersey, 1968.

Lombroso-Ferrero, Gina. "Criminal Man." In Joseph Jacoby, ed., *Classics of Criminology*. Waveland Press, Prospect Heights, Illinois, 1994.

Lunden, Walter A. "Emile Durkheim." In Hermann Mannheim, ed., *Pioneers in Criminology*. Patterson Smith, Montclair, New Jersey, 1973.

Longshore, Douglas, and Susan Turner. "Self Control and Criminal Opportunity." *Criminal Justice and Behavior* 25, no. 1: 81–98, 1998.

Lykken, David. *The Antisocial Personalities*. Lawrence Erlbaum Associates, Hillsdale, New Jersey, 1995.

Lynch, Michael J., and Paul B. Stretsky. "Radical Criminology." In Raymond Paternoster and Ronet Bachman, eds., *Explaining Criminals and Crime*. Roxbury Publishing Company, Los Angeles, 2001.

Mannheim, Hermann, ed. *Pioneers in Criminology*. Patterson Smith, Montclair, New Jersey, 1973.

Martin, Randy, Robert J. Mutchnick, and W. Timothy Austin. *Criminological Thought: Pioneers Past and Present*. Macmillan Publishing Company, New York, 1990.

Marx, Karl. "Class Conflict and Law." In Joseph Jacoby, ed., *Classics of Criminology*. Waveland Press, Prospect Heights, Illinois, 1994.

Matza, David. *Delinquency and Drift*. 1964. Transaction Publishers, New Brunswick, 1992.

McCord, William, and Joan McCord. *Origins of Crime*. Patterson Smith, Montclair, New Jersey, 1972.

McDonald, Lynn. "Theory and Evidence of Rising Crime in the Nineteenth Century." *British Journal of Criminology* 33: 404–420, Sept. 1982.

Mednick, S.A., W.H. Gabrielli, and B. Hutchings. "Genetic Influences in Criminal Convictions: Evidence from an Adoption Cohort." *Science* 224: 891–894, 1984.

Mednick, S.A., and E. Kandel. "Genetic and Perinatal Factors in Violence." In S.A. Mednick and T. Moffitt, eds., *Biological Contributions to Crime Causation*. Martinus Nijhoff, Dordrecht, Holland, 1988.

Megargee, E.I., and M.J. Bohn. *Classifying Criminal Offenders: A New System Based on the MMPI*. Sage, Beverly Hills, Calif., 1979.

Meloy, J. Reid. *The Psychopathic Mind: Origins, Dynamics, and Treatment*. Jason Aronson, North Vale, New Jersey, 1988.

Merton, Robert K. "Social Structure and Anomie." *American Sociological Review* 3: 672–682, 1938.

_____. "Social Structure and Anomie." In Joseph Jacoby, ed., *Classics of Criminology*. Waveland Press, Prospect Heights, Illinois, 1994.

_____. *Social Theory and Social Structure*. The Free Press, New York, 1949.

Merton, Robert K., and M.F. Ashley-Montague. "Crime and the Anthropologist." *American Anthropologist* 42, August 1940, pp. 380–384.

Messerschimdt, James. *Capitalism, Patriarchy, and Crime: Towards Socialist Feminist Criminology*. Rowman and Littlefield, Totowa, N.J., 1986.

Michael, Jerome, and Mortimer J. Adler. *Crime Law, and Social Science*. Harcourt Brace, New York, 1933.

Milinski, M., and T.C. Bakker. "Female Sticklebacks Use Male Coloration in Male Choice and Hence Avoid Parasitized Males." *Nature,* 344: 330–333, 1990.

Miller, Kenneth R. *Finding Darwin's God*. Harper Collins, New York, 2000.

Miller, Walter. "Lower Class Culture as a Generating Milieu of Gang Delinquency." *Journal of Social Issues* 14: 5–19, 1958.

Millet, Kate. *Sexual Politics*. Doubleday, New York, 1970.

Millon, Theodore, Erik Simonsen, Morten Birket-Smith, and Roger D. Davis. *Psychopathy: Antisocial, Criminal, and Violent Behavior*. The Guilford Press, New York, 1998.

Moffitt, Terrie. "Adolescence-Limited and Life Course Persistent Antisocial Behavior: A Developmental Taxonomy." In Alex Piquero and Paul Mazerole, eds., *Life Course Criminology*. Wadsworth, United States, 2001.

Moffitt, Terrie, Avshalom Caspi, Michael Rutter, and Phil A. Silva. *Sex Differences in Antisocial Behavior*. Cambridge University Press, Cambridge, 2001.

Monachesi, Elio. "Cesare Beccaria." In Hermann Mannheim, ed., *Pioneers in Criminology*. Patterson Smith, Montclair, New Jersey, 1973.

Murchison, Carl. *Criminal Intelligence*. Worcester, 1926.

Newman, Graeme. *Just and Painful: A Case for the Corporal Punishment of Prisoners*. Free Press, New York, 1983.

Overholser, Winfred. "Isaac Ray." In Hermann Mannheim, ed., *Pioneers in Criminology*. Patterson Smith, Montclair, New Jersey, 1973.

Partridge, G.E. "Current Conceptions of Psychopathic Personality." *American Journal of Psychiatry* 10: 53–99, 1930.

Paternoster, Raymond, and Ronet Bachman, eds. *Explaining Criminals and Crime*. Roxbury Publishing Company, Los Angeles, 2001.

Pavlov, I.P. *Conditioned Reflexes*. 1927. Reprinted by Dover, New York, 1960.

Pelfrey, William V. *The Evolution of Criminology*. Anderson, Cincinnati, Ohio, 1980.

Pollak, Otto. *The Criminality of Women*. University of Pennsylvania Press, Philadelphia, 1950.

Quay, Herbert C. "Intelligence." In Herbert C. Quay, ed., *Handbook of Juvenile Delinquency*. Wiley, New York, 1987.

_____. *Managing Adult Inmates: Classification for Housing and Program Assignments*. American Correctional Association, College Park, Maryland, 1984.

Quetelet, Adolphe. *Instructions populaires sur le calcul des probabilities*. Tarlier, Brussels, 1828.

Quinney, Richard. *Class, State, and Crime*. McKay, New York, 1977.

_____. *Class, State, and Crime*. 2nd ed. McKay, New York, 1980.

_____. "Class, State, and Crime." In Joseph Jacoby, ed., *Classics of Criminology*. Waveland Press, Prospect Heights, Illinois, 1994.

_____. *Criminal Justice in America*. Little Brown, Boston, 1974.

_____. *Critique of the Legal Order*. Little Brown, Boston, 1974.

_____. *The Social Reality of Crime*. Little Brown, Boston, 1970.

Raine, Adrian. *The Psychopathology of Crime*. Academic Press, San Diego, 1993.

Reid, Sue Titus. *Crime and Criminology*. 7th ed. Brown and Benchmark, Chicago, 1994.

Reuter, E.B. "Review of E.A. Hooten, Crime and the Man." *American Journal of Sociology* 45: 123–6, 1939.

Ritchie, Beth. *Compelled to Crime: The Gender Entrapment of Battered Black Women*. Routledge, New York, 1996.

Rose, Hilary, and Stephen Rose, eds. *Alas Poor Darwin! Arguments Against Evolutionary Psychology*. Harmony Books, 2000.

Rushton, J. "Race and Crime: International Data for 1989–1990." *Psychological Reports* 76: 307–312, 1995.

Rutter, M., and H. Giller. *Juvenile Delinquency: Trends and Perspectives*. Guilford, New York, 1984.

Sagarin, Edward. "In Search of Criminology Through Fiction." *Deviant Behavior* 2, no 1: 81, 1980.

Samenow, Stanton. *Inside the Criminal Mind*. Times Books, New York, 1984.

Sampson, Robert J., Stephen W. Raudenbush, and Felton Earls. "Neighborhoods and Violent Crimes: A Multilevel Study of Collective Efficacy." *Science* 277: 918–924, 1997.

Sandberg, A.A., G.F. Koepf, T. Ishihara, and J.S. Hauschka. "An XYY Human Male." *Lancet* 2: 488–9, 1961.

Sanders, Wiley, ed. *A Thousand Years of Juvenile Offenders*. University of North Carolina Press, Chapel Hill, N.C., 1970.

Schlag, Pierre. "Commentary: Law and Phrenology." *Harvard Law Review* 110: 877, 1997.

Sellin, Thorsten. *Culture Conflict and Crime*. Social Science Research Council, New York, 1938.

_____. "Culture Conflict and Crime." In Joseph Jacoby, ed., *Classics in Criminology*. Waveland Press, Prospect Heights, Illinois, 1994.

Sheldon, William H. *Varieties of Delinquent Youth*. Harper, New York, 1949.

Shoemaker, Donald J. *Theories of Delinquency*. 3rd ed. Oxford University Press, New York, 1996.

Simon, Rita. *Women in Crime*. Lexington Books, Lexington, Mass., 1975.

Smith, John Maynard. *Evolution and the Theory of Games*. Cambridge University Press, Cambridge, 1982.

Spencer, Herbert. *First Principles*. Originally published in six parts (1860–1862). Published as one volume, Williams and Norgate, London, 1862.

_____. *The Principles of Psychology*. Vol. I. D. Appleton and Company, New York, 1872.

Sterelny, Kim. *Dawkins vs. Gould*. Totem Books, U.S.A., 2001.

Sutherland, Edwin. "Mental Deficiency and Crime." In Kimball Young, ed., *Social Attitudes*. Henry Holt, New York, 1931.

_____. *White Collar Crime*. Holt, Rhinehart, and Winston, New York, 1961.

_____. "White Collar Criminality." *American Sociological Review*, 5, no.1: 2–10, 1940.

Sutherland, Edwin, and Donald Cressey. *The Principles of Criminology*. 7th ed. J.B. Lippincott and Company, Philadelphia, 1966.

Sutherland, Edwin, Donald Cressey, and David Luckenbill. *Principles of Criminology*. 11th ed. General Hall, Dix Hills, New York, 1992.

Sykes, Gresham M., and David Matza. "Techniques of Neutralization: A Theory of Delinquency." *American Journal of Sociology* 22: 664–670, 1957.

Tannebaum, Frank. "The Dramatization of Evil." In Joseph Jacoby, ed., *Classics of Criminology*. Waveland Press, Prospect Heights, Illinois, 1994.

Tarde, Gabriel. *Penal Philosophy*. 1890. Patterson Smith, Montclair, New Jersey, 1968. Originally published in 1890.

Taylor, Ian, Paul Walton, and Jock Young. *The New Criminology*. 1973. Routledge and Kegan Paul, Boston, 1979.

Taylor, Ralph. "The Ecology of Crime, Fear, and Delinquency." In Raymond Paternoster and Ronet Bachman, eds., *Explaining Criminals and Crime*. Roxbury Publishing Company, Los Angeles, 2001.

Thigpen, Corbett, and Hervey Cleckley. *The Three Faces of Eve*. Revised edition. Arcata Graphics, Kingsport, Tennessee, 1992.

Thomas, W.I. *Sex and Society*. Little Brown, Boston, 1907.

Thornhill, R., and N.M. Thornhill. "Human Rape: The Strengths of the Evolutionary Perspective." In C. Crawford, M. Smith, and D. Krebs, eds., *Sociobiology and Psychology*. Erlbaum, Hillsdale, N.J., 1987.

Time, Victoria. *Shakespeare's Criminals*. Greenwood Press, Westport, Connecticut, 1999.

Tittle, C.R., W.J. Villimez, and D.A. Smith. "The Myth of Social Class and Criminality: An Empirical Assessment of the Empirical Evidence." *American Sociological Review*, 43: 643–656, 1978.

Tittle, C.R., and R.F. Meier. "Specifying the SES/Delinquency Relationship." *Criminology*, 28: 271–299, 1991.

Toch, Hans. "Psychopathy or Anti Social Personality in Forensic Settings." In Millon, Theodore, Erik Simonsen, Morten Birket-Smith, and Roger D. Davis, *Psychopathy: Antisocial, Criminal, and Violent Behavior*. The Guilford Press, New York, 1998.

Tomkins, Silvan S. *Affect, Imagery, and Consciousness: The Positive Affects*. Vol. 1. Springer, New York, 1962.

Tooby, J., and L. Comides. "The Psychological Foundations of Culture." In J.H. Barlow, L. Cosmides, and J. Tooby, eds., *The Adapted Mind: Evolutionary Psychology and the Generation of Culture*. Oxford University Press, Oxford, 1992.

Trasler, Gordon. "Aspects of Causality, Culture, and Crime." Paper presented at the Fourth International Seminar at the International Center of Sociological, Penal, and Penitentiary Research and Studies, Messina, Italy, 1980.

Trivers, Robert L. "The Evolution of Reciprocal Altruism." *Quarterly Review of Biology* 46: 35–57, 1971.

Turk, Austin. *Criminality and Legal Order*. Rand McNally, Chicago, 1969.

U.S. Department of Justice. *Uniform Crime Reports*. Washington, D.C., 1994–2002.

U.S. Department of Justice, Bureau of Justice Statistics. *Source Book of Criminal Justice Statistics*. 1998.

van Bemmelen, J.M. "Willem Adriaan Bonger." In Hermann Mannheim, ed., *Pioneers in Criminology*. Patterson Smith, Montclair, New Jersey, 1973.

Vold, George, and Thomas Bernard. *Theoretical Criminology*. 3rd ed. Oxford University Press, New York, 1986.

Vold, George B., Thomas J. Bernard, and Jeffrey B. Snipes. *Theoretical Criminology*. 5th ed. Oxford University Press, New York, 2002.

Walklate, Susan. *Understanding Criminology*. Open University Press, Philadelphia, 1998.

Walsh, Anthony. *Biosocial Criminology*. Anderson Publishing Company, Cincinnati, Ohio, 2002.

Walters, G.D., and T.W. White. "Heredity and Crime: Bad Genes or Bad Research." *Criminology* 27: 455–485, 1989.

Washburn, S.L. "Review of W.H. Sheldon, Varieties of Delinquent Youth." *American Anthropologist*. 53: 561–563, 1951.

Watson, Frank. *Been There and Back*. J.F. Blair, Winston Salem, N.C., 1976.

Watson, J.B., and R. Raynor. "Conditioned Emotional Reactions." *Journal of Experimental Psychology* 3: 1–14, 1920.

White, Robert W. *The Abnormal Personality*. 2nd ed. The Ronald Press Company, New York, 1956.

Widom, C.S., and J.P. Newman. "Characteristics of Non-Institutionalized Psychopaths." In D.P. Farrington and J. Gunn, eds., *Aggression and Dangerousness*. Wiley, New York, 1985.

Wilbanks, William. *The Myth of a Racist Criminal Justice System.* Brooks/Cole, Belmont, California, 1986.

Wilson, E.O. *Sociobiology: The New Synthesis.* Harvard University Press, Cambridge, Mass., 1975.

Wilson, James Q. *Thinking About Crime.* 1975. Vintage Books, New York, 1985, p. 78.

Wilson, James Q., and Richard J. Herrnstein. *Crime and Human Nature.* Simon and Schuster, New York, 1985.

Wilson-Vine, Margaret S. "Gabriel Tarde." In Hermann Mannheim, ed., *Pioneers in Criminology.* Patterson Smith, Montclair, New Jersey, 1973.

Witkin, H.A., S.A. Mednick, F. Schulsinger, E. Bakkestrom, K.O. Christiansen, D.R. Goodenough, K. Hirschorn, C. Lundsteen, D.R. Owen, J. Phillip, D.B. Rubin, and M. Stocking. "Criminality, Aggression, and Intelligence among XYY and XXY Men." In S.A. Mednick and K.O. Christiansen, eds., *Biosocial Bases of Criminal Behavior.* Gardner Press, New York, 1977.

Wolfgang, M., R.F. Figlio, and T. Sellin. *Delinquency in a Birth Cohort.* University of Chicago Press, Chicago, 1972.

Wolfgang, Marvin E. "Cesare Lombroso." In Hermann Mannheim, ed., *Pioneers in Criminology.* Patterson Smith, Montclair, New Jersey, 1973.

_____. Introduction to Cesare Beccaria, *Of Crimes and Punishments.* Marsilio Publishers, New York, 1996.

Wonders, Nancy A. "Post Modern Feminist Criminology and Social Justice." In Bruce A. Arrigo, ed., *Social Justice, Criminal Justice.* West Wadsworth, Belmont, Calif., 1998.

Yaralian, Pauline, and Adrian Raine. "Biological Approaches to Crime." In Raymond Paternoster and Ronet Bachman, eds., *Explaining Criminals and Crime.* Roxbury Publishing Company, Los Angeles, 2001.

Yochelson, Samuel, and Stanton Samenow. *The Criminal Personality.* Vol. I. Jason Aronson, New York, 1976.

_____. *The Criminal Personality.* Vol. II. Jason Aronson, New York, 1977.

_____. *The Criminal Personality.* Vol. III. Jason Aronson, New York, 1986.

Young, Alison. "Feminism and the Body of Criminology." In D.P. Farrington and S. Walklate, eds., *Offenders and Victims: Theory and Policy.* British Society of Criminology and Institute for the Study and Treatment of Delinquency, London, 1992.

Young, Jock. "The Failure of Criminology: The Need for a Radical Realism." In J. Young and R. Matthews, eds., *Confronting Crime.* Sage, London, 1986.

Zelney, L.D. "Feeblemindedness and Criminal Conduct." *American Journal of Sociology* 38: 564–578, 1933.

Index